Robert Ainslie Redford

Christendom from the standpoint of Italy: proceedings of the ninth General Conference of the Evangelical Alliance

Held in Florence, 1891

Robert Ainslie Redford

Christendom from the standpoint of Italy: proceedings of the ninth General Conference of the Evangelical Alliance

Held in Florence, 1891

ISBN/EAN: 9783337107635

Printed in Europe, USA, Canada, Australia, Japan

Cover: Foto ©Lupo / pixelio.de

More available books at **www.hansebooks.com**

CHRISTENDOM

FROM THE STANDPOINT OF ITALY.

PROCEEDINGS

OF THE

Ninth General Conference of the Evangelical Alliance,

HELD IN FLORENCE, 1891.

PUBLISHED BY AUTHORITY OF THE COUNCIL OF THE
BRITISH ORGANIZATION OF THE ALLIANCE.

EDITED BY THE
REV. R. A. REDFORD, M.A., LL.B.,
(Prof. Emerit. New College, London).

London:
OFFICE OF THE EVANGELICAL ALLIANCE,
7, ADAM STREET, ADELPHI,
AND
T. G. JOHNSON, 121, FLEET STREET.

1891.

PREFACE.

In sending forth this volume, the Editor desires to explain the method which he has followed. Space would not permit of the entire insertion of all the Addresses delivered during the Conference at Florence. They have, however, been but little abbreviated wherever the whole Address has been forwarded by the Author. In some instances, the original not being forwarded, the Editor has been reluctantly compelled to avail himself of the report inserted in the pages of the monthly organ of the Alliance, *Evangelical Christendom*. Where abridgement has been deemed necessary, care has been taken not to omit anything that would seem to affect the substance of the paper, or injure by its abbreviation the general character of it.

An Appendix has been added, in which interesting information is given with respect to the Addresses and their Authors, and the Resolutions of the International Committee of the Alliance, which held its sittings during the Conference, are published, together with other Memoranda.

R. A. REDFORD.

Putney, October 1st, 1891.

TABLE OF CONTENTS.

	PAGE
PREFACE	V.
INTRODUCTION	1
RECEPTION IN THE SALVINI THEATRE, VIA DE' NERI—	
Address of Welcome by the Rev. Dr. Geymonat... ...	13
Description of the Meeting by the Rev. W. Sandford ...	17
OPENING OF THE CONFERENCE, MONDAY, APRIL 6—	
Address by the President, the Hon. and Rev. E. V. Bligh...	20
THE RENAISSANCE AND THE REFORMATION—	
By the Rev. Philip Schaff, D.D., LL.D., of New York ...	24
RENAISSANCE AND REGENERATION—	
By Pastor Baumann, of Berlin	37
FLORENCE AND THE ITALIAN REFORMATION—	
By the Rev. John Stoughton, D.D., of London	40
RELIGIOUS THOUGHT IN ITALY—	
Addresses by Professor Dr. Mariano, of Naples	51
and the Rev. Professor Geymonat, D.D., of Florence	58 & 330
THE OBSTACLES TO REFORMATION IN ITALY—	
By Professor Comba, of Florence	60
THE OBSTACLES WHICH THE REFORMATION ENCOUNTERS IN SPAIN—	
Address by M. A. Martinez de Castilla, of Spain ...	66
PRESENT SALVATION—	
Addresses by Pastor Theo. Monod, of Paris ...	68
and Rev. Principal Culross, M.A., D.D., Bristol ...	71

SPREAD OF THE GOSPEL—

	PAGE
Address by Rev. W. Park, of Belfast	76
„ „ Pastor Edouard Monod, of Marseilles ...	78

THE BEST METHODS OF EVANGELIZATION—

Paper by the Rev. M. Bowen, of Constantinople... ... 82

EVANGELIZATION IN ITALY—

Address by Rev. Cav. Prochet, D.D., of Rome	95
„ „ Rev. D. Borgia, of Milan	99
„ „ Rev. T. W. S. Jones, of Naples	106
„ „ Rev. G. B. Taylor, D.D., of Rome	108
„ „ Rev. James Wall, of Rome	112
„ „ Rev. William Burt, D.D., of Rome	115
„ „ Signor Varnier, of Messina	118
„ „ Rev. Gordon Gray, D.D., of Rome	123
Count Campello's Catholic Reform Movement, by the Rev. Alexander Robertson	125

THE DIVINE AUTHORITY OF HOLY SCRIPTURE—

By the Rev. Professor R. A. Redford, M.A., LL.B., of London 131

THE WORD OF GOD THE SOURCE OF SPIRITUAL LIFE—

By the Venerable Archdeacon Richardson, M.A., D.D., London 145

THE POSITION OF THE BIBLE WITH REFERENCE TO SCIENCE—

By Principal Sir J. W. Dawson, K.C.M.G., F.R.S., of Montreal 149

CHRIST, THE FOUNDATION OF THE AUTHORITY OF SCRIPTURE—

Address by the Rev. Professor G. Godet, of Neuchatel ... 160

THE WALDENSIAN BIBLE IN GERMANY BEFORE LUTHER—

By Pastor Baumann, of Berlin 164

POVERTY AND RICHES FROM THE GOSPEL POINT OF VIEW—
    PAGE
    Addresses by the Rev. Dr. Stöcker, Court Preacher, of Berlin   169
    Pastor Babut, of Nismes 173
    the Rev. William Nicholas, M.A., D.D., of Dublin 176
    and the Rev. Dr. C. C. Tiffany, of New York ... 186

CHRISTIAN TESTIMONY IN PRESENCE OF THE WANTS OF THE DAY—
    By Pastor A. de Loes, of Lausanne 194

THE RELIGIOUS AND SOCIAL NECESSITY OF THE OBSERVANCE OF THE LORD'S DAY—
    Addresses by Pastor T. Ehni, of Geneva 198
    and M. E. Deluz, of Geneva... 201

ON THE OBSERVANCE OF THE LORD'S DAY—
    Addresses by M. W. Meille, of Turin 225
    Rev. A. F. Buscarlet, of Lausanne ... 226
    and Rev. Signor Sciarelli, of Naples 227

CHRISTIANITY, A FAITH FOR ALL NATIONS—
    By the Rev. Donald Fraser, M.A., D.D., of London ... 204

THE RELATION OF THE CHURCH TO MODERN SOCIETY—
    By the Rev. G. Stringer Rowe, of Leeds 213

A NEW DEPARTURE IN EVANGELICAL ALLIANCE WORK—
    By the Rev. F. Russell, of the United States 219

FOREIGN MISSIONS—
    Addresses by the Rev. J. Murray Mitchell, M.A., LL.D., of Nice 230
    and the Rev. Dean Vahl, of Copenhagen ... 233

EVANGELICAL CHURCH IN EGYPT—
    By the Rev. J. K. Giffen 237

INTERNATIONAL CHRISTIAN CO-OPERATION—
    By the Rev. Dr. G. D. Boardman, of Philadelphia ... 240

CONTENTS.

BIBLE SOCIETY'S WORK AND TRACT DISTRIBUTION IN ITALY—

	PAGE
By the Rev. Signor A. Meille	246
and Rev. O. Jalla	248

THE DUTY OF EVANGELICAL CHRISTIANS IN REGARD TO THE SLAVERY QUESTION—

By Professor Ruffet, of Geneva ... 249

OUR YOUNG MEN AND YOUNG WOMEN—

By the Rev. Professor Charteris, M.A., D.D., of Edinburgh... 254

YOUNG MEN'S CHRISTIAN ASSOCIATIONS IN SWITZERLAND—

By M. Tophel, Pastor at Geneva ... 260

SUNDAY SCHOOL WORK—

Addresses by Bishop Walden, D.D., of the United States ...	262
Mr. Thomas Edwards, of the Sunday School Union, London	265
and Rev. Edward Clarke, of Spezia	272

CHRISTIAN WORK AMONG SOLDIERS AND SAILORS—

By the Rev. Cav. Capellini, of Rome...	275
and Rev. Donald Miller, of Genoa...	280

HOW THE POWER OF FAITH IS PERFECTED IN LOVE—

By Professor Dr. Fabri, of Bonn ... 286

THE PRESENCE AND POWER OF THE HOLY SPIRIT IN CHRISTIAN LIFE—

Addresses by the Rev. H. W. Webb-Peploe, M.A., of London	290
and Professor Barth, of Berne	292

THE TRUE UNITY OF THE CHRISTIAN CHURCH—

Addresses by the Rev. Dr. Gerth Van Wyk, of Holland ...	294
the Rev. Dr. L. T. Chamberlain, of Philadelphia	297
and L. Monod, Pastor of Lyons	303

CLOSING ADDRESS—

By the Rev. Cav. Prochet, D.D., of Rome ... 305

APPENDIX ... 311

difficulty, and so as to secure a very representative gathering of brethren from all parts of the Peninsula. Without disparaging any previous Conference, it may be said that there has never been held a more remarkable and influential series of meetings in connection with the Evangelical Alliance than those of which the following pages are the record.

Œcumenical, in the best sense of the word, the Conference certainly was, though it made no claim to be a Council. If all Churches were not represented, still the whole extent of Evangelical Christendom seemed to be brought into mutual touch and fellowship. Great Britain, France, Scandinavia, Germany, Switzerland, the Netherlands, Spain, the United States, Canada, Turkey, Greece, Egypt, Australia, and other lands, all were present through those who came together in the spirit of faith and love to declare publicly their common allegiance to the one Lord and Saviour, and to take counsel with one another for the glory of His Name. And while such a gathering from all parts of the world would be of great interest at any time, and in any place, it was especially influential in Italy at the present juncture. The changes which have been brought about in the relations between the Monarchy and Papacy, and the entirely new aspect of the Roman Catholic religion since the loss of the temporal power and the establishment of religious liberty, opened the opportunity for such a Conference to be held, and to draw a very considerable amount of public attention. But the effect produced upon the world in general was not the only result which it was hoped the meetings in Florence would bring about. The Evangelical Churches of Italy are at present but a feeble folk so far as numbers and appearance are concerned. They require to be aided by the sympathy and substantial help of brethren in other countries. And they would be likely in such gatherings to feel their own hearts lifted up with the inspiration of a common faith and love and brought into closer union with one another. "It was the confident hope of the Council," says the Rev. W. Sandford, Rector of Edlaston, in his paper on the Conference, "that if the very widely-dispersed Evangelical Christians of Italy could be brought face to face for even a few golden days of brotherly intercourse, and thus enabled to make personal acquaintance with each other as fellow servants in the 'household of faith,' they would go back to their several localities with increased power to promote the spiritual welfare of their common country. Such a result, even if no other should follow, seemed an adequate reward for the expenditure of time and toil and funds, which the preparation for a General Conference demands." Such a result has certainly been attained. Not less than one hundred and fifty Pastors and Evangelists from all parts of Italy joined in the meetings, and found in them such an opportunity of personal stimulus and fraternal fellowship as they never enjoyed before.

It is also well to point out that the subjects which came before the Conference were of the greatest interest, and the papers read and addresses delivered were frequently of special value, as the readers of this volume will be able to judge. *History* was well represented by such men as Drs. Schaff and Stoughton, Pastor Baumann of Berlin, Professors Comba of Florence and Mariano of Naples, and Dr. Geymonat, President of the Florence Branch of the Alliance. *The Spread of the Gospel and the best methods of Evangelization, The Authority of Holy Scripture, The Assaults of Modern Infidelity, The Circulation of the Bible, Christianity in its relation to great Social Questions, Home and Foreign Missions, Christian Faith and Christian Testimony;* not only were these subjects ably dealt with, but large assemblies of Italians were gathered to listen to earnest, practical addresses, and brethren of all nations united daily in most fervent prayer for the outpouring of the Holy Spirit. How is it possible to doubt that blessed results must follow from such meetings? We may think their influence is merely temporary and limited, but "God's thoughts are not as our thoughts" upon such matters. We cannot know what impetus has been given to the spread of evangelical truth in Italy. The fact that a magnificent theatre was filled to overflowing night after night with townspeople of the Roman Catholic city of Florence to listen to Gospel addresses, and that the same scene was witnessed for many weeks after the Conference was concluded and will probably be witnessed again shortly, surely speaks volumes. Earnest evangelical preaching has been carried on for a considerable time under the superintendence of the Florence Committee, but it may be well believed that such meetings as were held in April will do much to awaken the minds of the people and prepare them for the more continuous labours of Evangelists. The accounts received since the Conference was held of the eager and widespread interest in the services continued in the Salvini theatre are full of encouragement and may be regarded as a token of the blessing of God upon the work of the Alliance.

There was one incident at the commencement of the meetings which has had no little effect in drawing the attention of the world to them. In a Roman Catholic country it was not to be expected that any member of the Royal family should be present at any of the meetings. In Copenhagen not only did the King of Denmark express interest in the Conference which was being held in his country, but he and his family were present, and attentive listeners to the proceedings. This could not be the case in Italy. But it was well known that Cav. Prochet of Rome had had a very interesting interview with King Umberto, in which his Majesty had inquired fully into the nature and objects of the Conference, and expressed his good wishes for it. Indeed he had gone so far as to regret that it was not to be held in Rome itself. This, however, he saw to be undesirable, when it was explained by Cav. Prochet that it might cause unnecessary excitement and offence at the Vatican. His Majesty observed that such consideration for the feelings of others was much to be commended, but would not have been extended to the Protestants by the Papal party. Knowing the kindly feeling of the liberal monarch, it was a very suitable recognition of the peaceful and propitious atmosphere in which the Conference opened its meetings when Lord Kinnaird, representing the British Branch of the Alliance, proposed that a telegram containing the respectful salutations of the Conference should be forwarded to the King of Italy—a proposition which was at once and enthusiastically accepted. The telegram was worded as follows:—

"The Evangelical Alliance assembled from twenty different countries in its Ninth International Conference, and for the first time in Italy, sends respectful salutations to his Majesty King Umberto. The members of the Alliance praise God for the civil and religious liberty now enjoyed throughout this fair land, remembering that forty years ago they were pleading the cause of persecuted Christians in this city of Florence. They pray for peace and prosperity; for

Heaven's richest blessings to rest upon the Italian people and their beloved Sovereign."

This telegram when it was received by the King was handed over to a high official to draw out a reply for his approval. It was laid upon his table, but when he read it he tore it up as not cordial enough to please him, and with the help of his secretary drew out the following:—

"His Majesty the King has received, with great satisfaction, the wishes and homage of the representatives of a religion which is professed by a Piedmontese region, so dear to his soul and so loyal and true to his House. He thanks especially the foreigners gathered in Florence for the prayers they lift up to God for Italy, and is hoping that, on returning to their homes, they may take back feelings of sympathy for this country."

This interchange of kindly sentiment between the Conference and the Throne gave a delightful tone of pleasant confidence to all the meetings. It was felt that such a commencement assured the success of the Conference, and would procure for it a large amount of popularity. It would draw public attention to it both in Italy and in all other parts of the world, and it augured well for the cause of Evangelical Truth and Freedom on the Continent.

Before concluding this introduction it may be useful to place before the reader what have been some of the impressions of those who attended the Conference so far as they can be gathered from the testimonies of Christian brethren. First and foremost should be placed the conviction which is deepened by such a Conference, that whatever may be the differences which separate Evangelical Christians from one another in ecclesiastical forms and denominational distinctions, there is an ever-increasing desire to subordinate all other considerations to that which is supreme in the heart of every sincere Christian, faithfulness to the Lord Jesus Christ. In almost every address, and in some with very special emphasis, this was set forth as the uppermost feeling of our times. We must not suffer anything to hide from us the great fact that what the nations want is not our systems of theology, our forms of Church government, our rites and ceremonies, but the Spirit of Christ. The Gospel is Christ. It was delightful to hear the representatives of Italy proclaiming this supremacy of the Saviour in a country where a corrupt ecclesiasticism has done so much to rob Him of His glory, and hide His free grace from the people by exalting the power of the priesthood. "It is impossible," said one of the Italian deputies, who was once himself a Roman Catholic priest, but is now a devoted Evangelical preacher, "it is impossible to foretell what shape the Church of the future will take in this land; it is in vain to expect that Protestantism as Protestantism will obtain a hearing, but we may be sure that nothing will satisfy Italy but a gospel which preaches Christ as its essence." Professor Mariano, of Naples, dealt very ably with this subject—"We must not think," he said, "that the Papacy is soon to disappear, but it can never give redemption and holiness to the people. Nothing can do that but the grace of God by faith in Christ and in His Gospel. The Evangelicals alone have rightly understood the religious problem of Italy, and have set themselves to solve it." There are many elements of good mixed up with the corruptions of the Roman Catholic Church. No one can visit Italy without being impressed with the wonderful possibilities of the future, which lie there still shut up in the bondage of superstition; but that bondage can be broken, and the free spirit of faith called forth to a new religious life. As Dr. Schaff observed in his noble paper on Renaissance and Reformation, "God has great surprises in store for us," and one of those surprises may be the rapid spread of evangelical truth in the place of the dead formalism and heartless infidelity which at present hold the masses of Italy in the deep sleep of indifference.

Another prominent impression left by the Conference was the very decided growth of the spirit of charity and brotherly love, and its fervent expression in all assemblies of Christians. No doubt, at all such meetings of evangelical believers sentiments of brotherhood prevail, but there is an unmistakeable increase of warmth in such expressions. Whenever they were introduced into the Addresses at Florence there was a thrill of response through the audience which was very striking. The people seem to be longing to be lifted above their own prejudices into a higher atmosphere of spiritual fellowship. Unity in Christ is uppermost in their thoughts. They are ashamed of the divisions and dissensions which have disgraced the Christian

Church for so many centuries. They are feeling keenly the reproaches of unbelievers. They are longing to be able to manifest to the world that whatever appearances there may be, all those who love the Lord Jesus Christ in sincerity are one in Him. This realization of unity was very specially seen when the daily meetings for prayer bowed all heads before the One Throne of Grace. It was very delightful and very impressive to listen to the voice of the Spirit, as on the Day of Pentecost, uttering the various languages of men before Him to Whom they were all the same speech of the heart. The out-pouring of the spirit of prayer upon the churches will settle many a problem and overcome many a difficulty. The heat of Divine Love will melt down the Alps of division. We shall know and feel that we are "one body in Christ" when one Spirit pervades all our assemblies and absorbs all differences in a common devotion.

Reference has already been made to the state of the Protestant Churches in Italy. Professor Mariano spoke out very plainly mourning the want of union among the different evangelical denominations. The Council of the Evangelical Alliance wrought a good work when they set themselves to overcome, which they did most successfully, the obstacles which appeared in the way of hearty co-operation. There were many forebodings before the Conference which might have cast a cloud over it, but courageous faith and simple dependence on the Divine promise of spiritual guidance and blessing put such forebodings to shame. The brethren who came to the meetings wondering whether they would be drawn nearer to their fellow believers, or driven farther apart from them, went home with but one feeling in their hearts—that of devout thankfulness to God for a most inspiring and uplifting season of joyful brotherly intercourse. The atmosphere was not favourable to the germs of division. They were largely destroyed, and a healthier spirit, we may confidently hope, will prevail among the Protestant Churches of Italy.

And what, we may ask, is the outlook, the prospect of Evangelical truth on the Continent generally? Is it more favourable than it was when the Conference of the Alliance was held in 1884 at Copenhagen? No doubt when we endeavour to forecast the future we are very apt to think as our hearts prompt us. At the same time, it is better to be optimists than to be pessimists. The promises of the Gospel encourage us to search out the signs of hope, and not to dwell on the dark side. The progress of the world is not by the path of smooth things, but by the rough road of contradiction and conflict. The good overcomes the evil. The evil is destroyed by the manifestation of the good, which can only be by the positive and energetic development of holy principles in opposition to the falsehood and corruption of the world. Moreover, we were powerfully reminded in the city of Florence that the making of the soil in which Gospel Truth has to grow is not the work of God's people, but very largely of the forces which are arrayed against one another in the world. It was the fearful collision of 1870, the awful desolating conflict between two great nations which brought about the political and ecclesiastical changes in Italy twenty years ago. Those changes have made the new soil into which the seed of the Gospel is now being cast far and wide throughout the Peninsula. How can we doubt that all such changes are preparing the way for the greater triumphs of the Truth? The testimony of many brethren from different countries was to the wonderful openings now given to the people of God for preaching and spreading the knowledge of the Scriptures. There are crowded congregations listening to the Gospel in many of the towns of Italy, and the Rev. Dr. Kalopothakes of Athens spoke of the circulation of the Scriptures, in Greece, and of religious tracts and pamphlets, as most encouraging. There are many signs of revival among the Protestant Churches of Scandinavia. Rationalism is losing ground among the clergy, and Sunday Schools are rapidly developing something like a new life among the people. There are portions of the Continent, no doubt, where little encouragement is at present to be found; where a corrupt Church or a dead Protestantism still keeps the people in a state of spiritual slumber; but when evangelical Christians meet together from all parts of the world as they did at Florence, their feeling is not one of despondency but rather of glowing hope. Never let us forget that man is not alone in this warfare. The Lord of all power and might is working with His people. "Who hath despised the day of small things?" Why should we despair because there is a great display of worldly power and wealth on the side of those who hate the Gospel? What are these "great mountains" before the Lord of the whole earth? How easily He can shake them to dust as He did in the United States, when the time came for the destruction of slavery, as He did in Italy and France, when He had determined to bring to an end the temporal power of the Papacy. "The Lord of Hosts is with us, the God of Jacob is our Refuge."

> "Now, Christians, hold your own—the land before you
> Is open—win your way, and take your rest."

PART I.

ADDRESSES DELIVERED AT THE CONFERENCE.

SATURDAY, APRIL 4, 1891.

Reception in the Salvini Theatre.

THE following Address of Welcome was delivered by the Rev. Dr. PAOLO GEYMONAT, who presided:—

HONOURED AND DEAR BRETHREN—

It is an event, a benediction, a *festa* for the Evangelical of Italy, this solemn reunion of distinguished co-religionists from every land, from Greece, Turkey, Egypt, India, Australia, Austria, Germany, Russia, Belgium, Switzerland, France, Spain, Britain, North America and Canada.

Οἱ ἀπὸ τῆς Ἰταλίας ἀσπάζονται ὑμᾶς—*Those of Italy salute you*—and heartily bid you all welcome.

Languages distinguish us, but they do not divide us; rather they unite us, forming special groups. Permit us to place together the delegates of countries where the same language is spoken, and to address to each group a few words:

Honoured and dear *Brethren of the French tongue*, in you we salute, on the one hand, the descendants of the heroes of the Reformation, who with unheard-of constancy have fought and suffered for the cause of the Gospel; and, on the other hand, the sons of generous Switzerland, refuge of the persecuted and bulwark of liberty, who received with equal affection the emigrants of France and of Italy.

The Reformation did not become national in France, but its

effect has been universal. It founded the rights of man with respect to his fellow-man and to the State on the Sovereignty of God.

That principle, still worthily represented by you, is essential to Protestantism, and necessary to the Alliance. In the rainbow of various tints harmoniously blended, which the Alliance forms as a sign of peace, the brilliant French colours should not be lacking. The presence of a goodly number of brethren from France and Switzerland was desired, and your attendance is a good omen for our meeting.

Honoured and dear *Brethren of Holland*, which was also, and in fact pre-eminently, a refuge of the Reformation, with whom could we group you? In everything you are yourselves, only yourselves. Therefore we specially salute you. The absolute tenacity of the ancient faith is still seen in your Protestantism, while at the same time we behold the extreme daring of modern thought. You bring to the Alliance the benefit of two extremes, namely, constancy of faith and freedom of thought, both so dear to us all, and so needful for the times.

Honoured and dear *Brethren of the German tongue*, one of the richest of languages, in which the Gospel resounds with such force, and yet with such sweetness, in consequence of the Reformation of your Luther, who by the power of his speech was a true king without a crown, you form a vast group comprehending in language and doctrine brethren of various countries to the South, to the North, and to the West of Germany.

Your thought is as rich and complex as your language, and your immense periods. In your books and your Universities we all drink at the fountain of your profound knowledge.

Religion among you blossoms and abounds not less in erudite theology than in poetry and music, which proceed from the heart, and rise sublime.

Your good part, which shall not be taken from you, consists in heart, in sentiment, *im Gemüthe*, and it is this that brings a blessing and is your most precious gift to our Alliance.

Honoured and dear *Brethren of the English language*, you come from all parts of the world; your group comprises the Globe, now made small by your active enterprise. You cover the earth with

Bibles, translated and printed in all languages, and sow the seed of the Kingdom of God among all nations.

You have multiplied denominations, pushed individualism to extremes, and shown a divided Protestantism; yet, on the other hand, you seek after and manifest unity through the Evangelical Alliance, of which you are the strenuous and constant promoters. *Unity through liberty*, this is God's way, and it is also the way of the Alliance, of which you are the advance guard.

And those of us who are but *small minorities* in the midst of catholics, both Roman and Greek, and likewise in the midst of Turks and heathen, brethren of Italy and Spain, of Belgium, of Greece, of Turkey, and of other countries, we are all borne in the arms of the Alliance; we too are welcomed here, so much so that on this occasion we the last have become the first.

Honoured and dear Brethren, we have not yet in Florence a temple large enough to enable us to receive you in a consecrated place. Not unfrequently a temple is transformed into a theatre; for a few days let us prove that a theatre may become a temple. Let us begin by reading from the Word of God, the first five verses of Matt. xvii. :—

> "And after six days Jesus taketh Peter, James, and John his brother, and bringeth them up into an high mountain apart.
>
> And He was transfigured before them; and His face did shine as the sun, and His raiment was white as the light.
>
> And behold, there appeared unto them Moses and Elias talking with Him.
>
> Then answered Peter, and said unto Jesus: Lord, it is good for us to be here; if Thou wilt, let us make here three tabernacles: one for Thee, and one for Moses, and one for Elias.
>
> While he yet spake, behold, a bright cloud overshadowed them, and behold a voice out of the cloud, which said: This is My Beloved Son, in Whom I am well pleased; hear ye Him."

Our earnest desire and prayer, beloved brethren, is that by the presence of the Lord, by the Spirit of grace, by the joy of fraternal communion, you may feel that it is indeed good to be here, that you would even pitch your tents and abide with us, that no one will regret having come.

Is there less of blessing here than upon the Mount, whence the disciples were loth to descend? Nay, there is even more and better. Lifted up on high infinitely above all, behold the Master, our Lord Jesus Christ, in His present glory, His eternal glory, of which that which shone forth on the Mount was but a symbol, a momentary sign.

On the right, and on the left, behold Moses and Elijah, the Law and the Prophets, which testify of Him, and remind us of the golden Rule, to do unto others as we would that they should do unto us. Below, the disciples looking up humble, attentive, ecstatic, represent the attitude that becomes us in the presence of our Lord and of His Holy Word.

The souls of the three disciples exulted at the sight of the glorious spectacle. Here we are hundreds of disciples, representatives of thousands and millions, who, from all parts of the world, look up with us to Jesus Christ. Joyful day! Glorious spectacle! Should not our souls rejoice?

In the Transfiguration beheld by the first disciples, we see the ideal, into which the sad reality ought to be transformed, into which it has already in part been transformed; the ideal which is gradually being realized by the fulfilment of the Law and the Prophets, by the Gospel of Christ, Who with righteousness as white as the light clothes every soul that calls upon Him.

The Evangelical Alliance in its solemn assemblies represents that ideal, and by its labours is seeking for its realization.

The Alliance has principles which it must maintain, and ends which it must strive to attain. But these principles of Evangelical Protestantism, and these only, are universal, truly Catholic, common to Christianity, which holds the Lord Jesus Christ as the only Master, Mediator and Saviour; and these ends are all included in the universal application of that supreme precept of the Law and the Prophets, which suffices to establish and maintain the best relations between man and man, between family and family, between Church and Church, between nation and nation: "Whatsoever ye would that men should do unto you, do you even so unto them, for this is the Law and the Prophets."

Protestantism, founded upon the Holy Scriptures, rule of faith and life, has various forms, among which each one may find freedom and a suitable sphere of action, and it has no need to be transformed or reformed; it needs only to be transfigured, so that the glory of Christ may shine through all these various forms in justice, truth and holiness. Thus unity is manifested in diversity. Thus the ideal is realized. Thus the Kingdom of Heaven is advanced on earth.

May these re-unions strengthen our ties, leave among us blessed traces, and give fresh power to the Gospel everywhere, among all the churches, and in all lands.

Is it really in Italy, in Florence, only a few steps from Savonarola's wood-pile and the Bargello, that we are assembled for this work of liberty and faith? Is it really in Florence, where the Madiai for the sake of the Gospel in August of the year 1851 were arrested, and in June of 1852 condemned for years to the galleys, where an honoured deputation of the Evangelical Alliance came to implore from the Grand Duke their liberation, and could not obtain an official hearing, is it on this very spot that we open this free Conference of Evangelicals of all nations? Scarcely can we believe our eyes. Never did Italy in the times of her republics, never did this classic land, never did Florence, the most liberal and the most cultured city of Italy, ever enjoy religious liberty, the highest and the holiest form of liberty, until the entire nation rallied round the house of Savoy, which with firm hands holds the sceptre of justice.

Hence we could not inaugurate the present Congress, which to the eyes of all is a great event in the cause of liberty, and to *our* eyes greater still for the Gospel, without heartily exclaiming: BLESSINGS FOR EVER REST UPON THE HOUSE OF SAVOY AS IT NOW REIGNS AT ROME!!

"This admirable Address," says the Rev. W. SANDFORD, in his paper on the Conference, which appeared in the May number of *Evangelical Christendom*, "delivered with exceeding gracefulness, from time to time evoked hearty applause as the successive points of it caught the notice of the deeply-attentive audience. It had been previously suggested that, at its close, a telegram should be forwarded to the King of Italy, respectfully saluting him, expressing thanks to God for the liberty now enjoyed in Italy; also the best wishes of the Conference for the welfare of the King and the Royal Family. Any individual of the large assemblage of distinguished men of various nationalities might well have valued the privilege of proposing the sending of this telegram. It was, however, to Lord Kinnaird, who responded to the Welcome in the name of the British Organization, that the privilege fell, and in appropriate and hearty terms he accomplished his pleasant task. A few words of like character from Bishop Walden, one of the American delegates, followed, and then the resolution was carried by the whole assembly rising.

Then followed the acknowledgments, by various national representatives, of the touching and gratifying allusions to their several countries in the President's Address. As these spoke in their own native languages, with one or two exceptions, the audience could not fail to mark with interest the earnestness and gracefulness of these responses to an Address of Welcome which had touched all present. An event which occurred later raised the enthusiasm of the already enthusiastic meeting to a yet higher and, it may be added, a yet holier point. This was the arrival of a message from far distant China, informing the assembly how earnestly the Christians there had been for some time praying, and would continue to pray, for a great blessing on this deeply interesting and important Conference. Such a message could not but strengthen the confidence of the older members of the Alliance in the prospect of seeing large and golden fruits in due time from the present Conference. And it was under such impressions that this very happy preliminary meeting came to a close. Sunday morning witnessed a short English-speaking prayer meeting in the Scotch Church, which proved from beginning to end a fitting continuation of the prayerful frame in which the Saturday evening meeting closed. The brief address by Lord Radstock gave the right tone to the meeting, and the simple prayers which in quick succession followed, showed that the Spirit of adoption prompted them, and that those who offered them had a hold upon the 'exceeding great and precious promises.'

The next incident which calls for mention was somewhat remarkable. Circumstances, into which it is needless to enter, opened the pulpit of Trinity Church to the Rev. H. W. Webb-Peploe. And it came to pass that in a place where high-churchism has a home, many evangelical Christians had the privilege of hearing a powerful scriptural sermon, which, without containing aught to give offence, showed that nothing short of a man's finding out his own absolute need of a divine release from guilt and sin, and his learning to come himself to Christ as the Giver of this, can avail to save him from everlasting ruin. Mr. Peploe's thesis was that death is the way to life in the Christian's case just as Christ's death and resurrection were linked together when He performed His part as our Redeemer. It is hard to say which most distinguished the address—the logical power which pervaded it, or the deep affectionateness of its appeals to the heart and conscience."

MONDAY, APRIL 6, 1891.

THE HON. AND REV. E. V. BLIGH PRESIDED.

ADDRESS BY THE CHAIRMAN.

DEAR CHRISTIAN FRIENDS, AND MEMBERS OF THE EVANGELICAL ALLIANCE—

Owing to the absence of Count Bernstorff from circumstances beyond his control at Berlin, I find myself in the honoured position of presiding over the proceedings of the first Session of this International Conference of the Evangelical Alliance, held at Florence, in the Year of our Lord, 1891. I could have wished, indeed, that Count Bernstorff could have filled the position for which he was first, and most fitly, indicated. He is well known to most present as an able and distinguished member of the Alliance; but I have had the good fortune to be associated with him more particularly during the two Conferences of the International Committee held at Geneva in 1886, and at Berlin in 1888; and it gives me a peculiar pleasure, therefore, to have an opportunity of testifying to the loving spirit, and temper, and tact, which this dear Christian brother has continuously brought to bear upon the discussions of that Committee, and to which spirit indeed any success which has been obtained by it, has been, I venture to say, in a large measure due. I heartily regret Count Bernstorff's enforced absence, and I feel I may say, "So do we *all*," and we wish him heartily "God-speed."

But being where I am by stress of circumstances, I may, perhaps, find an apology in certain facts which should considerably counterbalance the diffidence which I, a foreigner, must naturally experience in presiding over the deliberations of so distinguished an assembly in an Italian city. It so happened that my first experience of Florence was, as an Attaché to the British Legation to the Grand Duke of Tuscany, in that memorable year, 1851, when Francesco and Rosa Madiai were imprisoned in the Bargello of this city. I was not immediately concerned with them; but I was so with an English gentleman (now a physician in Londy) who was detected in the act—Hear it! ye Evangelical and Protestant Christians assembled at Florence in 1891—"*en flagrant délit*"—I remember the expression—of reading the Holy Scriptures; hardly even that, for if my memory serves me rightly, this English gentleman was found lying on a sofa with a favourite Bible in his pocket, doing nothing at the moment, but merely awaiting the arrival of the Madiai (in their house, I think) to commence a Bible reading. The gendarmes were, in fact, a little too soon, and in rather too great a hurry. The Englishman was, however, searched and seized by them, and with the undeniable evidence of the Bible found upon him, he was marched off like a felon through the streets of this city of Florence, and imprisoned in the common gaol. I went to see him there the next day in the exercise of my official duty, and owing to the strenuous exertions of her Britannic Majesty's Legation this gentleman was released some twenty-four hours afterwards. The Madiai were not so fortunate, and lingered in imprisonment several months before the then misguided rulers of this country bent before the growing force of public opinion, which was aided not a little (we are thankful to be able now to say) by the prayers and efforts of the friends and founders of this great Evangelical Alliance. "One sows, another reaps!" After forty years' interval, "their works do follow them!" These noble pioneers of Christian love and union who founded the Alliance have now their reward. A marvellous change indeed! Then, a hostile ruler; a foreign domination, a dark intolerance. Now, a benevolent and beneficent king: Italy free, and a great Power of Europe; Religious Liberty supreme! I have thought I might be pardoned for dwelling thus briefly upon so remarkable a contrast—1851 and 1891! May I refer for one moment to the year 1877, which was the occasion of my next visit to this beautiful city in conjunction with my friends, the Rev. William Arthur—a name illustrious and beloved among the Wesleyans—and the Rev. Dr. Donald Fraser, a much honoured leader among the Presbyterians. As a miniature representation of the working of the Evangelical Alliance, we three—*quasi* three "reconciled irreconcileables" of Church, Kirk, and Chapel—had then the high honour of being entrusted with a fraternal mission to our dear Italian friends and brethren, who were then struggling manfully out of the toils and difficulties of the former dark period. If our visit, perhaps, savoured somewhat of the loving presumption of an elder sister, and if some of the fair daughters of your native Protestantism in Italy might have been inclined to question its expediency or its utility, we at least were free to admit that we found much to rejoice our own souls in what we saw, and that we learned a great deal which we could ill afford to lose. If we were "physicians" of an at all doubtful character, we at least "healed ourselves!" We went back to our own country fully persuaded that it was fully likely that in some ten or a dozen years Italy would be able to teach us another noble lesson. Fourteen years have not yet elapsed, and what do we see? What do we know? What may we not expect?

We have seen you in Italy gradually growing into the fuller appreciation of brotherly love and unity. We have watched your development—both particular and general—as component parts, and as a whole body. Our souls yearned with yours when leaders of the Waldensians held out the hand to the Chiesa Libera, when the revered and patriarchal Gavazzi threw even all his energy into schemes for closer union with the heroic Church of the Valleys.

Speaking now as an Englishman, and bearing in mind our own unhappy divisions—those sectional differences which have grown out of the very plethora of our religious liberty—I unaffectedly declare that we are quite ready to be taught by you. You, Italians, are now holding out the right hand of fellowship in a way which cannot be mistaken. It was no slight thing—we know well—to attempt to hold this Conference. We know the modesty and diffidence with which you continually regarded the possibility of assembling, even on your own classic ground, the various representatives of European and American Christendom. We trust you will be amply rewarded for the efforts which you have made, upon which the crown of success seems to be already settling.

Speaking now in the name of the whole Evangelical Alliance and for all countries, I should ill-discharge my pleasant duty as the president on this occasion, if I did not congratulate you upon having added Florence to that distinguished roll of names—London, Paris, Berlin, Geneva, New York, Amsterdam, Basle, Copenhagen—cities which have already received high rank—I may say true Christian nobility—as centres for our great International Conferences. May it please God that all who have taken part in previous Conferences shall more than ever realize, in our present sessions, that spiritual unity of heart and soul in Jesus Christ our Lord which is the *raison d'être* of the Evangelical Alliance, and which is expressed in its motto: *Unum corpus sumus in Christo!* May all our friends—the faithful ministers and labourers in the Gospel, and particularly those who have assembled here from the various parts of Italy—be enabled to take back with them into the midst of their seclusion, or of their bustle, as the case may be, into the busy town or into the isolated village, agreeable and profitable reminiscences of what they have seen and heard, and experienced here! May the result be a mighty awakening of the dry bones which have slumbered through centuries of darkness and superstition in Italy. May each pastor and each labourer, as he moves in his several orbit, spread light and radiance among his flock and people when he returns home again! reflecting the brightness of love and union and that care for our perishing brothers' souls, which we trust exists among ourselves, and will characterize this International Conference; reflecting, however humbly, some of the rays of the Sun of Righteousness Himself—even thus may we each and every one of us receive a blessing!

The Renaissance and the Reformation.

BY THE REV. PHILIP SCHAFF, D.D., LL.D., NEW YORK,

Honorary Foreign Secretary of the Evangelical Alliance for the United States of America.

RENAISSANCE and Reformation are significant words for two kindred, yet distinct movements of history: the one closes the Middle Ages, the other opens the Modern Age. Both are not simply past events, but living forces which control our civilization, and have not yet finished their mission. Renaissance, Reformation, Re-action, Revolution, Re-construction are the links in the chain of modern history.

The Renaissance was a revival of classical culture; the Reformation, a revival of primitive Christianity. The former was an intellectual and æsthetic movement; the latter, a moral and religious movement. The Renaissance drew its inspiration from the poets and philosophers of ancient Greece and Rome; the Reformation, from the Apostles and Evangelists. The Renaissance aimed at the development of the natural man; the Reformation, at the renewal of the spiritual man. The Renaissance looked down upon earth, the Reformation looked up to heaven. The Renaissance is the work of Italy, the Reformation is the work of Germany and Switzerland. The Renaissance prepared the way for the Reformation, and furnished the necessary intellectual equipment for it. Erasmus and Reuchlin, Melanchthon and Zwingli are the connecting links of the two movements. Without the Renaissance there could have been no Reformation, and the Renaissance is incomplete without a Reformation. For man is a unit, and his intellectual culture and moral character must be developed and perfected in harmony.

I.—THE RENAISSANCE.

The Renaissance was born in Florence, the City of Flowers and the Flower of Cities, "the brightest star in star-bright Italy." From Florence it passed to Rome, and from Rome it spread all over Italy and beyond the Alps. Cosimo de Medici and Lorenzo the Magnificent were the chief among the Mæcenases of literature and art. Pope Nicolas V. and several of his successors down to Leo X. followed their example. Florence gave birth to a brilliant galaxy of poets, statesmen, historians, scientists, architects, sculptors and painters, and yields to no city in the world, except Rome, in wealth of historic reminiscences and treasures of art.

The Renaissance began with Dante, the greatest son of Florence, and the greatest Italian poet. His power extends over the civilized world, and is growing with the advancing years. A poor exile, he could not eat his own bread, nor ascend or descend his own stairs; but how large is the number of those whom he has fed and taught to descend the steps of his *Inferno,* and to ascend the mountain of his *Purgatorio!* His *Divina Commedia,* conceived in the year 1300— noted for the first papal jubilee—is a mirror of the moral universe viewed from the standpoint of eternity, a cathedral of immortal spirits, a glorification of the Christian religion, and a judgment on the corruptions of the secularized Church and papacy of his age. It is at once autobiographical, national, and cosmopolitan, a song of the Middle Ages, and of all ages, a spiritual biography of man as a sinner, a penitent, and a saint. It is a pilgrimage of the soul from the dark forest of temptation, through the depths of despair, up the terraces of purification, to the realms of bliss, under the guidance of natural reason (Virgil) and divine revelation (Beatrice). Dante was and still is a prophet rebuking tyranny and injustice, avarice and pride in high and low places of Church and State, without fear or favour, and pointing to the eternal issues of man's actions. He stands on the transition between the Middle Ages and Modern times. He broke the monopoly of the clergy for learning, and of Latin as the organ of scholarship. He proved that a layman may be a philosopher and theologian, as well as a statesman and poet, and that the *lingua toscana* may give expression to the deepest thoughts and emotions, as well as the language of Virgil and Cicero. He proved that one may be a good Catholic Christian, and yet call for a thorough Reformation. If he had lived in the fifteenth century, he would have sympathized with Savonarola; in the sixteenth he would have gone half way with Luther and Calvin; in the nineteenth he would advocate the unity of Italy and the separation of religion and politics, of Church and State, on the basis of equal freedom and independence for both in their different spheres. Such is the power and bearing of his

> " Sacred poem
> To which both heaven and earth have set their hands."

Petrarca and Boccaccio are far below Dante for depth of genius and extent of influence, but they share with him the honour of being the fathers of Italian literature and promoters of liberal learning. Petrarca, "the poet of love," was also an enthusiast for classical literature, and the pioneer of humanism in the technical sense of the term. He spared no pains and money for the recovery of old manuscripts from the dust of convents. He was the first collector of private libraries of classical authors, and studied them as a means for intellectual and æsthetical culture. Cicero and St. Augustine were his patron saints.

His friend Boccaccio followed his example in the search for manuscripts, though he is better known as the master of Italian prose, the author of the *Decamerone* and the first biographer and commentator of Dante.

In the fifteenth century, the enthusiasm for classical literature and humanistic culture spread with irresistible force through all the cities of Italy, and even crossed the Alps as far north as Poland, and as far west as England and Scotland. The discovery of the classics was the revelation of a long-forgotten civilization, and created as much sensation in the fifteenth century as the discovery of the hieroglyphics and cuneiform inscriptions and the excavations of Troy and Mycenæ in our age. Italian scholars travelled to Greece and Constantinople in search of Greek manuscripts, and translated them into Latin. Greek scholars who left their native land before and after the fall of Constantinople, brought with them the literary treasures of the East.

The discovery and reproduction of classical literature was followed by the discovery and reproduction of classical art, which revealed the beauty of the human body, as the former had revealed the strength of the human mind. At the end of the fifteenth, and the beginning of the sixteenth century, the masterpieces of Greek sculpture, such as the Laocoon group, the Apollo of the Belvidere, the torso of Hercules, were dug from the ruins of palaces and villas of old Rome, and kindled an enthusiasm for similar achievements.

What do we owe to the Renaissance of letters and arts? What is its permanent contribution to the civilization and happiness of mankind? The Renaissance raised Greece and Rome from the dead, recovered and collected the ancient classics, created a taste for the humanities, for literary and artistic culture, produced the national literature of Italy, and the greatest works of art, adorned churches, and filled museums and picture galleries, which will attract admiring visitors from every land to the end of time. The Renaissance destroyed the clerical monopoly of learning, and made it accessible to the laity; it emancipated the mind from the bondage of tradition, and introduced the era of intellectual freedom. It substituted for the monastic seclusion from the world, the social duty of transforming the world and the institutions which God has founded. It taught the value of man as man; and showed the finger of God in reason, in nature, and art. Humanism made the literature of Greece and Rome repeat the preparatory service which they had accomplished at the first introduction of Christianity by furnishing the language and the framework for its divine contents.

But man is a moral and spiritual as well as an intellectual and æsthetic being. And here we must not be blind to the defects of the Renaissance. Some of the first humanists and artists of Italy were sincere and devout Christians. But many of them were indifferent or secretly hostile to religion, while outwardly conforming to its ritual. Not a few were pagans at heart, and disciples of Zeno and Epicurus rather than of Peter and Paul. They substituted the worship of beauty for the worship of holiness. The revival of pagan art was to a large extent also the revival of pagan immorality. Savonarola, undazzled by the splendour of Lorenzo's reign, preached with prophetic zeal from the pulpit of San Marco the necessity of a moral reformation, but was publicly burned on the Piazza della Signoria.

The corruption centered at the metropolis of Christendom, and culminated in the highest dignitaries of the Church. Alexander Borgia practiced vice as an art, and turned the Vatican into a den of prostitution and murder. Julius II. was a warrior rather than a Churchman. Leo X. delighted in the chase and in comedies more than in the duties of his high office, and although his saying about "the profitable fable of Christ" is probably a myth, it characterizes the sceptical atmosphere of the Vatican at that time.

When Erasmus, as the literary monarch of his age, visited Rome in 1506, he was charmed with her culture and refinement, her freedom of discourse, the honeyed conversation of her scholars, and the magnificence of her arts, but at the same time shocked by "the abominable blasphemies," uttered by priestly lips at the papal court. And when Luther, four years later, went to Rome as an humble monk and pilgrim, he visited the tombs of the apostles and martyrs, and climbed up the Scala Santa on his knees, but was horrified by the sight of the prevailing worldliness, frivolity, and ill-disguised infidelity of priests who hurried through the mass, and were heard to say over the consecrated elements: "*Panis es, panis manebis; vinum es, vinum manebis.*" Machiavelli, the great statesman and historian of Florence, asserts from his own observation that "in proportion as we approach nearer the Roman Church, we find less piety," and that, "owing to the bad example of the papal court, Italy has lost all piety and religion, whence follow infinite troubles and disorders." Guicciardini, another distinguished historian of Florence, who was secretary and viceregent of the Medicean popes, makes in his "Aphorisms" (1529) the startling confession: "My position at the court of several popes has compelled me to desire their aggrandizement for the sake of my own profit. Otherwise I would have loved Martin Luther myself— not that I might break loose from the laws which Christianity, as it is usually understood and explained, lays upon us, but that I might see that horde of villains *(questa caterva di scellerati)* reduced within due limits, and forced to live either without vices or without power." We have even the contemporary testimony of a pope, Adrian VI., a Dutchman, who was elected after Leo X. as a reforming pope, but reigned less than two years (from Jan. 9th, 1522, to Sept. 14th, 1523). He admitted through his legate, Francesco Chieregati, at the Diet of Nürnberg, March, 1522, "that for some time many abominations, abuses, and violation of rights, have taken place in the Holy See; and that all things have been perverted into bad. From the head the corruption has passed to the limbs, from the pope to the prelates; we have all gone astray, there is none that doeth good, no, not one." The Council of Trent, so loudly called for, and so long delayed by the policy of the curia, was confessedly convened for the reformation of morals as well as for the settlement of dogmas.

Who can doubt, in view of these contemporary testimonies of the most competent observers and judges, the necessity of a Reformation?

II.—The Reformation.

The Reformation began during the pontificate of the last pope of the Renaissance, who was a cultivated pagan, and fairly represented the secularization of the Church, which from a kingdom of Heaven had become a kingdom of this world. It was at first an indignant protest against the sale of indulgences, which degraded religion to an article of merchandise; as had been done by the profane traffickers in the temple at Jerusalem, whom the Saviour expelled at the beginning of His public ministry. Leo X. condemned Luther, and the monk answered by burning the pope's bull. This was the fiery signal of separation. Since that time Western Christendom has been divided into two hostile armies.

The Reformation was neither a revolution which destroys but cannot build up, nor a reaction which restores a former state of things without vitality and permanency. It had a positive and a negative side. It was constructive as well as destructive, conservative as well as progressive. It emancipated the half of Europe from the spiritual tyranny of the papacy, and cleared away the rubbish of mediæval traditions, which obscured and "made void the Word of God," like the rabbinical traditions of old (Matt. xv. 6), and which obstructed the access to Christ, the only Mediator between God and man. It brought every believer into direct communion with Christ and His Word. This of itself is an inestimable blessing, which can never be surrendered.

The Reformation kindled an unbounded enthusiasm for primitive Christianity; it produced the most faithful and idiomatic versions of the Scriptures, German, Dutch, and English, which occupy the position of first classics in modern literature; it enriched worship with a treasury of hymns of faith and praise which are a perennial fountain of edification and comfort. It taught the supremacy of the Bible in matters of faith and practice, justification by a living and ever-active faith, and the general priesthood of believers. It secured liberty of conscience and private judgment, which in legitimate development led gradually to full liberty of conscience and public worship within the limits of public order and peace. Protestantism has been a propelling force in modern history, and a stimulus to every progress in theology, philosophy, science, and politics.

The Reformation was so deeply rooted in the necessities of the Church, and was so thoroughly prepared, that it broke out almost simultaneously in different countries, and marched with irresistible force through Germany, Switzerland, France, Holland, Scandinavia, England and Scotland. It was making progress even in Italy and Spain till the middle of the sixteenth century. Pope Paul IV. is reported by Onuphrius to have declared that the only firm support of the papacy in Italy was the Inquisition with its prisons and funeral piles.

Some distinguished scholars and orators of Italy, as Bernardino, Occhino of Siena, Pietro Martire Vermigli of Florence, and Pierpaolo Vergerio, bishop of Capo d'Istria and nuncio of two popes, renounced Romanism, and had to flee from the Inquisition. Others who occupied the highest positions, like Cardinals Sadoleto, Contarini, Morone, Reginald Pole, favoured at least a moral reform, and came very near the fundamental evangelical doctrines of the supremacy of the Bible and justification by faith. Vittoria Colonna, the most cultivated lady in Italy, and her greatest poetess, equally illustrious for genius, virtue, and piety, together with her friends Michelangelo, the Duchess of Gonzaga, and the Duchess Renata of Ferrara, were in sympathetic contact with the semi-Protestant reform movement. This distinguished group forms a connecting link between the Renaissance in its best type, and the Reformation in its evangelical character. That remarkable little *Trattato utilissimo del beneficio di Giesù Christo*—the work of a monk of Naples, Don Benedetto of Mantova (a pupil of the Spanish nobleman, Valdés), and the poet Flaminio of Imola—teaches the Pauline doctrine of justification by faith, and the union of the soul with Christ, as clearly and strongly as the writings of Luther, and was spread in many thousands of copies throughout Italy. It was first printed at Venice, 1540, and publicly burned at Naples in 1553.

The Counter-Reformation and the Inquisition extinguished the rising flame of the Reformation in Italy, and at the same time sounded the death-knell of the Renaissance by charging it with immorality and irreligion. The last representative of the philosophical Renaissance was condemned as a heretic and burnt on the Campo de Fiore at Rome, but on the same spot the friends of liberty of thought and speech erected a statue to Giordano Bruno in 1889, three hundred years after his death. What a change! The Renaissance has risen from the dead, and is as strong in Italy now as it was four centuries ago. Yea, it is stronger and more widely spread among educated men and women who will not go back from the light and liberty of the nineteenth century to the ignorance and superstition of the dark ages.

III.—ITALY AND THE FUTURE.

By repudiating the Renaissance and burning the Reformation, Italy and Spain lost their front rank among the nations of Europe, and reaped the Revolution as a chronic disease. In the sixteenth century, Italy was the most civilized country, and Spain the most powerful monarchy in Europe; while Prussia and England were far behind them and just emerging from the semi-barbarism of the Dark Ages. Now the case is reversed. The same change has taken place in America; the United States and Canada, which are Protestant to the back-bone, have far outstripped the older Catholic settlements of Central and South America.

But in our age, Italy has made vast progress and undergone a political and social regeneration. She has achieved the incalculable temporal blessing of national unity and independence, in spite of the protest and obstruction of the papal hierarchy which finds it more easy to rule Italy divided than Italy united, according to the maxim, *Divide et impera.*

The unification and emancipation of Italy and Germany from the selfish misgovernment of petty tyrants, are among the greatest events in the nineteenth century. Many of us remember the time when none but Roman churches were allowed within the walls of Rome, when Protestant Bibles were confiscated at the Custom House, and when the Madiai family was put in prison at Florence for the innocent crime of holding meetings for prayer and reading the Holy Scriptures! Now religious liberty is established throughout the kingdom of Italy as fully and firmly, we may say, as in England and North America.

It was the great Italian statesman, Cavour, who spoke the winged word " A free Church in a free State," as the key to the solution of the vexed question of the relation between the ecclesiastical and civil powers. It is true, the *Statuto fondamentale* of March, 1848, which has since 1870 become the law of all Italy, still recognizes the Roman Catholic Church as the sole religion of the State (*la sola religione del stato*), and gives only toleration to other existing modes of worship (*gli altri culti ora existenti sono tolerati conformamente alle leggi*); but in point of fact, toleration has become liberty, which is an inalienable right, and cannot be taken away. A return to the ages of persecution for conscience sake is impossible. The papal Syllabus of 1864, which declares war against civil and religious liberty, is an anachronism, and about as effective as a bull against the motion of the earth, which " still moves." Every Italian may now proudly say, I am no more a Sicilian, or a Neapolitan, or a Lombard, but an Italian citizen, and am free to worship God according to my honest convictions.

What will be the next chapter in the history of Italy? Will she complete her political reform by a religious revival and ecclesiastical reconstruction? No mortal eye can penetrate the future, but one thing is certain, revolutions never go backwards. The past cannot be undone. History, although it does not move in a straight line, is yet moving forward, like a sailing vessel, now turning to the right, now to the left, according to the wind, and is steadily advancing towards the destined harbour. For God is the unerring Captain of the ship, and makes winds and waves the servants of His omnipotent will.

We cannot expect or wish Italy to become Protestant, but we do hope and pray that she may become evangelical and Christian in the best sense of the term. She will not and ought not to turn the back on her glorious past, to disown the immortal works of her literature and art, to break with her Catholic traditions, and to import a foreign religion which is not congenial to her genius and taste. She wants a religion that will in some way combine the best elements of the Renaissance and the Reformation with the best features of Catholicism.

The liberals of Italy are dissatisfied with the Church of their ancestors, and have no leaning to the sects of foreigners, but they are not on that account destitute of religion; they have a religion of their own, which will kindle into a flame of enthusiasm when the Spirit of God, through some inspired prophets, shall blow the breath of life into the dry bones and clothe them with flesh and blood.

There must be a possibility of harmonizing the highest civilization with the highest virtue and piety. There must be a way of reconciling the Protestant, the Catholic, and the Rationalistic rules of authority. The Bible, the Church, and enlightened reason are not necessarily antagonistic. The Bible, as containing the Word of God, is and must remain the supreme rule of faith; the Church of God is and will remain the guardian, propagator and expounder of the Bible; reason, the greatest natural gift of God to man, is the organ by which alone we can understand and appropriate the teaching of the Bible and the Church. These are the ways which lead us to God, Who is the source of truth. In this threefold light every man must decide for himself what to believe and how to live according to his conscientious conviction and personal experience. This is the awful responsibility which God has laid upon every rational being made in His image. "Let each man be fully assured in his own mind." (Rom. xiv. 5.) "Prove all things; hold fast that which is good." (1 Thess. v. 21.)

IV.—CATHOLICISM AND PROTESTANTISM.

The Catholic Church has been greatly benefited by the Protestant Reformation and forced to an abolition of many abuses. She shows to her best advantage in Protestant countries where she is put on her defence and feels the impulse of modern life and progress. She is still the largest body of Christendom, and nearly equals, numerically, the Greek and Evangelical communions combined. She is the best organized body in the world, and "the prisoner of the Vatican" commands with infallible authority an army of priests and monks in five continents. She is backed by inspiring memories as the *Alma Mater* of the Middle Ages, the christianizer and civilizer of the Northern and Western barbarians, the Church of the Fathers, the Schoolmen, and the Mystics, the Church of St. Chrysostom and St. Augustine, of St. Benedict and St. Francis, of St. Bernard and St. Thomas Aquinas, of Tauler and Thomas à Kempis, of Pascal and Fénelon. She is still full of missionary zeal and devotion, and abounds in works of charity. She embraces millions of true worshippers and followers of Christ, and has the capacity for unbounded usefulness. We honour her for all she has done in the past, and wish her God's blessing for all the good she may do in the future. We do not pray for her destruction—God forbid!—but for her reformation.

On the other hand, Protestantism is by no means perfect in any of its forms. With the great merits which we have set forth in the previous section, it has also its defects, and is liable by the abuse of individualism to run into sectarian division, rationalism, scepticism and agnosticism. It has, fortunately, never claimed infallibility in any of its numerous confessions of faith, and hence admits of constant progress, rectification and improvement. It ceases to be Protestant if it ceases to move. Its mission is far from being completed. It has to grapple with problems which lay beyond the horizon of the Reformers, but press themselves upon the attention of the present generation. Protestantism is bound to investigate and re-investigate every theological and philosophical problem; to search and re-search the Scriptures in the light of modern discoveries and advances in philology, archæology and science; to harmonize faith and reason; to grapple with social problems; to improve the condition of the working classes; to preach the gospel to every creature, and to bring the Word of God as a lamp of life into every household.

V.—The Duty of Protestants in Italy.

Evangelical religion has now fair play in Italy, and numbers in a population of 30 millions about 60,000 professors, including the foreign residents. In Rome and in Florence alone, there are about a dozen Protestant congregations, representing nearly as many denominations. Two of these denominations are of native growth (the Waldensian, which is by far the strongest of all, and the Chiesa Libera); the others are of foreign importation, and chiefly supported by friends in England and the United States. They all do good in their respective fields of labour, and far be it from us to underrate their usefulness on account of their numerical weakness. The Kingdom of Heaven itself began as small as a mustard seed, and Paul, when a prisoner in Rome, was mightier than Nero on the throne.

At the same time we should not be blind to the danger of the centrifugal tendency of Protestantism to excessive individualism and division, which hinders its progress among Catholics brought up in the tradition of a centralized church organization, and unable to discern the essential spiritual unity which underlies the variety of external forms.

There must be liberty in non-essentials, but there ought to be unity in essentials and charity in all things.* Liberty we have as much as we desire, and divisions only too many. Unity and charity are the greatest needs, and necessary conditions of success for evangelical missions in any country.

First unity. It is the burden of our Lord's sacerdotal prayer. It is enjoined over and over again in the Epistles. "A house divided against itself cannot stand," says the highest authority. Let the Protestant pastors in Italy, let all evangelical churches on the Continent, in England and North America, unite on the immoveable rock which is Christ, and emphasize above all minor differences their common faith by which we all hope to be saved.

The deepest and strongest tendencies of our age, which by its wonderful inventions almost obliterates the distances of time and space and brings the ends of the earth into instantaneous connection, is not towards division but towards re-union. A task as great as the conversion of the world, and apparently as impossible. But all things are possible with God Almighty. He has great surprises for us in store—reformations purer, deeper, broader, than that of Luther and Calvin ; yea, pentecosts with more flaming tongues than that of Jerusalem. His wisdom and love will bind together what the folly of men has put asunder. He will heal the wounds of Christendom, and melt the hearts of the Churches in the sorrow of a common repentance and in the joy of a common forgiveness, and bring once more a beautiful cosmos out of chaos, as in the days of creation. The Creeds of the Militant Churches will be merged into the one Creed of Christ, Who is the prince of peace and the divine concord of all human discords. There must and will be one flock and one

---

* "*In necessariis unitas, in dubiis (or non-necessariis) libertas, in omnibus caritas.*" A famous motto of irenics, usually ascribed to St. Augustine, but dating from a Protestant divine in the seventeenth century.

Shepherd, as sure as Christ, Who promised it, is the truth. The sacerdotal prayer must and will be fulfilled. "I in them and Thou in Me, that they may be perfected into one; that the world may know that Thou hast sent Me, and lovedst them even as Thou lovedst Me."

Renaissance and Regeneration.

BY PASTOR BAUMANN, OF BERLIN.

RENAISSANCE and Regeneration are two synonyms, and at the same time they are opposed to one another and can never be identified. Their contrast is as old as the world. It is prefigured in the people of Shinar building the tower of Babel, while Abraham called upon the name of the Lord; and in Solomon building the temple, while David prayed for a new heart. Renaissance finds its representative in the time of our Lord in Herod the Great, who is rebuilding the temple for the glorification of his name, while Nicodemus learns from the Saviour the meaning of Regeneration. Renaissance is the classical expression for earthly rejuvenescence. Regeneration: the exact designation for renewing of the heart by the Spirit of God. Renaissance celebrates its highest triumphs in Italy. Regeneration seeks its energetic formation in the Reformation works of Luther, Zwingli, and Calvin, which complete each other. The former is received forthwith with enthusiasm by the Church of Rome, although it is but a repetition of Paganism, and contrasts, by reason of its nature, with the holy life in God. In it, God is treated as Sommo Giove, and the Pope as Mercurius. Outward splendour, immorality, vice, complete religious degeneration, go hand-in-hand with Renaissance as well as with the Church of Rome. She, blinded by its worldly splendour, by her fatal alliance with it, dies inwardly. To this day she suffers under its ban, and Italy is choked with the rubbish of this unchristian and, therefore, immoral blending.

Reformatory attempts in Italy to bring about Regeneration by the Holy Ghost have been in vain. Savonarola was near the goal, but he lacked the indispensable force of evangelical regeneration and renewing of the Holy Ghost. Giordano Bruno was altogether an alien from the Spirit of Christ. Philosophical axioms and lascivious derision against Rome do not help to regenerate the national soul lying in mortal disease, nor does it accomplish a healthy reformation of decaying times. Let us not laugh at Rome, let us rather pray that God may give her the spirit of true regeneration.

Wherever the Reformation has triumphed it has brought with it the regenerating energy of the Divine Spirit; wherever it has reached the heart and conscience there it has transformed and blessed peoples and states. *Luther*, the man of mind; *Zwingli*, the herald of the believing intellect; *Calvin*, the hero of the force of will, represent through the continent of Europe the *thought* of Regeneration. "*Faith alone*" was their watchword, and hence it was that at first they showed themselves indifferent and passive, and subsequently hard, cold, and repellent to the Renaissance. They did not despise the good gifts of God in art and in science, but they made it their object to permeate them with the fear of God, with morality, and the sound sense of spiritual regeneration. "*Ye are Christ's*," therefore "*all things are yours*."

First Regeneration, *then* Renaissance. The former the bread of life, the latter that which is eaten with it as a relish. As a Christian I can live without Renaissance, but not without Regeneration. As the Reformers have had little time to devote to matters of Renaissance, the Evangelical Church has always maintained towards such matters a cautious and critical reserve, and rightly so, for the Renaissance has gone aside from religion, and carried with it the modern life of the people. It has adopted methods which deviate continually from spiritual Regeneration. Science, industry, politics, society, have all fallen under the dominion of naturalism and irreligion—the upper classes have neither faith nor reverence, and the working classes despise and neglect religion. Socialism boldly scorns both religion and morality, and takes no account of anything but worldly possessions, enjoyments, and the rights of man—it thinks care for eternity a useless trouble because there is no such thing. Where shall we find salvation? The Christian Church, is it in a position to save and bless humanity? But, alas! it is not as it should be. It is full of division and discord. Well might Victor Emmanuel, looking at such divisions in the Church, exclaim in Naples, "*Quante tinte!*" What a variety of colours! Which of all these Churches has the Holy Spirit? Which exercises the greatest influence upon its own members? Rome boldly claims to be the only Church which is able to Christianize the people, and unite them under one bishop. But however brilliant the influence which she exercises in Germany, she is losing power in Roman

Catholic countries themselves, in Italy, in Spain, in Brazil, and in Peru. Externally there is still the same splendour and earthly wealth, but in the heart there is indifference.

Can the Evangelical Churches renovate the heart of humanity with pious faith? Certainly in Evangelical Christendom there is a powerful movement of culture, of morals, a renovation of the laws, and yet, even there, religious matters are relegated to the second line. The real power of religion is hindered by the State, and the people are not regenerated. There is no Church which we have yet seen which can bring back what has been lost simply by its own power.

Help can alone come from above, by the pouring out of the Holy Ghost upon all flesh. And we can only pray for His coming. If the Evangelical Churches were ever to be the bearers of the religious regeneration of the nations, the Evangelical Alliance would have to accomplish a great stroke of work before then. The Alliance has been called the grandest thought of the nineteenth century. Very well! but that thought would need the gravest realization, and the most energetic extension in all evangelical spheres.

Florence then—a new step in its working out! Florence—the first attempt to influence a Catholic population! What will be the result? If the concentration of all evangelical parties for united action becomes a fact, then its influence will be irresistible, and not only Italy, but the Christian world will recognize the power of the watchword: Not Renaissance, but Regeneration by the Spirit of God.

Florence and the Italian Reformation.

BY THE REV. JOHN STOUGHTON, D.D., OF LONDON.

> "Of all the fairest cities of the earth,
> None is so fair as Florence."

Those who are here assembled feel the truth and beauty of these words. No one can look down from the Bridges on the Arno, with its lines of time-stained buildings, and its banks in the distance covered with lofty trees, or upon the wide surroundings of the ancient capital of Tuscany—as the eye sweeps round prospects, seen from the porch of the Miniato—and other elevations upon the spurs of the Apennines, prospects marked by fields and pastures

> "Where the dove-coloured steer
> Is plowing up and down among the vines"—

without being charmed, beyond expression, with this land of corn and wine, flowing with milk and honey, like Canaan of old, the garden of the Lord. We think of the palmy days of Florence at peaceful intervals when the city flock lay down at noon to rest, and when at eventide each Florentine could sit under his vine, and under his fig tree, none daring to make him afraid. Now, whilst we are all touched by these sights and associations, when we come to think of certain objects close by, and to connect with them histories of the past, we are struck to find how they furnish a number of standpoints from which we may study the subject before us. No part of this rich country could have been selected for our meeting more germane to our purpose, more helpful for illustrations of our theme. I purpose conducting you to certain local points round which we may gather persons and incidents bearing on the Italian Reformation.

1. Let us begin with the *necessity there was for reformation* towards the close of the Middle Ages.

There are two centres in the city whence we may look at this striking fact: the first includes the home and haunts of Italy's "Altissimo Poeta," Dante; the second, that magnificent duomo where the Council of Florence assembled in the middle of the fifteenth century.

In the middle of the preceding one Dante lived in Florence. Go to the street which bears his name, and look at an old doorway belonging to the house in which he was born; then enter the Church of St. Martin—a small dark building—where he worshipped as a child; and next visit the Palazzo Salviato, occupying the site of his beloved Beatrice's home; afterwards repair to the Duomo Piazza, where a stone is seen identifying the spot where the poet sat and gazed on Giotto's bell-tower rising into the blue sky. Then, when you have realized the personality of the bard, as depicted in the fading lines on the Bargello Wall, open the "Divine Commedia" and see what he said about the state of Italy in his days; mark how he indicates the state of the Church, how he paints the Popes, and exposes the existing scandals of Christendom. On this subject study what he says in book after book, canto after canto, line after line. "Rogues and traitors," he declares, "are not so numerous in Florence as are fables repeated every year in pulpits, so that the flocks who know no better come back famished, only fed upon the wind. Men go forth with jests and drolleries to make people laugh. He exclaims:

> "The Church of Rome,
> Mixing two governments that ill report,
> Hath missed her footing, fallen into the mire,
> And there herself a burden much defiled."
> *Purg. Canto* xvi. 127-9.

> "Of gold and silver ye have made you god,
> Differing wherein from the idolater,
> But that he worships one, a hundred ye?"
> *Inferno* xix. 112-114.

This is not the language of a modern Protestant but of a mediæval Catholic, sincere in faith, a reformer full of ideas bearing on the political, moral, and religious condition of his country, with nothing like what we should call a sectarian bias. One idea, as a patriotic Italian, he brings out again and again, is that Rome at the time was "a sink of evils." He exposes corruption with a view to its removal, and points out the cure, "through Moses, the rapt Prophets and the

Psalms, the Gospel written by those gifted of the Holy Ghost." Dante read his Bible. His wonderful poems afford ample proofs of it. At that period, with all its sins and miseries, there were those who repaired to Holy Writ for wisdom and instruction. Dante was one of them. He was a politician, no doubt, mixed up with city quarrels, a man of impassioned nature, not free from prejudices, full of absorbing love and burning hate, but a Christian notwithstanding up to the light he had; studying nature, science, history, the fathers, the schoolmen, and bringing all to bear on men and things. He paints them with amazing vividness. As we read his pages we are transported to the Italy and the Florence of the fourteenth century, and we see plainly enough how they needed a thorough reformation.

A second proof of that necessity we discover in the history of the Florentine Duomo, a hundred years later. Within its walls a Council assembled at the beginning of the year 1439. Then came the Pope and Cardinals from Ferrara, where they had been similarly employed amidst inextricable confusion. For some years disorder had prevailed. Pontiff was against Council, Council was against Pontiff, more Holy Fathers than one appeared at the same time. A Pope was deposed by an assembly of this kind, and such an assembly was pontifically dissolved. The Duomo, as you see, is a magnificent structure embodying an idea which led to its erection—namely, that the highest and the best of what the city had should be devoted to divine worship. The Florentine Republic was never infidel. It did not resemble the Republic of the French Revolution. It never had a pantheon, never worshipped the Goddess of Reason.

The Council here opened with state and splendour. The Latin and Greek Churches were represented with a view to re-union after centuries of strife. The city kept holiday, people crowded the pavement of the temple to gaze on gorgeous vestments worn by Pope and Cardinals, and on the quaint ancient attire of Greeks from Constantinople. During the sittings of the reverend fathers, discussions arose on points of doctrine with a view to settling the old feud between east and west; suffice it to say, after a too hasty supposition, that union was established, the old rent remained, only made worse. Points in dispute I have not space to discuss. I can only say, Rome had long hated Constantinople, and Constantinople had responded to Rome in like manner. The mutual hatred continued till Constantinople was taken by the Turks.

Rome, after the Council, acted towards Italy and Europe has it had done before. The disposal of crowns, the accumulation of wealth—these were its main objects. Supremacy over France and Germany, as well as over the kingdoms and states of the Peninsula, was the coveted prize of those who wore the tiara; and, while the order of Friars regarded poverty as the holiest of earthly conditions, many thought, that if it were so, the Father of Christendom would do well to get rid of his enormous wealth. He himself thought otherwise, and continued to fill his coffers to the brim. It is said at such a time hatred of the clergy was a common thing. No wonder. Hence necessity for reformation at that crisis is sufficiently apparent.

2. We proceed to glance at certain intellectual and literary preparations made for an ensuing reform of theology and religion.

Think of the movement which went on in this way in the middle of the fifteenth century. "In a villa," says Mr. Hallam, "overhanging the towers of Florence, on the steep slope of that lofty hill crowned by the mother city, the ancient Fiesole, in gardens which Tully might have envied, with Ticino Landino and Politian at his side (the author is speaking of Lorenzo de Medici), he delighted his hours of leisure with the beautiful visions of platonic philosophy, for which the summer stillness of an Italian sky appears the most congenial accompaniment." That villa of Carreggi, on the way to Fiesole, was a cradle for nursing a study of that language, in which the New Testament is written. It had, in Europe, been long neglected. There was a dark spell of ignorance in this respect over our part of the world for many centuries. The fall of Constantinople, the consequent scattering of Greek MSS., served to break the spell. First came the study of Greek classics: in this study Lorenzo and his friends became absorbed. In the first instance, many literary enthusiasts turned away from Christianity to Platonism; but to devout minds, the restoration of Greek knowledge became a priceless aid in studying the original Gospel of our Salvation. The learned came to listen to Apostles and Evangelists in the tongue they used. Such studies, carried on in this neighbourhood and elsewhere, helped many to understand the records of our faith as they never did before.

These workers prepared the way for Erasmus, Melancthon, and others to whom you and I are indebted when we read our Bibles far beyond what we are accustomed to remember. One of these pioneers often overlooked was Berni, who died in Florence, 1536, author of the famous "Orlando Innamorato"—a poetical work of genius, but spotted with licentious stains too common in those days. By the grace of God, this poet underwent a spiritual change. He embraced evangelical truth; and wrote religious verses, expressing the doctrine of Christ, as distinguished from prevalent dogmas in that age, and teaching the reader to place himself in Divine hands for salvation, acknowledging God's Word and not fearing the denials of men. A tract was printed by Signor Panizzi, of the British Museum, containing the verses now referred to and he remarks: "The more we reflect on the state of Italy at that time, the more we have reason to suspect that the reformed tenets were as popular among the higher classes in Italy in those days as liberal notions in ours." Let me add, however that may be, and perhaps the deduction goes too far, certainly enough was published to shake faith in the existing state of things. Petrarch followed Dante in exposing ecclesiastical scandals. "I am at present," he writes, "in the western Babylon, than which the sun never beheld anything more hideous, and beside the fierce Rhone, where the successors of the poor fishermen now live as kings." The Papal Court then resided at Avignon.

Boccacio, with characteristic humour, dwelt on the worldly and unpriest-like life which went on there and elsewhere. Bracciolini joined in describing ecclesiastical vices, at the same time pathetically alluding to the recent martyrdom of Jerome, of Prague, which he had witnessed with his own eyes. Laurentius Valla also condemned Papal abuses, and effectively prepared for a coming age by his "Scholia on the New Testament" and his Correction of the Vulgate, founded on a comparison of it with the Greek original.

3. I must now call attention to a typical prelude of what was near at hand. I refer to Savonarola, of whom you have so many mementos, his cell in the monastery of San Marco, the Duomo itself where he preached to crowds standing, in the early morn, on the cold marble pavement to await his sermon; also the spot where, under the spell of his eloquence, people burned to ashes "the pyramid of vanities."

For awhile he was the spiritual lord and master of Florence, which, in the name of Christ, he claimed as a Divine kingdom, to be governed by His Divine law. He was not a Protestant in our sense of the term; he held no such conceptions of the Gospel as did Martin Luther. He condemned the action and policy of the Pope, but he adhered, on the whole, to the dogmas and ceremonies of the Roman Catholic Church. There was, however, a spiritual power in his ministry which laid strong hold on devout hearers. They were convinced he was one who brought to them a Divine message. Even Lorenzo de Medici said, "he was a true monk, the only one he knew who acted up to his profession." I have seen and read, in part, a translation of some of his MS. sermons; they were mystical expositions of prophecy, full of fervid eloquence— and nothing in the Magliavecchian Library has interested me so much as the Bible he used to carry under his arm, containing copious notes in his own hand. He was infamously tried and condemned to be burnt; and, in the Chapel of San Bernardo, under the roof of the Palazzo Vecchio, at his last sacrament, he uttered this prayer: "Lord, I know that Thou art that perfect Trinity invisible, distinct in Father, Son, and Holy Ghost. I know that Thou art the Eternal Word, that Thou didst descend into the bosom of Mary, that Thou didst ascend upon the Cross to shed blood for our sins. I pray Thee, that by that blood I may have remission of my sins, for which I implore Thy forgiveness for every other offence or injury done to this city, and for every other sin for which I may unconsciously have been guilty." He was burnt to ashes, in front of the Palazzo Vecchio, and we are told that two brethren from Bohemia, sent on a visit to the Waldensian valleys, travelled to Florence, where their faith and courage were strengthened by Savonarola's memorable martyrdom.

4. *The extent to which the Reformation advanced in Florence and other parts of Italy.*

The names of three native Florentines occur in the list of Italian reformers—Peter Martyr Vermiglio, Carnesecchi, and Antonio Brucioli.

Peter Martyr's father is said to have attended the sermons of Savonarola, to have seen into the corruptions of the Church, and to have disapproved of the superstitions attendant on Monarchism; but, notwithstanding, the boy determined to follow a monastic life. There still exists an Augustine monastery on the descent from Fiesole, which

I remember visiting some years since, when the building was used as a college for art students. There Peter Martyr entered, and spent three years within the walls, when he left the place to study in the monastery of St. John, near Padua. There he became a Doctor of Divinity, a popular preacher, and a student of the Holy Scriptures. Preferment in the Church followed, but, as he embraced, through careful ponderings of St. Paul's Epistles, the Gospel doctrine of Justification by Faith, he was silenced by the superiors of his Order. Protestantism became more and more apparent in his opinions and habits; enemies laid snares for him, but ultimately he came out an avowed Protestant. He returned to Florence, where he had "steady friends;" subsequently we meet with him as a distinguished advocate of the reformed faith. After zealous service in Italy, he came over to England, and accepted the Regius Professorship of Divinity in the reformed University of Oxford.

Carnesecchi, who had been attached to the interests of the Medici family, had been protonotary to Pope Clement VII., became connected with some Italian Protestants in different parts of the country, was accused of heresy and consequently fell under the ban of the Church. At last he suffered martyrdom at Rome, having been basely delivered up into the hands of the Papal Inquisitors as he was dining at the table of the Grand Duke of Tuscany, who then occupied the Palazzo Riccardi, at the corner of what is now the Via Cavour.

Antonio Brucioli was a republican, opposed to the Medicean policy and rule, and, being involved in a conspiracy against them, had to escape for his life to Venice, whence he went to reside in France and Germany. He was a brave man, saying, "If I speak truth I cannot be wrong." He was denounced from the Dominican pulpit of St. Mark's, by a preacher, who playing on the Italian name Brucioli (which means twigs or shavings) exclaimed "Brucioli is only fit to be burned." This reformer, in a preface he wrote to the New Testament, maintained it would be praiseworthy if the peasant learned to sing psalms in his native tongue, as he guided the plough, the weaver as he worked at his loom, and the boatman as he steered his rudder.

But these reformers do not appear to have been successful in their native city, as the tide of thought and feeling, on the part of the authorities, ran decidedly in the opposite way. The Inquisition sat at Santa Maria Novella, and, in December, 1551, twenty-two penitents, wearing cloaks painted with crosses and devils, were marched to the Duomo, where, in the piazza, heretical books in the possession of those thus disfigured were publicly burnt. In 1559 there was a similar book burning before the doors of the Santa Croce.

5. We must now leave Florence to see how reformatory work went on in other parts of Italy. There is room only for a hasty glance at its centres of activity, its means of operation, and at the suppression of the cause.

1. The following were principal centres, not far from the Vaudois Valleys, where the reformed faith in simplicity had long existed— Milan, on the western sweep of the Lombard plain stretching from the foot of the magnificent Gothard Pass; Venice, in the eastern and opposite side of the Peninsula, amongst the lagoons of the Adriatic Gulf; Ferrara, on the road to Florence across the edge of the picturesque Apennines; Bologna and Modena, which lie on the way between; Lucca, on the south side of the range just named; Siena, romantically perched on a high hill in the heart of Tuscany; and, last, Naples, situated far to the south near to Vesuvius, more than 150 miles away from Siena. Together with Naples we may mention a Vaudois settlement in Calabria. I mention these positions and distances to show how scattered were these centres of reforming influence, and how far removed from one another. Then you sail round the south point of Italy, and all round the gulf of Saranto, and up the shores of the Adriatic till you reach Venice again, without identifying one port or place connected with the history of the Reformation. Protestant work was limited to a few spots far asunder.

2. But the means employed were considerable, and in several instances efficient. I can only name some of them.

Already notice has been taken of the impetus given to Greek Testament study by the literary movement on the part of Lorenzo Medici and his friends. The printing press at Venice followed up this kind of preparation by the issue of numerous religious works, favourable to reform. A Franciscan friar living in Padua wrote an apologia, dedicated to the Venetian Senate, and vindicated the Lutheran standpoint of Justification by Faith, explaining faith to be the living roots of salvation, implanted in the soul by the Holy Spirit. Books by German and Swiss Protestants were consigned to merchants, who transported them to various parts. Attractive Scripture readings were carried on by Juan Valdes, in his villa on the shore of the Mediterranean, "set in verdure," with an open view of the Neapolitan Bay. Such meetings were held morning and afternoon, and the host, who presided, spoke to his friends in addresses as instructive as they were eloquent. Some of them are printed in his well-known "CX. Considerations." That book was originally composed in Spanish, but has been of late translated into English. Another book written in Italian, and entitled "Il Beneficio di Christo," had an immense circulation, and was the means of doing much spiritual good. The authorship has been matter of controversy; perhaps Valdes had some share in it, and I think another Italian Reformer, Aonio Paleario, an eloquent orator residing in Siena, had a share much larger. Preaching was a powerful instrument in evangelizing the people, wherever it might be possible; and Bernardino Ochino stood chief amongst his brethren in this respect. Charles V., Emperor of Germany, said "Ochino preaches with a power that can draw tears from stones." Bembo, writing from Venice to a friend, said, "Our Fra Bernardino is literally adored here : there is no one who does not praise him to the skies." Epistolary correspondence and social intercourse were further means of promoting the cause. Letters were not then, as they are now, comprised in a few words—they were often long homilies. Of the effect of social influence I must give an example.

In the quaint old city of Ferrara there still stands a fortress-like palace, which, in the age of the Reformation, was inhabited by the Duchess René, daughter of a former French king, sister to the reigning one. To the characteristic qualities of her race—intellectual and emotional, eminently gifted, and of determined will—she added superior culture, indeed extensive learning, also a charitable dispositon, and much social sympathy. Educated in the faith of Rome, without imbibing its intolerant spirit, she became acquainted with Protestant opinions, and decidedly shared in some of them. Moreover, she had a strong dislike to the reigning Pontiff, Julius II. Her household for a time included the French hymnologist, Marot, and Olympia Morata, one of the most accomplished women of her age :

both on the side of reformation, the lady especially so. Amongst the guests of the Duchess were Peter Martyr and Ochino, already particularly noticed, and other leading reformers. Chief amongst such visitors was John Calvin, a confidential correspondent and adviser, who conducted worship within the palace. A room with an altar in it, where he is said to have ministered, I saw a few years ago. Rome regarded with stern displeasure the approaches to Protestantism made by the noble lady of Ferrara. Threats modified her zeal in that direction, without extinguishing the flame. How many people in the city adopted her views I cannot say; but mention is made of several preachers in 1528 sympathizing with her. I find no evidence of an organized Reformed Church in the place; but the history of a man named Fanino, a native of Faenza, is preserved, who laboured for the conversion of his neighbours, and for so doing was seized by the fangs of ecclesiastical power, and committed to a dungeon under the Duchess' castle. She would have no power to prevent this under the constituted government of that period; but Olympia Morata and another lady visited the prisoner; and whilst they sympathized in his sufferings, were strengthened by his heroic constancy. Intercessions were made at Rome on his behalf, but all in vain. He was first hanged, and then burnt. To the last he conversed with those permitted to visit him, insisting upon salvation by faith.

3. One word touching the suppression of Protestantism in Italy, and I have done.

The division of the country into so many sovereignties and republics was unfriendly to any national reform, such as obtained in England, France, Germany, and the Netherlands. The reformatory movement in the Peninsula made way more with the upper and highly-educated classes than amongst the mass of the people. A fact not to be overlooked, but deeply to be regretted, is that unevangelical opinions arose in the Northern States, amidst opponents of Rome, much to the detriment of Protestantism. Also the departure from Italy of some leading advocates on that side is much to be lamented; and to this we may add, that from the beginning there was a want of mutual understanding and social consolidation amongst the reformers. Each worker was too much "like a star, and dwelt apart."

The ultimate suppression of the good work, however, was owing to the institution of the holy office at Rome, in 1542. Inquisitors were invested with a right to delegate power to other ecclesiastics, to decide all cases without appeal, to imprison the suspected, to punish the convicted—in short, their authority had only one restriction, they were not to pardon. His Holiness alone can do that.

The result was as might be expected. Heretics were burnt at the stake, or sentenced to imprisonment and penance. Such cruel tyrannical acts caused numerous families to leave the country, and a minute account of these religious emigrants is given by Dr. Galiffe in his interesting book, entitled "Le refuge Italien de Genève."

Religious Thought in Italy.

BY PROFESSOR DR. MARIANO, OF THE UNIVERSITY OF NAPLES.

For two reasons I have accepted the invitation to speak at the Conference; first of all in order to show that I am not ashamed of the Gospel of Christ, and in the second place because I have thought it desirable that an independent and objective voice should be heard on this occasion. Born in the Roman Catholic Church, and a fervent Catholic from infancy, I have been convinced by the study of Hegel's philosophy that the Pope and his Church are incapable of giving redemption and holiness, and that these can only be obtained through a mystical transformation of the heart, under the influence of the grace of God, and by faith in Christ and in His Gospel. I have not joined any particular evangelical denomination, because I have felt called to urge my country to reform itself religiously, not in the name of some Church, but in the name of the Gospel only.

[1. Having explained thus his personal position, Professor Mariano goes on to define the question he is to treat of. He speaks of the paramount importance for every nation of the religious question. Everything must be governed by religion in the life of human beings. His conclusion is that "the religious problem, which is in reality the eternal problem of the world, is the vital problem of Italy. Upon it depends the present and the future of the country. All the difficulties that besiege us at the present moment can all be traced to the religious question."]

2. Italy is not an irreligious country. Erasmus was wrong in saying, "*Itali omnes Athei.*" The Italians, to the outward observer, may appear to have retained much of Paganism, but their inward social organization is moulded on Christianity. In the Christian firmament Italy can boast of stars of the first magnitude: Cassiodorus and Benedict of Norcia, the Abbot Joachim and Francis of Assisi, Anselm of Aosta (or of Canterbury), and Thomas of Aquino, Dante and Savonarola, Beato Angelicus and Michael Angelo. These men of

faith, full of spiritual ideals, have given the world sublime examples of divine religiousness.

Unhappily, religious thought in Italy is Catholic-Popish thought; indeed, emulating Spain, Italy has fallen asleep religiously in the Roman Catholic doctrine. Now Catholicism is of all historical incarnations of the Christian idea the most immediate, the one which, subordinating the internal and intelligible to the outward and sensible, leaves no entrance, in the apprehending of Christian truth, to the true and direct action of the Spirit. True it is that Catholicism is much improved since Reformation times. Still its distinguishing feature is that it teaches Christian truth as a letter, not as spirit; as a precept from outside, as a formal law which obliges from without. With the sacraments reduced to mechanical acts, with purgatory and pecuniary offerings to be free from it, with festivals, indulgences, jubilees, pilgrimages, relics, miracles, adoration of saints and madonnas, Romanism has inoculated in the Christian religion the forms of a magical and idolatrous naturalism.

On the other hand, it makes salvation of the soul to depend upon outward practices and works more than from internal conversion of the will. And the worst of all is that Romanism makes the sacerdotal hierarchy the only and indispensable mediator of the religious and moral life. The atonement of Christ and the repentance of the sinner become a monopoly of the priests. It is the priest who must procure merit and justification to the people without the people even thinking about it. He reconciles with God. Without him no mercy, no grace can come from God to mankind.

In this way faith is destroyed. The *fides generans intellectum* of Anselm becomes the *credo quia absurdum*, and well might a witty, though devout French lawyer say: "*Si je suis dans l'erreur c'est l'Eglise qui portera la responsabilité.*"

From all this we must conclude that Romanism is the very opposite of that duty which distinguishes the human soul, and in obedience to which every man must seek his own salvation, and conquer it himself, in the intimacy of his own will, trusting of course to divine grace, but through the free activity of his own mind.

3. This religion may have had its days of glory and usefulness, but it has now become a pure formalism; it has no power over the

morals of the people; it does not attract, or educate, or edify the masses; but simply holds them under its sway by force of habit, by inert traditionalism, and its ultimate result can only be ignorant credulity in the midst of ignorant incredulity.

True it is that even superstition is better than incredulity. "With superstition," says Vico, "nations have become great; not one was ever founded with atheism." But what a difference between the nations that have conceived Christianity in its true spirit, and those who have reduced it to something very akin to idolatry and fetish worship.

4. And yet we must not be too severe on this miserable religious conscience of the Italian people, for when did the leading classes take the trouble of illuminating and raising it up? It pains me to have to confess it: the religious condition of the upper classes is in Italy much more troubled than those of the common people. With a few honourable exceptions, they present to us a large army of minds whose existence is a perpetual moral somnolence; unable to believe, they have not moral strength enough to disbelieve anything seriously. They are Catholics for social convenience or opportunism. They boast that they have minds strong and free; but whilst they attack religion, they send their children to Jesuit schools. They have no convictions, and laugh at everything; but you see them on every occasion ordering masses and priestly funerals. They deride the priest, but in the solemn moments of life they throw themselves, body and soul, into the clergy's arms.

To this class our politicians mostly belong. These men think that the contest between Italy and the Papacy is simply a political one, and is now settled by our going to Rome. As to the religious question they either deny its existence or maintain that the State cannot do much to solve it, except perhaps by the formula: a free Church in a free State. In reality their aim is a conciliation with Papacy, whose political power they would like to enlist on their side; a clever calculation, but a very aerial one! A Pope that places himself at the service of Italy, helping to make it great, would be a suicidal Pope, and that phenomenon is yet to be seen. As to the political problem, what an illusion to think it solved by our going to Rome! Let us rather say that the problem has been formulated on the very day we entered Rome, for Europe, which recognizes at present our right to stay there, might deny it to-morrow. Rome is not a town to be stormed with artillery. It is a system, a faith, a religion. Against the dangers of a religion we can only be insured by religion. Will the Italians have the wisdom and the courage to turn their backs on the spiritual authority of the Pope? That is the important point. Then, and only then, our right to Rome will be respected.

5. It is a cause of immense surprise that Italy's best thinkers, even Bonghi, Spaventa, and such-like minds, have no higher conception of religion. Anything in their writings that still retains some reminiscence or sentiment of religion bears the stamp of Romanism, whilst they totally misunderstand and despise Protestantism. But where would their freedom of thinking and writing be if the Reformation had not been? As for the religious problem some of them hoisting the obsolete banner, *Intus ut libet, foris ut moris est*, pretend that since we have the Pope, we must keep him; others say that nothing is to be done, that no reform is needed, that we must not divide the people for questions of faith, that *Inertia, Sapientia* must be the motto of the Italian nation, for so there will be peace amongst the people, and liberty to the Church.

This is fatalism and indifference; worse still, it is scepticism regarding the moral world. It is easier, of course, to shake from us all that requires an effort, in order to live quietly; but that is *Propter vitam, vivendi perdere causas*. In the religious sphere a nation must not aim at impossible things, but it must have the courage to face living and present problems, and do something towards solving them.

6. And what of the clergy? Here, indeed, Romanism has worked the greatest destruction. Under the whip of the Papal system our clergy lies now prostrated in a senile and servile lethargy, which deadens mind and soul. It is enough to enter a Roman Catholic Church to perceive that the faith and the religiosity of the priests themselves have become deadened and mummified in formalism and outward rites. The ignorance and the haziness in which they rejoice it is easier to deplore than to measure. With a few remarkable exceptions, their studies are such a mean, sterile, and decrepit thing, that we can quite understand the saying of a Bavarian

schoolmaster: "A drop of holy water is better than all philosophy." The despotic power of the hierarchy, centred in the Pope, has caused the priesthood to become morally apathetic, and to turn their eyes from heavenly to earthly things. Enforced celibacy is the reason why immorality and hypocrisy have become the dominant traits of their lives. And strange to say, as if the Pope was not powerful enough, the Italian State, by renouncing almost every jurisdiction, such as might have been a protection for the lower clergy, has made the bishops and the Pope himself more powerful than ever over the inferior priesthood.

7. It will be easy to understand now that the Evangelicals are the only ones who have rightly understood the religious problem of Italy, and have set themselves to solve it. They are few, but their small nucleus is the column of fire in the wilderness. They alone have secured peace to their consciences, in which the truths of Christianity are united with the rights of morality and culture, with respect for freedom and patriotic duties. They are the same in private as in public; as believers and as citizens they feel the same men. What they think they say; they speak as they believe; and they act in accordance with what they believe, think, and say. They have freed themselves of that machiavelism and liberal scepticism which proclaim that the country must be preferred to the soul. They love their soul not less than their country, and prove that the love of the soul is the root of strong and fertile patriotism. No enterprise is more worthy of praise than that of the evangelical missions. Their followers are few, but each one of them is a conscience freed from the tyranny and the terror of Romanism, and restored to the liberty of the Christian soul.

8. But have we no fault to find with them? Allow me to speak with all frankness.

The Evangelicals are wrong to break up into so many different denominations. I know that these divisions are an intrinsic consequence of personal sincere religious convictions; I understand, also, that in spite of these divisions faith may be fervid, and the Church really united. But all that must be taken *cum grano salis*. Let the Italian denominations remember that each of them is only a part of the one Church, that what makes them Christian Churches is not the things in which they differ as to rites and forms, but rather the great principles which are found in all their creeds.

In a purely Protestant country the movement and the working of different sects is inevitable, and may be useful. But in Italy all these denominations appear to us like a chaotic vortex of individual atoms. And that is to be avoided. One would almost think that the evangelizers of Italy have not rightly understood that they have to confront Papacy. Against a power so formidably compact, your ranks could never be too firmly knit together. May the time soon come when the Evangelicals will no more say: "I am of Peter, or of Paul, or of Apollos;" nor even content themselves with the motto: "*Unum corpus sumus in Christo;*" but will, through Christ, form one single Church—the Church of God. This meeting is a good omen for it.

Another thing I must say. The evangelical churches—so cold, so bare, look like places of business rather than churches. The excess of outward symbolism in Romish churches must not lead us too far. The Anglican and Lutheran churches have retained symbolism in just proportions, giving thus satisfaction to an invincible want of the human heart.

9. And now shall the evangelical missions be the leaven which leavens the whole lump? or must we desire in Italy a more intrinsic, more historical, more organic religious revival?

It would be an illusion to think that Papacy is soon to disappear. Its political character, its supreme ability in the diplomatical sphere, the mass of traditions it represents, the strength and help it gives European conservatism, and, lastly, the divisions of Protestants— these will make Romanism last much longer than we think. The world is full of people who do not want the trouble of thinking for themselves; and, more than all, there will always be many minds willing to accept a religion of traditions, of legalism and of outward forms. For such minds, the proclamation of the infallibility of the Pope, outrageous as it may appear to us, has rather strengthened than otherwise the edifice of the Romish Church; whilst the liberty of criticism in the Protestant world makes them afraid.

Another thing, also, must be considered. The great contest is now no more between Romanism and Protestantism. Christianity, as a whole, is now attacked on every side. Positivism, naturalism, materialism, united in a common league, assail the treasure of divine truth. Is this a moment to despise the moral authority of Catholicism, and throw away the help it can give? We must not desire the death of the sinner, but rather his improvement. Purified from its defects and its sores, Catholicism may still be of great value to defend the Christian principle, and to maintain the moral basis of society.

Let us remember, also, that the ills of Romanism are due principally to its ambition to be the only master of souls and consciences. Where it has had to fight against Protestantism in Germany and England it has undergone a remarkable change. The words of Luther to the priests of his day: "My name will trouble your peace for ever, until you are either gone to ruin, or have become better men," has to a great extent become true in his own country. German Catholicism is not, as with us, a mixture of credulity and incredulity, a mass of outward and magical forms, but an inner and spiritual life. Unity is servitude, languor, indifference, corruption; religion is life, spirit, movement, fight. What we need is a contest which will revive things and men.

What we suffer from is the heavy, leaden atmosphere which the uncontrasted empire of Romanism has generated in Italy. This it is which prevents any movement of thought in the laity as well as in the clergy, and this can only be remedied from within. It is in the religious conscience of the nation that must arise, by its own inner power and initiative, the movement of reform, rather than by foreign importation. If such a movement was to be produced, some would be drawn in its current, others would resist it; hence a contest that would wake us all to action, from the Pope downwards. The Pope himself might be led to see that the syllabus, the Vatican decrees, the infallibility, the intolerance, the superstitions of the Romish Church, are simply a negation of Christianity; and the clergy would again acquire that religious culture, and those graces of the Spirit of which they are now wanting.

So it has always been. Moral and religious controversies are an element of life. That has been the great power of Reformation. The discussions between Calvin and Luther, and between the different Protestant Churches have made them living and vigorous.

Christ Himself has inaugurated in the world the greatest contest the world ever saw—the everlasting contest between the mind and matter, the human and the divine.

ADDRESS BY THE REV. PROFESSOR GEYMONAT, D.D., OF FLORENCE.

WE have preferred that the aspect of religious thought in Italy, the very seat of the Papacy, should be stated by the learned Professor of the University of Naples—a fervent Catholic prior to his enlightenment, and at the present moment unattached to any communion. We have reserved for ourselves the part of putting before you official Roman Catholic thought, if we may so call it, and contrast the same with Evangelical thought.

We have no intention of entering upon the various phases and changes which have passed upon it, and which may be traced in history, but we shall confine ourselves to showing what are the noteworthy changes of phases as set forth by one Pope and another.

To take Pius IX. and Leo XIII. These two appear to be opposed to each other; nevertheless the thought and opinion of the latter is a logical continuation of that of the former. The one proclaimed the dogma of Infallibility, and exhibited the negative side of it by continual anathemas against all liberty; the other puts the dogma in practice, showing its positive side, and endeavours to do this by making use of philosophy, history, and a persistent issue of encyclicals, and thus to influence and control the minds and souls of *all*.

The inevitable consequence of the proclamation of the dogma of Infallibility is that truth is not to be sought for and found in dogma, nor in the faith which demands unity and uniformity, but only in the thought and mind of the Pope.

By reason of the Pope continually harping upon the subject of the temporal power, he is in perpetual collision with the national aspirations. And it is for this reason, perhaps, that he has less influence in Italy than elsewhere. We are free to propound Evangelical thought, which is the positive antithesis of Papal thought.

An ideal drawn from the Middle Ages, and worked out by the Jesuits, such is the programme adopted by the Vatican. To this imaginary ideal, there must be opposed the true ideal—the ideal of the truth. *Reality* must be substituted for these fictions and illusions.

Let us ask ourselves "What is this Church—one, holy and indivisible, directed and governed by one head alone?" It is an imaginary ideal, accredited by ancient tradition and by wonderful monuments, by an imposing order, but disfigured by errors and arbitrary conditions, by dissensions and hatred, by political and perfidious subterfuge, a theocracy based upon texts wrongly interpreted, and which sustain nothing more than false and vain pretentions.

To all such fictions and inventions, Protestantism has placed the true and the real in juxtaposition.

To an imaginary ideal there should be shown another ideal in opposition, a *true* ideal; an ideal which is not the outcome of the imagination, but one which has been revealed by Jesus Christ, and which by Him, both in His person and His work, has been already realized, but which has, as yet, to be universally accepted and carried out.

The ideal realized in the person and work of Christ, is the living and life-giving substance of the faith, and also the object of religious thought and of dogmatic investigation. By means of the latter, it is reduced to precise formulæ. There is also the study of the æsthetic involved therein, with its conditions of beauty and its results. The realization of this ideal is the aim and end of religious investigation and study. It should determine the line to be carried out practically—first in morals, and then for the general welfare of mankind. But whether it be science or the arts, whatever may be proved to be the foundation, the forces, and the laws which affect the welfare of mankind, they must all bear upon and tend to the glory of God, and the making of His will to be done on earth as it is in Heaven.

Religious thought ought not to be exclusively theological or ecclesiastical. The ideal should merge into the real, or rather the ideal and the real should be one and the same thing; like truth, that truth which religious thought seeks for, and must find. This ideal, we say, should be applied to everything. Perfection should be sought after in all directions, and above all in seeking the Kingdom of God and His righteousness. Such is religious thought as in opposition to the theocracy of the Vatican.

The Obstacles to Reformation in Italy.

OUTLINE OF A PAPER READ BY PROFESSOR COMBA, OF FLORENCE.

WHEN the voice of Savonarola, on the banks of the River Arno, proclaimed the necessity of reform it seemed to be near at hand. But it was delayed. Three long centuries have passed away. And now what is the prospect? Here and there are signs of a revival. The seed is springing up. But at present we labour among the thorns. Our hope is that we shall lighten the toils of our successors.

One chief object in this paper is to notice the greater obstacles. We cannot undertake to exhaust so large a subject. The *political obstacles* come first. It has been said that the Protestant Reformation had not only a religious origin but a political as well. It was a rising against the predominance of the Latin race and traditions. The nation itself was at last involved, for the cause of Church and State was one. Reformation would not have come forth victorious if it had not had a helper, and at last patron and defender, in the political world. Who can say how long it might have struggled for existence? In Germany, in Great Britain, in Switzerland, it was the political barrier which kept back the power of Rome, and in the titanic conflict of that period the principles of the Reformers would not have prevailed without the help of the political arm. True "the blood of the martyrs is the seed of the Church;" but persecution has sometimes absolutely prevailed, as we see in Bohemia and in Spain, not to say in our own land. Religious liberty can be suppressed like all other liberty. If the Waldenses had not fought for it in their valleys it would have been destroyed. Italy had no desire to promote religious Reformation lest it should be hindered in political progress. People of all classes were too much absorbed in their multifarious political interests to care for it. The Reformation encountered armed resistance all along the line. Venice was an exception, because the Doge would not permit Rome to repress heresy within his dominions, but the Queen of the Adriatic only differed from other Italian cities in the form of the persecution. The other cities burned the heretics, Venice drowned them. From Geneva the Reformation spread into the valleys and cities of Piedmont, and subsequently into Calabria and Sicily, but by its connection with political movements it brought terrible and innumerable severities upon the converts. All through the times of the Reformation the saying of Machiavelli might be illustrated—"All the fighting prophets will conquer, and those who are disarmed will be ruined." But next to the political obstacles there are the ecclesiastical. Reform, regarded as an individual work, has been wrecked upon the rock of Latin, Roman, Catholic unity. The faith which was received from Jerusalem, and the theology which came from Greece, has been remoulded by Rome in accordance with its own peculiar genius in priestly laws and institutions. Ecclesiastical unity was established by the Pope in imitation of the Empire. The good work which was done by Rome in the time of chaotic ruin was followed by a sterile uniformity and the suppression of liberty. The Latin spirit would not bear differences of opinion. It must be supreme. There were storms which shook Rome itself, but it was only to strengthen the oak in the ground. Even such a man as Savonarola declared his desire to disarm the power of Rome. His martyrdom showed that it would be vain to hope to reform the Church without destroying its unity. It was the passion for unity which led to the enormous persecutions of the Huguenots. It was the feeling of unity that kept France faithful to Rome notwithstanding that the monarch said that the unity of the State was in himself, and he held forth as her motto—"one faith, one law, one king." Roman unity is the guardian angel of the Catholic faith. It was then its Cerberus, and its bark was, "Non prævalebunt." Then, thirdly, there is the moral obstacle. It is a well-known fact that the Revival of Letters had no moral character. Savonarola's reform in such an atmosphere was a mere soap bubble. It was the testimony of the German Reformers, when they visited Italy, that our people were blasphemous and depraved, and Calvin exhorted our martyrs to give an example of sincerity to "a crooked and perverse nation." Such were the obstacles to Reformation three centuries ago. And now let us note the fact that all such obstacles are centred in the Papacy. Everyone knows that the political obstacle was impersonated there. And the ecclesiastical obstacle is now seen more than ever to be identified with Roman usurpation, which received its coronation in the dogma of infallibility. The moral obstacle was also there. Machiavelli said, "The people nearest the Roman Church have the least religion. If we follow the example of the Church, and of Italian priests, we shall be irreligious and wicked." And the worst feature of the case was that the Pope was regarded as bearing all the "responsibility." The people saw no necessity to repent. Worldly ambition in the Church covered it with infamy and error.

So it was in the time of Luther. And it is not to be wondered at that to the Reformers the Pope seemed to be the Antichrist of the Apocalypse. We have laid aside such a reproach in these days. Thanks to the growth of liberty, we can now unite the spirit of Reform with the spirit of Liberalism, but if we are to be delivered from the power of Papal absolutism, we must revive not only the spirit of the Renaissance, but the spirit of the martyrs of a free evangelical faith. The work of the Reformation has been resumed in this age, if not by Italy herself, at all events by Italians, and under the auspices of different Protestant Churches. What then are the obstacles which in the present day hinder the work from being accomplished better than in former times?

Politically the Italians have become Protestants. Cavour, a son of Geneva, at his mother's side once received a letter from his aunt, Cecilia di Bude, in which she said: "Vinet did not know that you will be his instrument." Yes, we are Protestants. The syllabus has declared it. The separation between Italy and the Pope is complete as a fact, but not yet fully worked out. But the obstacles to Reform are not in our political condition, except that there are still those who think that it is the duty of the State to hasten the fulfilment of Catholic aims. So far as the ecclesiastical obstacles are concerned, our position is little changed. Roman unity prevails everywhere, like a strong wall without munitions and arms, with a few publicans sitting at the receipt of Custom, waiting at the gates for the tolls of the penitent, a true wall of China preserved by the credulity and traditions of its defenders. It is impossible to say how many Italians hold the Creed of Rome with sincere conviction. But whatever Reform worthy of the name is made, the liberty which we have obtained must be its indispensable condition. And is there any hope that the Romish Church will be reformed, and that the unity which is a unity of mere appearance will yet be broken up? No, Latin civilization is irresistibly carried forward in the path of freedom, both by its own intrinsic character and by the working of events. Roman unity has had its day, and must give place to that which is true and living. The motto of the future is "*Through Liberty to Unity.*" But many cannot distinguish between unity and uniformity. The Roman Catholic will rather remain where he was born, than separate and isolate himself from others, yea, even though the tower of his unity be a Tower of Babel.

Morally the situation is decidedly improved. Such scenes at the Vatican as were possible in the time of Leo X. are not possible under Leo XIII. Now the laity would express their abhorrence. Is it not a sign of the times? Both justly and in charity, the contrast which not so many years ago might have been drawn between Catholic morality and Protestant morality would not now be openly proclaimed. But there are many witnesses who could be called to show that still there is a sad moral defect. When Father Curci found little response to his zeal in translating and publishing the New Testament, he said: "The Christian conscience is more than half destroyed, and it is only through the divine mercy that any portion of it remains." As Renan has observed, the blood of Italy is impoverished. Our generation is anæmic in religion. Surely we owe it to the memory of the martyrs and to our country to carry forward the Evangelical Reform.

But the question demands a solution. Seeing that the obstacles are diminished, how is it that Reform accomplishes less than in former times? With all our liberty of action, after forty years, we cannot show a number of new converts equal to those who in the sixteenth century went boldly to the stake. How is it? So far as the Catholic Reform is concerned it moves in a vicious circle. All change must be subordinated to Roman Unity, to the Papacy. Is Reform to be expected in the head and therefore in the members? Only those who are obstinately blind to history will believe that Catholic Reform is sincere. The ideals of that Church are expressed in doctrines of which only blind eyes cannot see the absurdity. Some have entertained the hope that Italy will be saved from the dualism which is destroying it by a Reform originating in a Catholic sphere and cleansing its seat, so spreading through the country, bringing the Papacy within proper limits. But the hope is not sound. We shall never see the Catholic School rise to the ideals of a new life. It has not the moral and intellectual independence which the time, as well as the dignity of man, demands. It is owing to Roman Catholicism that Italy is in the state of moral weakness in which it is. It is the Evangelical Church which must supply the want.

But why is the Evangelical Reform so slow? We do cry out, "*Mea culpa*," if we do not say, "*Mea maxima culpa*." Hesitation and uncertainty, as every one knows, attended the first efforts at Reform, as we knew not whence would come the means of success. We did not clearly understand how it was best to present Christ to Italians. The best intentions are not all that is required, nor is it enough to cry out, Christ, Christ. "The living word which alone can awaken the conscience must be drawn from the Gospel." So said Father Curci himself. But it is one thing to repeat the name of Christ, and another thing to teach men to love Him truly and in the spirit of self-sacrifice, and to teach them in that spirit of charity which made the Apostle of the Gentiles a Jew to the Jews and a Gentile to the Gentiles.

The Evangelical Reform has failed for lack of internal and social union, which is so specially required here. It is not so much the land of Italian martyrs, which has been represented in our various missions, but rather different churches. Unintentionally the theological or ecclesiastical views of Calvin, Wesley and Whitfield have been proclaimed rather than "the mind of Christ" and the ideals of an Italian Reformation. Would any one pretend that in order to be Christians we must accept the theology of Thomas Aquinas? Old it is, but is Calvinism much more modern? We must here in Italy unitedly labour for an ideal which, if not yet above the horizon, will at last appear—a Christian ideal, but a new one—which will allow many theological and ecclesiastical strifes to fall, which will unite the elements of Culture and Reform, Catholicism and Protestantism; will unite faith, thought and action, liberty and unity, religion and patriotism, and diffuse the spirit of charity over our social miseries.

This, I know, is no new thing to say, but *repetita juvant*. The same sentiments which were heard and approved thirty-five years ago in our Conference at Paris find favour here in Florence. You desire, like Savonarola and like Paleario, that Jesus Christ alone should bear the sceptre of the Evangelical Church in Italy. Jesus Christ is risen, and is reigning, and Italy has in Him the ideal which she needs, in faith, love and hope. May He be our only Master and Leader, and then the shadows, great and small, will vanish before the brightness of His Light.

The Obstacles which the Reformation has encountered and still encounters in Spain.

ADDRESS BY M. A. MARTINEZ DE CASTILLA, PASTOR AT REUS, SPAIN.

MR. President and Members of the Central Committee and brethren of the Evangelical Alliance, met together in this city where Savonarola and other Christians have suffered martyrdom for the Gospel, and thus given blessed testimony to the Faith, I must first greet you in the name of the young Church and its connexions, over which the Lord has placed me in the province of Tarragona to carry on there the work of evangelization among my countrymen. I wish to thank you for all that you have done and are doing for Evangelical Christians in Spain. Especially in the time of Matamoros and his companions, in persecution, in prison and in exile, who were rescued from the galleys through the intervention of the Alliance, delegates being sent to intercede for them, through whose efforts their sentence of nine years' imprisonment was commuted to banishment. In 1863 they were received with much Christian love in France, and afterwards in England, Holland, Switzerland and Germany. At that period it was that I was led to the knowledge of the Gospel, being then in a College at Bayonne for the training of young men from Spain as teachers, pastors or evangelists, and now for the last seventeen and a half years I have been a pastor in my dear country, where in the town of Reus I have been blessed to establish a Church and two evangelistic stations at Tarragona and Pont d'Armentera.

The obstacles to the Reformation in Spain in the sixteenth century were different from those of to-day. At first it was in Cathedral chapters that the Gospel was received. *Diego Sarmiento* was a very distinguished theologian and literary man, and *Cipriano di Valera*, who gave to Evangelical Christians (1) a Version of the Bible which we still use in our services, schools and families; (2) a Translation of Calvin's Institutes; (3) a Treatise on the Pope and the Mass; (4) the Arts of the Inquisition in Spain, and other edifying treatises, to strengthen those who were in the dungeons of the Inquisition, or in prisons, or in the galleys, because they had embraced the Gospel. I may mention *Perez Diaz* who was murdered by his brother, *Valdés, de Vargas, de Leon,* and *Juliamillo,* the faithful, clever and indefatigable colporteur, who carried the Word of God even into the convents, and whom the very exciseman helped in passing his heretical goods. The monarchy, the clergy, the Inquisition, and the people were all against the new doctrines, and by means of their terrible persecutions succeeded in suppressing the work of the Reformation in Spain until 1868, when to our great joy it was opened to the preaching of the Gospel. We have enjoyed liberty of conscience and of worship up to the time of the restoration of the Bourbons. At present our position is that of half-toleration. We have to struggle against indifference, spiritualism, want of union among the different churches and committees, and the terrible opposition of the Church of Rome, still very powerful, and giving no quarter to Evangelical Christians.

Ten years ago I was called to go and preach in a village of my province, and speak to more than two hundred and fifty people. I was arrested, tried and condemned to two months' imprisonment, and a fine of 250 fr. and the costs of the trial. But, thank God, during the time of my imprisonment I was able to make the Gospel known to the prisoners in prison with me, and thus found access to many villages where I can preach the Gospel frequently, and had I the means at my disposal, by the help of a colporteur I could evangelize ten villages a month. The villages are well disposed to the Gospel, and could we evangelize them we should see a great advancement of the kingdom of God in our dear country. There are more than a hundred Churches and as many Evangelical Stations, at least two hundred Evangelical Schools, and as many Sunday Schools. There is a Bible Depôt and five Evangelical Journals. We have two, or rather three, Protestant hospitals at Barcelona, Madrid, and Figueras, and an Educational Institute for pastors and teachers. At San Sebastian there is a Governesses' Institution. We should be ungrateful not to recognize all these advantages. May the Lord bless the Alliance and all its represented Churches, missions and families.

PUBLIC MEETING IN THE EVENING.

LORD RADSTOCK PRESIDED.

Present Salvation.

ADDRESS BY PASTOR TH. MONOD, OF PARIS.

Suppose I should inform you that it has been my privilege this afternoon to save a man, you would at once inquire from what great peril I have saved him. The very fact of my using the expression, *he is saved*, would imply that if not saved he would have been lost. Likewise, when we speak of the salvation of men, we point to their perdition. To say that God has given His Son that we "should be saved," or that we "should not perish," is to express the same fact in different words.

The work of our salvation may be considered in the past, in the present, and in the future. We may speak of our *having been saved* (Titus iii. 5), and of our *being* saved (Eph. ii. 8), and also of our salvation as yet *to come* (Acts xv. 11). Just so, a drowning man might be told of the lifeboat ready long ago for his salvation; or of the happiness he will enjoy when restored to his home; or, lastly, of his being saved at the very moment. And I dare say that the latter point, his present salvation, is to him by far the most interesting.

It is with our present salvation that we have to do this evening. Of this salvation the Apostle speaks in these words: "If, when we were enemies, we were reconciled to God by the death of His Son, much more, being reconciled, we shall be saved by His life." (Rom. v. 10.) Or we might quote the words of the Lord Himself: "Because I live, ye shall live also." (John xiv. 19.) A present salvation means a present Saviour. To speak of an absent Saviour and a present salvation would have no meaning. Present salvation alone can bring to us Christ Himself, and with His real presence (for we also believe in the real, though not in the material presence of Christ) all strength and victory, all peace and joy, are ours. This is not always understood. A Christian will look back and say: "I have been saved by Christ;" or he will look forward and say: "I shall be saved!" and yet he dare not, will not, does not say: "Christ is saving me now." Had we to give advice to an anxious soul, we would point it to Christ, and say: "Believe in Him, and thou shalt be saved." Had we to administer comfort to a dying saint, we would speak the very same words. But between conversion and death—that is to say, during the whole course of the race that is set before us—we often forget that the one thing to do is to believe in the Lord Jesus Christ and be saved. We take Him to be "the first and the last, the beginning and the end:" but does He not fill the whole interval? We call him "the Alpha and Omega," but do not these very names teach us that He is, so to speak, every letter in the alphabet of salvation?

Suppose you had to go across a wide and deep river, and could not do so except by a bridge; and suppose one of the arches of that bridge reached to the shore where you stand, while another arch touched the further shore where you intend to go; but suppose, finally, that between those two arches the middle arch was wanting, so that your way should be suddenly interrupted by empty space, letting you look down upon the mighty river rushing at your feet, of what use would such a bridge be to you?

And yet that bridge fairly represents salvation, such as it is understood by many; they believe that they *have been* saved, that they *shall be* saved, but not that they *are being* saved. They believe in converting grace; they believe in dying grace; but between this and that they have merely to gather as best they can the fruits of converting grace, and get ready for dying grace. Even on their own ground they should believe in present salvation, for who can tell but that they may need dying grace to-day? When the Apostle writes: "Whom He *justified*, them He also *glorified*," does not the very omission of the word *sanctified* imply that sanctification is included, as a matter of course, between justification and glory? What the Saviour gives us when He forgives our sins is not merely a title—I had almost said a ticket—to Heaven, but Himself, the Living Guide. We cannot afford to leave any part of our salvation out of sight. To forget that it has been accomplished in the past is to lack the very foundation of our hope; to forget that it is yet to be accomplished in the future will easily lead to blind presumption, if not to fatal delusion; to overlook present salvation is to cut ourselves off from the main spring of power, of victory, of happiness.

The men of our generation are being, with increasing rapidity, driven to the conclusion that the only possible basis of every social progress lies in the moral renovation of the individual. Men will not believe in a salvation for the future that gives no evidence of its present power to save. A man of the world once said to me: "I am acquainted with some persons who profess to be saved, but I am tempted to put the question to them, What are you saved from?" We need to be saved from selfishness, from pride, from hardness of heart, from the lusts of the flesh, otherwise the world will not believe in the saving power of the Gospel. One of the most remarkable religious movements of the age, the Salvation Army, owes the greatest part of its power to the fact that it proclaims, manifests, and offers to all, a present salvation.

Such a salvation is necessary as an example to the world, and also as the only power that can act upon the world. A man thus saved has, in the words of an American evangelist (Mr. Inskip, I believe), both hands free to work for God. Or to mention another example, that of a saint of God, belonging to the ancient Church, prior to the Reformation (Catherine, of Siena), whose memory I rejoice to honour in her own land : The Lord, she said, commanded her to banish from her heart all anxiety in reference to her own salvation, so that she might be able to labour for the salvation of others. The dying words of that faithful servant of God in the fourteenth century show how fully she had received salvation as the gift of God: "O Lord, Thou callest me and I come to Thee, not because of my merits, but because of Thy mercy; and to that mercy I have appealed, O Jesus! in the name of Thy precious blood."

In truth, to proclaim salvation as past, present, and future, is the same as to bear witness to "Jesus Christ, the same yesterday, to-day, and for ever."

ADDRESS BY REV. PRINCIPAL CULROSS, M.A., D.D., OF BRISTOL.

It is one of the painful things to which no Christian man can shut his eyes, that so many immortal beings around us are living only for the present world. The things that they believe in and seek after are things that they can see and touch. Invisible realities surround them, unperceived. God is not in all their thoughts, except when they cannot help it, and then He seems an intruder. At best they treat Him with a kind of reverent neglect.

And yet a dull, uneasy feeling haunts them of something wrong in their condition—they scarcely know what. They do not like to speak about this feeling. A stranger might never suspect its existence. They themselves at times forget it in the hurry of business, the excitement of pleasure, the delights of social intercourse; but it comes back upon them at the most unexpected moments in the very midst of their gaiety, or when they wake at midnight and the darkness is full of God.

What does this haunting uneasiness mean? It is the Saviour saying: "Awake, thou that sleepest, awake from the stupor of carnal security." You are dowered with the awful capacity of saying "yes" or "no" to the living God. You have said "no" to Him. Your life has been a prolonged "no." You have not loved Him. You have set up your own will against the holy and blessed will. In this way you have broken the first law of your being. Here is the deepest thing wrong with you—the very root of evil living and misery.

When Jesus began to preach in Galilee, His first word was: "Repent, for the kingdom of heaven is at hand." It is the word He speaks by His Spirit to-day. It is one of the profoundest words in human speech. It marks no mere superficial and temporary pain, such as many reduce it to. It marks no mere resolution formed in the glow and flush of excited feeling to live another life. In its deep Bible sense repentance is the heart's sincere acknowledgement of having been sinfully in the wrong, and its turning trustfully to the God of Grace for pardon and renewing. It is the man taking God's side against his own sin. It is the man humbling himself before God on that kneeling place which mercy has provided. It is the prodigal saying to God: "Father, I have sinned." Without repentance pardon would be no blessing to us. Without repentance no life can be right, but must go on from bad to worse. Without repentance Heaven itself would only be a place of misery to us. Do not shrink, then, when the Lord carries His candle into the secret places of the heart and shows you what you are in the light of His purity. If there is pain in His dealing—bitter pain and shame and humiliation—there is also love in it and hope. It shows that He has not given you up, or said the awful words, "Let him alone."

Then, further, He who deals with you that you may repent brings to you the gift of a free pardon. You look back over your past life. There may have been no shameful hour in it over which you pray: "Let darkness and the shadow of death cover it." It may have seemed blameless, even virtuous, in the eyes of men, as well as in your own. But now, in the light of eternal purity, how black and stained it appears! And there are black spots in it that all the water of the ocean could not wash out. As you look, and your brow grows crimson with secret shame, a voice cries out, or whispers awfully within your breast, awaking a dull agony, "It is done, and can never be recalled." And God answers, "Even so; it is done and cannot be recalled." No tears, even of blood, can wash it out; but it may be forgiven, at once, frankly, freely, righteously, eternally forgiven. "For He hath made Him Who knew no sin to be sin for us, that we might be made the righteousness of God in Him." Not by works of righteousness that we have done, but through the ever-availing sacrifice of Calvary, there is pardon for the very chief of sinners. That is how God puts sin out of the way. He forgives it, blots it out, and sheds abroad the blessed assurance of pardon in the heart; and so we learn to say, "Abba Father," and to live in the joy of His love.

> "I the chief of sinners am,
> But Jesus died for me."

Now, this forgiveness is not a blessing deferred and held back until the Day of Judgment. It is given now and here. Just recall what Scripture says. In Psalm xxxii. David tells how for long he kept silence before God about his sin. Silence brought him no peace—

only misery. At length he humbled himself before God, and made a clean breast of it. This is what followed: " I said, I will confess my transgressions unto the Lord"—I had got no farther, I had only *said* it—"and Thou forgavest the iniquity of my sin"—so swiftly did pardon follow. Again, our Lord tells how a certain publican, a man whose sin could not be denied, went up to the temple to pray. He stood afar off; would not lift up his eyes to Heaven; smote upon his breast, while one short, sharp, broken cry rang out, " God be merciful" (God be propitious) " to me the sinnner!" How did he fare? " I tell you," the Lord Jesus says, and He knew, "this man went down to his house justified." He had gone up with a black, shadowy burden on his shoulders, which he could not get rid of; he went down to his house "justified"—in God's meaning of the word—cleared, acquitted, accepted, clothed in a righteousness not his own, able to say with the calm assurance of faith: "There is, therefore, now no condemnation" *to me*. This is the grace which the Lord Jesus invites you to share. "Behold," He says, " I bring near My righteousness." He asks no price either beforehand or afterwards. He does it all freely, for His name's sake. The grace is yours for the taking.

You break in: Ah, if you knew what a sinner I am, you would not speak as you do. I do not know what a sinner you are. The person sitting at your elbow does not know. You do not yourself know. But God knows; knows the very worst about you, all the sin you have done, all the sin you have imagined, and desired to do, and would have done if He had not held you back; and He Who knows the very worst about you says: "Come, now, and let us reason together; though your sins be as scarlet, they shall be as white as snow; though they be red like crimson, they shall be as wool."

There is another thing—the craving of the heart for something unattained. Just listen to the wail, "Who will show us any good?" It comes up in all lands, in all ages, in all ranks of society, in all forms of speech, in articulate groanings, or the dumb misery of despair. Not from the poor only, the friendless and forlorn, the men beaten down in the struggle of life; but from the most fortunate and envied. Even in the hour of success, when the hand closes on the coveted prize, the disappointed heart will exclaim, "*Is this all?*" and the unquenched longing burns as fierce as ever. The stir and tumult around us, the restlessness and agitation of society, the eager rushing after excitement, and pleasure, and change—what is it all but just the world's exceeding great and bitter cry, "Who will show us any good?" *Things* cannot satisfy. The heart must have God.

And God suffices. The proof lies in experience. They who can look up, though it be from the depths of poverty or pain, and say: "But God is my Father; He has cast all my sins behind His back; He loves me; He has won my heart; I belong to Him"—these men find the heart's need met. It is not that desire is quenched; but in God all good is found. "O taste," the Gospel calls aloud to the weary and heavy-laden, "O taste and see that the Lord is good; blessed is the man that trusteth in Him"—blessed, indeed, in God's great meaning of the word, and blessed already.

Think just of one thing more—prevailing sinfulness. We all know something about it. We have seen the wrong, and resolved against it, and then committed it. Reason has pointed one way, and desire has drawn us the opposite. Conscience has said, "Thou shalt not," and passion has answered, "But I will." The heart needs God, and cannot do without Him, and yet turns from Him. "The good that I would I do not; and the evil which I would not, that I do." Ah, there is no room for human pride. Flattery of human nature has a bitter and terrible irony in it. Man can subdue the earth and have dominion over it; can rule the elements; can tame and control the fiercest natures; but he cannot subdue the lawlessness, or tame the lusts, or curb the passions that rage within his own breast.

Now, Christ is Saviour because He delivers those who trust Him from the law of sin and death, subdues our iniquities, and introduces us into the liberty of the children of God. His redemption is no mere breaking of bonds and delivering from death. It is not as when one comes on some wild animal caught in a snare, and undoes the snare, and lets the panting, struggling thing return to its wild freedom again; but, as if he tamed it, and made it love him, and follow him, and do his will. So Christ does with us. We are the glad captives of His love, and our will learns to stand and wait on the Blessed Will, like an angel continually beholding the face of God. I cannot explain how, because I cannot explain the secret working of the Holy Spirit, but, as a matter of experience, whosoever surrenders to Divine grace finds a living power within his breast, delivering him from the old thraldom, and moulding him to a new and heavenly life, so that he can say with triumphant joy, "I thank God through Jesus Christ our Lord."

There is much more to be said, but time forbids. I sum up by saying, "There is no difference, for all have sinned and come short of the glory of God." There is no guilt so great and shameful but it may be forgiven; no soul so sin-stained but it may be restored to purity; no breast so demon-haunted but it may become a temple for the Holy One; no man so deeply lost but he may be saved by the omnipotence of grace, and made "an heir of God and a joint heir with Jesus Christ." To you is the word of this salvation sent. The Gospel points to the Lamb of God Who taketh away the sin of the world, and calls aloud to sinful men, in tones of tenderest pity, of holiest love, of most solemn urgency: "*Come straight back to God!*" May every soul here answer to the call *by consenting;* "And I will receive you, and will be a Father unto you; and ye shall be my sons and daughters, saith the Lord Almighty." Amen!

TUESDAY, APRIL 7, 1891.

PASTOR BAUMANN, OF BERLIN, PRESIDED.

The Spread of the Gospel.

ADDRESS BY THE REV. W. PARK, OF BELFAST.

A SPEAKER from Ireland may be reminded that his own country seems to need missionaries, instead of proposing to send them to other lands; and this is true in part. Much mission work is being done in Ireland by the circulation of good literature and of the Word of God by colportage and other ways, and there is much ground for encouragement and hope at this moment as to results. The 17th of March has for some years past been set apart by the Alliance as a day of prayer for Ireland, and the speaker mentioned some facts which show these prayers are being answered. Speaking in Italy about Missions, one is surrounded with scenes which awaken happy memories. The great Apostle of the Gentiles laboured here, and his Epistle to the Romans occupies in more ways than one a central place in New Testament Scripture. We are in the footsteps of Paul the Apostle here, the great missionary; but how changed is the world since his day! This gathering from all the Churches of Christendom in one of the great cities of Italy, to discuss, among other subjects, the spread of the Gospel in the world, is proof enough of the change, and may well fill us all with hope and courage. The mention of the Apostle Paul and of his Epistle to the Romans reminds us how much there is in the Word of God about Missions (on this the speaker lingered a little, tracing the golden thread of prophecy and promise from the days of

Abraham to the glorious scenes pictured in the Book of Revelation). No subject is more appropriate on an Alliance platform. For, first, the necessity of alliance is most felt by our Evangelical Churches, as we study the map of the world, and see how vast is the work remaining to be done before Christ's last command is obeyed. Only earnest and united effort can overtake it at all, and it is a shame to let this, our chief work, wait till every little point of difference between us at home be settled. And, secondly, it is, I think, through foreign missions that the object of the Evangelical Alliance is likely to be attained. The problem of how to secure brotherly recognition and even corporate unity is solving itself in the foreign field in the happiest way. (The speaker referred to some cases—Japan in particular.) The Home Churches must soon feel the effects of these movements abroad; seeing that God's blessing seems to rest about equally on all the Churches of Christ in mission work abroad, and that union is so easy and necessary in presence of the Heathen, the question will be soon felt pressing, " Why not more unity at home?" The Gospel is spreading. Note some facts: The great missionary work of the nineteenth century has been foundation work—the translation of the Bible into the tongues of earth; one Bible Society (the British and Foreign) advertises close on 300 versions, and has added 53 in the last ten years. There are few countries and provinces not now attacked by the missionary army, God's providence, in our own day, having opened doors on every side, and His grace having roused and prepared the Churches to enter in. In some countries the success has been so great as to make us feel that the age of miracles is not over. (The speaker here referred to the Fiji Islands, Madagascar, Uganda, &c.) The missionary movement gathers force continually; our workers do not rely on one plan, but try every plan to reach and move all classes in Heathen lands; not preaching only, but teaching, the press, medical missions, and Zenana work—all focussed on one point, the winning of hearts and homes and lands for Christ. (The speaker after saying something of these various plans, went on to speak of native agency, especially of the establishment of a native pastorate, and gave instances in which the work is being more and more entrusted to qualified and trained natives to carry on; the development of a self-sustaining, self-governing native church, full of missionary zeal, being the chief end of all missionary enterprise everywhere.) He concluded by showing the need of the Churches rising to new conceptions about giving to Christ's cause, expressing the hope that this Evangelical Alliance would soon be an alliance not only of those who hold the great fundamental truths, but of men and women who are prepared to sacrifice much to spread the knowledge of them the wide world over.

ADDRESS BY M. EDOUARD MONOD, PASTOR AT MARSEILLES.

I.

THE present moment appears to me to demand the most strenuous efforts of a public character, with a view to the propagation of all evangelical thought and principle. The press must be made use of, and in every way it should be rendered conducive to the putting forth of articles and notices in favour of the truth. Protestantism is somewhat in fault in this respect—it is too diffident, it is too apprehensive (in France at least), too much afraid to speak out, to lift up its voice in high places, and to call public attention to itself. We are too scrupulous. Let us have the courage of our convictions, and lay hold of the resources of publicity, and place them at the service of the Gospel. Let us not hide our light under a bushel on any pretext whatever. Let us sow our own newspapers and publications broadcast, and invade those of others. The shop windows of booksellers, the kiosks, railway stations, placards, advertisements, conferences—all should be pressed into the service in such a way as shall be best suited to the end in view. Then, let us put the Cross of Christ as the first and foremost object. Let us put it over the frontal of our churches. It is a visible emblem, another form of publicity, and not the least eloquent or the least striking either in a Catholic country, where we are accused of not being Christian men and women—we, forsooth, who are determined not to know anything save Jesus Christ and Him crucified.

II.

I think there should be a more popular style adopted by speakers and writers among the Evangelicals. I do not mean by that that there should be clearness in exposition, simplicity of language only—perhaps Protestants are somewhat too simple in their style, almost hard and bare so to speak; their meaning is presented baldly, and there is little consideration for the taste and culture of the educated classes.

By popularity, I mean, principally, the beauty of form and elegance of style suited to the taste of the times; a taste which has been nursed and fed by writers, who have, so to speak, pushed their anxiety regarding the colour and richness of language almost to excess. Let us become all things to all men. It may be objected that such was not the method of St. Paul, who declared to the Corinthians that his speech and preaching "was not with enticing words of man's wisdom," as though he dispised the resources of human eloquence. But it should be remembered that St. Paul was not alone among the great teachers of the Church. There was Apollos, and, after him, Clement (of Alexandria), St. Basil, Gregory (of Nazianzus), St. John Chrysostom and others, who all placed the fruit of their Greek culture and their beautiful language at the service of their Saviour and ours. See what an influence Bersier—the most classical and the most gifted of our contemporary Protestant preachers—has exerted on his times. Oh, that men would take as much pains and trouble about the glory of God and the salvation of souls as they do about their own honour! Oh, that we could show Christian poets, Christian novelists, Christian literary men, Christian journalists, Christian members of the academy! We can, indeed, boast of a few such, but not enough; and those few even are not so well known as they ought to be, and are scarcely able to compete with our secular writers.

By popularity, likewise I mean actuality. Our publications, issued on the lines for evangelizing the people, take too little notice of passing events, of what is said, of what is written. There is no Christian comment on these matters, and no consequences drawn from them, which might affect the cause of religion. We live too much in the past or in the coming eternity, not enough in the present; the present, however, will tint and colour the future. Let us be men of our own times; men of the present day, to the end that we may the better serve Him, Who is the same yesterday, to-day, and for ever.

III.

Finally, let us have wider sympathies. We must do so, if we wish to take in more fully the multitudes who are perishing around us. Our compassion must not be circumscribed. My ideal would be to extend the Evangelical Alliance to pious Catholics, who, like us, "love the Lord Jesus Christ in sincerity." I hear someone saying, "That is a dream, a thing which can never be realized." It may be so, but at least we might aim at it—see whether it could be effected or not. It is possible that that which our Roman Catholic brethren theoretically assert to be impossible might little by little be realized in practice. Do not let us ever neglect an opportunity of showing our fraternal sympathy to any who represent any of the various communions throughout the whole world—anyone who represents the true Catholic Church in the widest sense of the word. Why is it that we do not recognize and even salute each other in the streets and highways, pastors and priests, deaconesses and sisters of charity? .... Why not create an immense freemasonry of faith and piety in spite of the innumerable divergencies both intellectual and ecclesiastical? Why not found a grand Evangelical Alliance newspaper, or a grand enlarged *Christendom* in which should be inserted all that is done for the defence of the faith, for the salvation of souls, and for the struggle against sin? Again we are dreaming do you say? May be we are, but if a dream is a noble one, let us accept it—believe in it—for surely that is the way to merge it into a reality !

It may be objected that faithfulness to truth and conviction is opposed to certain ecclesiastical concessions. Any concessions of this kind ought to be regarded in the light of a compromise. Take care, under pretext of fidelity to your especial church, you may possibly become unfaithful to Jesus Christ! you may end by being faithful only to yourself! Had we not better lay aside our rivalries, in order that we may strangle the materialism of to-day? Materialism is our common foe !

Let us avoid public controversy, save in exceptional cases, let us confine our discussion to private conversation. Controversy always irritates and is seldom helpful. It is the proclamation of the Gospel pure and simple (and that in itself refutes all that is opposed to it) which edifies. The McAll Mission in France has adopted this principle and mode of action, and it would seem that, up to the present time, it has had no occasion to repent of it.

To sum up in three words: publicity, bolder and more aggressive; popularity with regard to form and actuality in the subjects treated of; larger-heartedness and expansion of views. These appear to me the principal desiderata demanded for evangelization among our beloved fellow countrymen, and these, I believe, will prove the best condition of victory and success.

The Best Methods of Evangelization.

BY THE REV. M. BOWEN, OF CONSTANTINOPLE.

EVANGELISTIC effort in Turkey is of necessity confined to non-Moslems. It includes the Jews, but is especially active among the nominal Christians, mainly Armenians, Greeks, Bulgarians, and Syrians. This puts the work at once, in the minds of many, under the ban as a system of proselytism in its bad sense. This prejudice is not confined to the people aimed at. Probably its most intense form is among certain classes of resident foreigners, who are known as Protestants. It is to some extent shared in by good people in England and America, who in general are friendly to missionary enterprises. The prejudice as we meet it in Turkey, often asserts the opinion with extravagant emphasis, that men should always remain in the faith in which they were born, and that any influence to the contrary is an outrage. This prejudice it is difficult to overcome. It grows out of a misconception of the objects of the work. A great advantage would be gained if these people could be convinced, that mere numerical results are not aimed at; that evangelism abhors a mere nominal change; that the spiritual power of Christianity in the land of its birth has decayed and ought to be rekindled; and that however imperfect the human agents may appear, the inspiring motive of evangelistic effort in the East, as everywhere, is divine, and that its chief concern is not with names or with systems or creeds, but with human hearts, and the loftiest ideals of character. It were to be desired that these people, at least so far as they are sincere, might acquaint themselves with the history of the evangelical movement in Turkey. They might, if they would, easily ascertain the facts, as to the early policy of the missionaries; that no pains were spared to avoid the slightest appearance of a sectarian propagandism; that every energy was put forth for the development of the evangelical spirit and life within these Eastern Churches; that if that effort failed, the responsibility does not lie with Christian missions; and that the native Evangelical Church of Turkey to-day is due to Providential orderings, which missionaries could not resist and still be true to their Master.

The cry of proselytism is strengthened by the antagonism of the people aimed at, an antagonism which owes its chief bitterness to the intense nationalism so prevalent. The religious system is simply another expression of the national life. A Greek is not a man of Greek parentage, but an adherent of the orthodox Greek Church. Inquire of a Greek or an Armenian papist his nationality, and he informs you he is a Catholic! Protestants have insisted upon the distinction between nationality and faith. Fortunately they have had some opportunities of proving the genuineness of their *race* loyalty. The fact is becoming patent, that the Greek and Armenian nationalities have no better patriots, and the Sultan no more law-abiding subjects than are found among the men of evangelistical sentiments. It is noteworthy that this nationalism does not assert itself with equal emphasis against Romanizing influences. Antagonism is less. Denunciation is more under control. Is not the reason obvious? An Armenian Bishop in Conia (the ancient Iconium where St. Paul did good missionary work) does not hesitate to say to his people from the pulpit of the Armenian Church, "You may love the Greeks, you may love the Catholics, but you must hate the Protestants." It is the common sentiment of the three. They are bound together by the instinct of self-defence, all standing in equal dread of the enlightening power of Evangelism. Not all ecclesiastics in these old Churches, it is true, antagonize gospel influences. On the contrary, many openly welcome them. But the prevailing influence of the clergy is anti-evangelistic. It would not be difficult, but it is unnecessary to uncover the selfishness of this antagonism. Whatever its motive, its quality is bitter; and its strength lies in fostering the prejudices of nationalism. Another singular manifestation of the prevalent nationalism is this, that a man may be an avowed infidel, and yet retain good standing as a Greek or an Armenian. But the moment he shows evidences of moral and spiritual life, he is suspected of Protestantism and disloyalty. Rationalism is developing rapidly, under nominal adherence to the old churches. It is often of the most ignorant kind, but it is not without support in educated quarters. Singularly enough while recognizing the intellectual superiority of Protestantism, it easily joins the coalition against truth, of bigotry, and mistaken nationalism.

Are we to expect that the Churches of the East will ultimately be Protestantized? If by this we mean a formal turning *en-masse* from those Churches to another Church, no. But if we mean the development of a truly evangelistic power, emphasizing loyalty to Christian life as well as to the Christian name, yes! Much has already been accomplished in the line of such a development. It would be a shock to faith, if three-quarters of a century's toil exhibited no fruits. We expect fruit and we find it. There has been an immense change in the attitude of the people towards evangelical institutions. This is especially noticeable in districts where Protestantism has flourished. Its power and its worth are recognized. Respect is manifested and courtesies are exchanged, where not many years ago violence would have been fashionable. Armenian bishops can now unite with American missionaries in an effort for the formal recognition by Imperial firman of an evangelical college. Evangelistic labourers not infrequently are permitted to teach evangelical sentiments within the precincts of the national churches and schools. Children are sent in large numbers to Protestant schools, for the avowed reason, that in those schools more attention is paid to religious teaching. Skilful teachers, thoroughly evangelical in spirit, are in some cases employed in the national schools, in which also the study of the Bible in the vernacular is becoming more and more general. In Constantinople a school paper is published by Armenians which unfolds various courses of study, prominent among them a course of Scriptural study. There is an increasing demand for the Bible, not only for use in the schools, but also in the shop and in the home. The demand for a clergy of a higher moral and intellectual calibre grows more emphatic. With increased intelligence, the grip of superstition upon the masses has weakened. The illustration of the power of the Gospel in the Protestant community has developed a demand for Gospel preaching and teaching. This demand is so emphatic that the clergy have not been able to ignore it. Iconoclastic tendencies are strong. Pictures and images are disappearing. The Gospel is heard from unwonted pulpits. In some places this spirit expresses itself still more positively. There are here and there bands of men who refuse to Protestantize;

they refuse to leave the Church in which they were born. In some cases they take excessive precaution to avoid being confounded with Protestants. But they form themselves into congregations, and choose for themselves leaders, whose responsibility is to expound the Gospel. The Gospel they insist upon having. They rebuke their own Churches for hiding it. They labour and pray for a new spiritual life in those Churches.

All this leaves unsaid anything of what exists under the *name* of Protestantism. The problem of evangelism to-day in Turkey includes the fact of a large evangelical constituency. There is a great number of active evangelical Churches, enrolling their thousands of members. There is a still larger Protestant civil community. There are a great many schools, and seminaries, and colleges, aiming at a high education for both sexes. In these schools Christian training is paramount. There are Bible and Christian associations for women; associations for young men, and associations for children. There is no doubt about the fact of a Protestant constituency. It is a constituency, too, from which work is to be demanded and expected. It has demonstrated its evangelistic power. The revivals of which we have heard in various parts of Asia Minor during the last two years, especially the still recent outpouring of God's Spirit upon the Evangelical Churches of Central Turkey, are suggestive of the good that may be expected, and of the responsibility that must be laid upon this constituency. The policy of evangelical missions in Turkey has been to foster in every way self-reliance and aggressiveness. The difficulties have been immense, but the effort has not been unsuccessful. Larger results were aimed at, but we must not minimize the results achieved. There is a working evangelical constituency, and one which should surely feel responsibility. But we cannot ignore its *poverty*. Their resources are incommensurate with the demands made upon them. They become disheartened also by the cry of retrenchment from the missionary societies. The time has not yet come for the withdrawal of those societies. Their assistance will be needed yet for many years. Would that instead of chilling cries for retrenchment, evangelical work in Turkey might be kindled by the command to enlarge and advance!

In passing we may make regretful mention of the fact that this work in Turkey, as in too many other places, represents the spectacle of apparently divided ranks. Turkey, like other missionary fields, is intolerant of that kind of effort which emphasizes mere denominational tenets, rather than truths essential to eternal life. The cause of Christ in this land will welcome any symptoms of progress, which this great Alliance may make, in the good work of assigning to the proper agency each particular part of the field. It will respond quickly to the stimulating influence of any measure which aims at the harmonious presentation of Jesus Christ as the world's Saviour.

Such being some of the general circumstances conditioning the work in Turkey, we may enquire now as to the more important agencies to be employed.

The Native Ministry.

Experience has confirmed the view, early adopted in missionary effort in Turkey, that the Gospel must be preached principally by a body of well-trained and competent natives. And the raising up of such a ministry must remain as in the past a prominent factor in the accomplishment of the work. To realize what is involved in such an undertaking, it is only necessary to remember the different classes of people to be reached, and the variety of language to be employed.

This Native Ministry, as well as the Missionary labourers, need to be thoroughly endued with spiritual power.

This will tell far beyond mere intellectual culture, in breaking down the barriers, removing unreasonable prejudices, and harmonizing the sentiments of loyalty to nation with the dictates of conscience. Oriental human nature does not differ from human nature elsewhere in feeling marvellously the power of a life, which they easily recognize as a God-inspired life.

Christian Education.

Too great emphasis cannot be laid upon the need of a more ample provision for Christian education, as one of the most essential of evangelistic forces. The Christian teacher can go where the Evangelist finds closed doors. Christian schools break down barriers, where preaching would excite antagonism. An experienced pastor in a large town of Asia Minor one day said to me, "For a long while evangelistic effort has busied itself in seeking to enlighten the adult adherents of the old Churches. The more important work now before us is the religious training of our own children, and the bringing of wholesome religious influences to bear upon the other children also, whom we are able to gather together in well-ordered schools." The records of the schools as to the conversions of young men and women give ample testimony to the spiritual value of this department of work. Certainly only the most pessimistic notions of education could fail to anticipate rich spiritual blessings from schools in which the Gospel of Christ is an essential part of the curriculum.

Religious Literature.

The paramount importance of Religious Literature as an evangelistic agency is ever receiving new illustrations. The increasing demand for the Bible in Turkey is stimulated both by the intellectual training of the schools, and by the spiritual training of the pulpit. It must be met on the part of the Bible Societies with enlarged schemes for the dissemination of the printed Word. That Divine Word goes into many villages and many homes, unaccompanied by any human comment, and exercises there its redemptive influence. The Bible colporteur finds villages, never visited by any other evangelical agency, and leaves the seed which is to develop into eternal life. He, too, like the Christian school teacher, prepares the way for the more systematic and persistent effort of the evangelist.

The increasing intellectual life among all classes of the people, suggests the imperative need that evangelical enterprise should at least keep abreast with the times. The astonishing spread of atheistic literature throughout the country emphasizes this need. Evangelism should make itself felt in the intellectual life of the people by wholesome religious literature. Illustrations are not infrequent of the work accomplished by some good book, where no other visible agency has been at work. In the pushing of this department of work also, the missions are crippled by the economy which they are obliged to practise. We expect, of course, to hear of such a censorship that it tolerates absolutely no books, that have as their distinct object the enlightenment of Moslems. Its intelligence and spirit may be imagined from facts of actual occurrence like the following: Astronomical articles in the newspapers have been prohibited because of the use of the word for *star*, which in Turkish is the name of the palace of the reigning sovereign. Geographies have been condemned for containing the name and picture of Mt. Ararat, as located in Armenia. The use of Shakespeare in the schools as a text-book could not be tolerated, because Shakespeare teaches the possibility of overthrowing sovereigns. The biography of Livingstone is not allowed to pass the custom-house, because Livingstone was a missionary to Africa, and no Christian missionary had any business to go to such Moslem peoples. The story of the Prodigal son is objected to, because it will be supposed by some to refer to family disturbances at the palace. Christians have been refused permission to publish the phrase that Christ is the Saviour of the world. The use of individual texts of Scriptures has been forbidden by censors, although knowing that the words are taken exactly from the Christian Bible, the publication of which is authorized. Tracts of small size have been objected to on the ground that they were so convenient for dissemination. Hymns familiar to Christendom have been expunged, because containing the word for soldier. The publication of a work on "Spiritual Awakening" was recently forbidden, because of the term Evangelical applied to Protestant Churches. It is only just to Turkish authorities to say that in this case, and in many of the most ridiculous cases, the censors are from the Christian nationalities.

The difficulties do not cease, even after the rigid press laws have been complied with. Books are published and put into circulation with the due authorization of the Ministry of Public Instruction at Constantinople. They are packed in cases and submitted to the usual examination at the custom-house. They go to the province, and are there confiscated by local officials on the ground that some obnoxious sentiment is discovered, which the censor at Constantinople had overlooked! No reliance, they say, is to be placed upon the imprimatur which appears upon the title-page. Nothing is to be trusted except the official seal of the censor. Ignorant upstarts insist that even this is of no value unless it appears upon every page of the book. The difficulties are not over after the books have gained an entrance into the vilayet. Colporteurs are arrested and books are seized, notwithstanding all the tribulations through which they have already passed. In some cases delays of months are interposed before the work can be resumed.

Here, again, it is only just to remark that the most unreasonable interferences emanate from petty officials, acting oftentimes under instigation from Armenians and Greeks, of that kind zealous for the liberty of all except Protestants. The central government has manifested a disposition to right matters, and correct the blunders of provincials. It is a matter of regret, however, that so long a time should be necessary, and such persistent pressure also, before securing the plainest rights.

Notwithstanding awkward embarrassments of this nature, it is a matter of profound gratitude that the missionary organizations, and also the Bible Societies of Great Britain and America, are able to accomplish the mighty work they do, in the publication and circulation both of Scriptures and other religious literature.

The Political Status of Protestantism.

That the civil and political status of Protestantism should have an important bearing upon evangelistic effort grows out of the peculiar constitution of things by which the Turkish government is administered through the religious communities. Thanks, we believe, to most timely pressure from the British government, the claims of Protestantism to civil existence have again been formally recognized, and we have now at the head of the Protestant Chancery a man pre-eminently well qualified to maintain its dignity and meet its responsibilities. He has before him an almost superhuman task to bring order out of chaos, and put Protestantism as to its civil status where it ought to be. In order to meet the financial burdens of the office he needs the cordial support of the Protestants of Turkey. This he is likely to receive, if we may judge from the sense of need which has been so repeatedly and so emphatically expressed. But it would be visionary to hope that in the present material condition of things these burdens can be very largely met by the community. And so the cordial indorsement of the missionary societies will sustain the Protestant Chancery, in an earnest appeal at no distant day, to the Protestant nations, for material aid in putting the civil welfare of evangelical Christianity, in this land, on a sure foundation.

The Social Status of Protestantism.

There is another great need relating to the material stability and also to the spiritual welfare of evangelical institutions in Turkey. One hesitates in speaking of it, and yet it cannot be ignored in an honest presentation of the demands of the work. I refer to the need of a heartier sympathy and championship in influential quarters. I refer not now to the financial help, but to that moral support, so essential to any religious system in maintaining its dignity and respectability. Why should not Protestant institutions have as enthusiastic a championship as that accorded by their influential men to Greek, Armenian, and Catholic institutions? There are those from whom Protestantism might experience a more cordial treatment, and that to the great encouragement and advancement of its institutions.

Evangelistic workers in Turkey are conscious of being influenced by the highest motives; they are exceedingly scrupulous in observing the laws of the land; they are fully aware that the great Christian pulse of the home lands beats in sympathy with their own. But their character is often vituperated, their motives are impeached or misunderstood, their deeds are misjudged. It is not surprising that they should long for a more emphatic endorsement at least from those men of influence, who accept and love the same faith with themselves.

The Moslems.

Organized effort in Turkey for Moslems is impracticable. This was the decision reached at a missionary conference in Constantinople, so far back as 1856. The decision was afterwards confirmed by the action of both an English and an American Society, in formally withdrawing from organized effort for Moslems. The passing years have wrought great changes in the Turkish empire. Concessions have been made to broad and enlightening influences. The evidences of progress in almost every line are numerous. But the feasibility of evangelistic movements among Moslems is to-day apparently what it was in 1856.

It will, however, be interesting at this time to note some features of the Moslem attitude toward Christianity.

1. It would be entirely gratuitous to suppose that Moslem opposition to Christianity is simple obduracy. We are not to think of Mohammedans as opposed *per se* to the spiritual ideals of Christianity. The phrase "unspeakable Turks" is misleading. Moslem Turks are a religious people. From infancy they are trained to reverential habits and modes of thought in relation to God and eternity. They are stern anti-idolaters. The conception prevalent among them of Christianity is that it is idolatrous. This idea is the natural product of their centuries of contact with those forms of it which they have known. It is difficult for them to interpret otherwise what their eyes have seen and their ears heard. Protestant Christianity puzzles them, but it pleases them. The Protestant chapel, free from anything suggesting idol worship, pleases them. Protestant forms of worship please them, as contrasted with the pomp which they associate with Christian worship. Moreover the Moslem mind is pleased with the earnest spiritual teaching of the Protestant pulpit and the Protestant class room. There may be some suspicion about its sincerity. The truth approved may be regarded as taken really from the Koran. But the fact remains that the essential features of evangelical Christianity please, rather than antagonize the Moslem mind.

2. There is, however, a powerful opposition to Christianity as such, emanating in the first place from the Oolema, or ecclesiastical class. The attitude is that simply of lofty disdain. Christianity, as they understand it, is vastly inferior to their own faith. Their comprehension of both systems may be very limited. But their training, their traditions, and the whole existent order of things makes contempt for the other faith perfectly easy and natural. Neither is it the contempt of mere political superiority. It has the positiveness of honest conviction.

3. There is also a literary opposition which is by no means insignificant. Intelligent Moslem minds understand very well that evangelical Christianity can not be sneered out of existence. The intellectual activity of Protestantism tends to develop in no inconsiderable degree an attempt to imitate it, and compete with it in the interests of Islam. And so we find rapidly coming into existence a body of Mohammedan apologetics. But this enterprise is not merely defensive. It reaches out in ambitious and unsparing attacks upon

Christianity. Not only newspaper and magazine articles appear, but books, exhaustive treatises, are published.

4. There is finally an opposition, the most decisive of all in its results, which centres in the governing class. It is political, rather than religious or intellectual. There are many nominal *Christians* whose religion is not embarrassing to them in the relations of this life. And so Turkish Pashas, as such, need not be suspected of feeling very deeply the religious authority, or even the intellectual superiority of Islam. But Islam, as a political power, seems tied up with its religious security. And disloyalty to the Moslem faith becomes confounded thus with political treason.

A mere reference will be sufficient to the constitution of the Turkish army, tolerating only faithful Moslems in its ranks. This of course strengthens the disposition to give a political interpretation to any movement which might contract their recruiting territory.

The impression is certainly very strong among the ruling class that all missionary effort in that land must have eventually a political object. Protestant missions are not responsible for this impression. The predilection to such a notion was confirmed by the large issue years ago of passports from Catholic powers which followed the operations of Jesuit Missions. Protestant missionaries have had numerous applications for foreign passports, as a reward for the profession of the Protestant faith. Though the missionaries have with emphasis rebuked this conception of their aim, still to this day the average Turkish official is suspicious. The professions of the missionaries do not suffice to undeceive him.

In closing, then, it is to be remembered that all statements in regard to religious liberty in Turkey should be qualified. The following are facts, which it is not likely Turkish authorities themselves would think of disputing.

1. The Turkish government permits and protects other religious systems than its own. It leaves its non-Moslem subjects free to follow the dictates of conscience. At the same time, however, it makes distinctions that are oppressive, as to civil and political rights, upon which we may not linger at this time.

2. The Turkish government nominally permits to every religious

community, schools, and churches. Great practical difficulties however are interposed. Severe restrictive laws are enforced.

3. The Turkish government permits a non-Moslem to change his faith, and eagerly opens the Mosque doors to such as elect the faith of Islam. It does not however allow the same freedom of choice to its Moslem subjects. Many, probably in this assembly, will remember the time when death was the penalty for desertion from Moslem ranks. In 1843, the Sultan gave a written promise to the British ambassador that from that time no one should be put to death on account of his religion. Such a declaration does not modify the law, but only suspends it, and that in violation of Moslem conscience and public opinion.

The Holy Law says that when a Moslem adopts another religion he is to be killed. He is unworthy to live and is already virtually dead. Hence his possession of property rights and conjugal rights terminates. Such a renegade is nevertheless to be dealt with mercifully. He is to be imprisoned during three days with such suffering as may make him realize the gravity of his situation. At the end of that time, if he still refuses to recant, he is to be decapitated and his property is to be seized. It is doubtful whether the Turkish government at the present time would venture to execute a man for accepting Christianity. But it would not be obliged to spare such a man's property, even if it spares his life.

Islam asserts also as strong a grasp upon the converts which it makes from Christianity as upon its born followers. Recently in one of the provinces, a little Armenian girl of 12 years of age, it is reported, was seized by her brother, who had become a Moslem, and put in the family of a Turkish Pasha, where she was persuaded to acknowledge herself a Moslem. Afterwards, she ran away, and returned to her father's house, and claimed his protection as a Christian. The local government decides that having once declared herself a Mohammedan (although the Armenian Bishop protested that a 12 year old child was not competent to change her faith) the proposition of her becoming a Christian cannot be entertained, and so summarily dismisses the case. We shall be glad if we hear that the enlightened central government at Constantinople has reversed this action, and announces its willingness to allow freedom of conscience, at least, to such Moslems as have previously been Christians.

More might be said, but this is enough to illustrate the fact that plans for evangelistic effort in Turkey must be limited. The day has not yet come, when we may, without hindrance, invite all men without distinction to the faith of Jesus Christ.

Evangelization in Italy.

ADDRESS BY THE REV. CAV. PROCHET, D.D., OF ROME.

With intense attention and delight I listened, yesterday, to all that was so eloquently said. But, I must say the truth, I have been sorely disappointed in one thing—I was expecting to hear a word . . . . the speakers succeeded to one another, and the word did not come. That word I feel bound to say, though it may take me out of my subject.

I heartily concurred in what our worthy chairman (Hon. Mr. Bligh) told us when he evoked the souvenir of the Madiai, who suffered in this very city for conscience sake; but there have been other Evangelicals that have preceded us and them in this land, to whom, as an Evangelical Alliance, it seems to me that we owe at least a thought at this stage of our proceedings. . . . So far back as 1218 we read that they held a Synod in the neighbourhood of Bergamo, and that they were numerous in all the provinces of North Italy. From 1350 to 1550 they founded many a town and village in the South of the Peninsula, and their messengers who went from the northern to the southern brethren left traces of them in all the Italian cities they crossed. I do not need to name them, nor do I intend to trouble you with the recital of their long sufferings. Anyone but slightly acquainted with history knows the wholesale butchery that destroyed thousands of them and annihilated the Calabrian colonies, and cannot ignore how they were driven from the other parts of the Peninsula (those at least who could escape the claws of the Inquisition) to the secluded valleys of the Cottian Alps. Who has not heard of the thirty-three bloody persecutions that visited even these, the descendants of the refugees? By thousands, by tens of thousands, they fell for no other crime than that of their persevering and undaunted attachment to Christ and to His Gospel . . . . Now, am I to believe that all those sufferings, those tears, those groans, those rivers of blood, have passed unnoticed by Him Who sitteth on the grand throne and judges according to justice? No, my whole being revolts at the mere supposition. He who took notice of Abel's death cannot have paid no attention to the slaughter of the thousands of confessors of His only begotten Son. Whatever philosophers may say about the connexion between cause and effect in the events of this world, we Christians know that the blood of the martyrs "speaketh to the Lord," that their tears are numbered by Him, nay, that their "very dust is precious to Him." . . . God alone can tell how much we are indebted to those martyrs for the privilege of holding our Conference in a town of the land they have watered with their blood; but I feel sure that no one of us will deny what a debt of gratitude we owe towards them, and that consequently it is not out of place to give a thought to their memory. . . . Impartial history will tell fifty years hence how much Italy itself is indebted to them for the liberty she now enjoys, and how it comes to pass that the land of the Pope has to envy no country of the world so far as freedom of conscience is concerned. . . . A striking fact, but *a fact*—as long as Italy behaved as a bad, heartless stepmother to the Waldenses, she was herself trampled down and trodden upon by all kinds of tyrants. The very year (1848) in which, at last, the emancipation of the Waldenses was proclaimed, that very year, I say, saw the first dawn of the new era of liberty. But mark, it was but a dawn, in point of liberty of conscience, for the first article of the Statute says: "The Roman Catholic apostolic religion is the religion of the State, the other worships are *tolerated* according to the laws." To this day the letter of the law speaks of *toleration.*

How is it that, notwithstanding—I would almost say against the letter of the law, we enjoy full and complete liberty? What may have induced the greatest Italian statesmen, thirty years ago, to give the strangest of all commentaries to the first article of the Statute, and to proclaim in the Subalpine Parliament the grand principle, "Chiesa libera in libero Stato" (Free Church in a Free State)? One of the speakers yesterday referred to the connection of Cavour with some Protestant family of Geneva; but that is not sufficient for an unprejudiced mind to explain the attitude assumed by Cavour. . . . Among his friends there was a deputy to the House of Parliament whose name will long be revered by all those who have known him (I mean Signor Giuseppe Malan, a Waldensian). It is by him, and through him, that the great Italian Minister learnt to know and to appreciate the only Italian Evangelicals then living in Piedmont.

How much Signor Malan had to do with the rapid growth in the concession of liberty of conscience in Italy I have no time to describe, but an anecdote will give an idea of it. In 1860, soon after the annexation of Tuscany to Piedmont, there was in Leghorn an evangelist who is with us to-day. The priests feeling instinctively that the preaching of the Gospel would put an end to their uncontrolled power over the people, did what they could to check his mission. They excited the mob—created disturbances—so much so that the life of the evangelist was more than once in real danger. The Prefect, under the influence of the priests, refused to provide for and protect Signor Ribetti in the exercise of his functions as evangelist. Signor Giuseppe Malan was written to, and went straight to Cavour. I am glad to see you, said the latter; I much wanted to have a talk with you. I hear that one of your pastors is the cause of unpleasant tumults in Leghorn. I am annoyed at it and vexed. I expected better things from the Waldenses. . . . Signor Malan let the great man give vent to his feelings, then very calmly contradicted the statement, and showed that the Waldensian pastor in Leghorn was preaching exactly the same doctrines that the Waldensian pastor of Turin was proclaiming in the Church of Corso Vittorio Emmanuale, the difference in the results depending on the fact that the inhabitants of Turin (priests included) understood what liberty of conscience was, whilst in Leghorn everybody (including the Prefect) seemed to ignore its meaning. "Can you answer for your man in Leghorn that matters stand as you describe them?" "As for myself"—"All right then." . . . And a few hours afterwards a telegram—such as Cavour knew how to write—went to the Prefect of Leghorn, and in twenty-four hours the disturbances were a thing of the past. In a similar way hundreds of officials have learnt what liberty of conscience was, and the whole nation has risen to a higher appreciation of it. . . . Italy being opened, brethren from other lands have come to evangelize it. Following the chronological order in which they have come successively, I name the Plymouth Brethren, the Wesleyans, the Baptists Open Communion, the Baptists Close Communion, the Methodist Episcopals, the General Baptists. In the year 1820 thirty congregations, formed by Plymouth Brethren, united together and founded the Chiesa Libera (Free Church). Some years after Count Campello began his movements towards the formation of the " Italian Catholic Church." All these brethren will speak for themselves. I wish only to say this in regard to them. I have been nearly thirty years in the field; for twenty years, through no merit of mine, I have been honoured by the Waldensian Synod with the presidency of its evangelization work, and I can boldly say that no brother of another denomination coming to me has met with a refusal when he offered the hand of Christian fellowship. I have visited Protestant Churches of many countries, delivered hundreds of public speeches, and I can challenge any man to point out a word less than courteous, in any one of those speeches, towards the brethren of other denominations working in Italy. . . .

And now I should tell of the progress of our Evangelization work, but my time is nearly up, and I don't want to take that of the brethren that have to follow me. So I shall simply say that we received 581 new members last year, and have had this winter about 600 men and women in our Bible classes, and nearly 3,000 scholars in our Sabbath schools. . . . But what is all that compared with an army of 30,000,000 of people? Looking at it, one's arms are ready to fall down in discouragement; but if we turn round and look at the way already travelled, then we can thank God and take courage. Two tableaux will enable you to understand what I mean better than many words. In 1862 the little town of Rio Marina was presenting one fine summer evening a very striking sight. Hundreds of men and women were rushing towards one house, shouting, yelling, and actually piling wood around it to burn it. What was the matter? Who was there? A murderer fled from the penitentiary of Porto Ferrajo? No, in that house were sheltered two theological students of the Waldensian Church, who were utilizing their holidays by preaching the Gospel; the mob, fanaticized by the priests, wanted to burn them alive, and would have done it had it not been for the energetic interference of some men of influence, who fortunately saved the lives of the evangelists and the Church of Rome from another bloody stain. Go *now* to Rio Marina, and you will find in the Waldensian schools 180 pupils, 160 of whom are children or grandchildren of the same people who wanted to burn the first evangelists of the island. . . . May the Spirit of the Lord breathe upon our people and awaken the thousands, the millions of consciences lulled asleep in superstition or infidelity, and we shall see still greater contrasts in the future.

ADDRESS BY THE REV. D. BORGIA, OF MILAN.

Honoured Brethren in Christ—

I gladly respond to the request to give a short statement as to the Evangelical Church of Italy. To the most of you I can say nothing that is new, especially to my fellow-labourers and friends here present, who have been eye-witnesses of the birth and development of this infant work in Italy, but to so many illustrious friends and brethren, gathered from every part of the world, who cannot be expected to know about us, it is right I should explain who we are, and what we should desire to do, with God's blessing, in our native land.

First of all, what is the Evangelical Church of Italy ? It is the Union of the separate evangelical Churches, which sprang up all over Italy in the early days of liberty, through the reading of the Word of God.

These various Churches, moved by the desire of united action in the work of Evangelization, met in General Assembly at Bologna in 1865, and laid the basis of their organization, under the title of the " Free Christian Church in Italy."

But it was only in Milan in 1870 that, properly speaking, the movement took shape and initiative, for it was in that second General Assembly that the compact of Union was ratified by the adoption of a Confession of Faith, or Declaration of principles common to all the congregations.

In 1871, at Florence, the Third General Assembly sanctioned the accomplished Union by means of a Constitution or body of Rules for the work of Evangelization.

Finally, in 1889, by unanimous consent of all the Churches, in order to respond to the ardent desire of the pioneers in the work, and also to the history and special disposition of our Church, the General Assembly by acclamation assumed for itself and for those

Churches which might hereafter be joined with it, the name of the Evangelical Church of Italy.

This Church has for its sole and infallible Head, Jesus Christ and Him Crucified,—for doctrine and rule of faith and conduct, the Word of God contained in the canonical books of the Bible,—for motto in all its actions, "Truth in Love," and for its guide in all social and civil life, "Honour all men. Love the brethren. Fear God. Honour the King."

The great aim of this Church is the salvation of souls and the welfare and prosperity of our beloved country, by means of the preaching of the Gospel.

Such is the Evangelical Church of Italy and such her noble purpose, with the divine blessing! It is a young Church, with little more than 20 years of life, but it has the conscientious conviction of having accomplished much good, by carrying the message of redemption into many towns and villages, and bringing many souls to the foot of the cross of Christ.

Nor has this been achieved without serious difficulties. If you, my hearers, had been present in many a Meeting of our Committee here in Florence, you would have seen us gathered together with sad thoughts, amid uncertainty and discouragement, amid earnest prayer and supplication to God. You would have seen us all, from the lamented Gavazzi to the Rev. Mr. MacDougall, on to the humblest member of the Committee, who has now the honour of addressing you, with tears in our eyes, like a father when he sees his beloved children without bread. Yet God has always heard our prayers, and brought us out of all our difficulties, so that the Evangelical Church of Italy goes on its way as if nothing had happened.

All these trials have done us good, because they have strengthened our faith and brightened our hope in the promises of God. The victory achieved over so many difficulties has convinced us still more that our Church is of God and that He has called us to do His Work. Hence, our greater activity and more lively zeal, hence the increase of the spirit of self-sacrifice in all our Churches and the ever growing desire for the wider diffusion of the Gospel.

I will say nothing about the sufferings endured by the individual Churches, and by the members of the same, for the sake of the truth. We enjoy much liberty in Italy, but the Clericalism of the Vatican is still very powerful and wages continual war against us, and raises up mountains of difficulties to the progress of the Gospel cause. But God is with us, and despite all the persecutions suffered, the testimony for Jesus is maintained by all, and the banner of our salvation is everywhere floating in the breeze.

After these general considerations, I shall now give you a few particulars as to the past and present condition of the Evangelical Church of Italy:

1. *The past.* When our Church presented itself to the Christian World, it was a very poor stripling indeed. The first two or three years were consecrated to the work of harmonizing the various elements in our union and of study and preparation, while we were carrying the Word of God far and near throughout Italy. But soon we found ourselves in presence of three great difficulties:—1. The want of a good Theological College for training aspirants for the Ministry. 2. The need of suitable places of worship, if possible our own property. 3. The opening of day and night Schools in connection with each of our Churches.

To provide at one and the same time for so many necessities was no light matter. But it is written: "Seek and ye shall find." We sought and God has blessed us, and in this wise:

Theological College. To tell the truth, there was always a small College in our Church from its earliest origin. In 1867, thanks to the help of Rev. Wm. Clark, of America, a College was opened in Milan, from which excellent labourers went forth, among others the lamented Zucchi, Girola, Manin and others.

In 1870, this first effort was closed, and immediately another was opened in Pisa, under the direction of Professor Paolo De Michelis, where several faithful servants of Christ were trained, among others Mariani and the lamented Pierallini, who founded the Church at Airolo, on the St. Gothard, and later on the Evangelical Italian Church in Marseilles.

In 1873 the Pisa College was closed and a more thoroughly equipped establishment was opened in Rome, directed by Gavazzi, with whom was associated in 1876 the excellent Henderson, whom God saw fit so soon to take to Himself. Among the Professors we may mention

Rev. Cav. Karl Roennek, Chaplain of the German Embassy, and Rev. Henry Piggott, Superintendent of the Wesleyan Mission in the North of Italy. A directing Council, presided over by the Rev. Mr. MacDougall, watched over the progress of the Classes, and as a result many Pastors, Evangelists, and Teacher-Evangelists were sent forth, a goodly number of whom have passed into other denominations. This has caused no regret. The principal aim of preparing able Evangelists has been attained. If some of these are enrolled in other regiments, we are comforted by the thought that we are all soldiers of one army, guided by one Leader, fighting under the same banner, and called to defend the same great and holy cause.

Owing to circumstances which we could not control, the Roman College has been closed for a time, to be soon re-opened either there or in some other city. The sad loss of Gavazzi, and the decreed demolition of our building in the general plan for the improvement of Rome—these are the reasons for the momentary closure of the College. In the meantime the students are placed under the care of Pastors in different towns. We hope, through God's blessing and the sympathy of friends, that the decision to re-open a Seminary in Rome, Florence, or elsewhere, will soon be carried out, and that many will be prepared within its walls who shall be worthy of the high Mission and of the Gospel, as well as of the Church and of Italy.

. *Places of Worship.* The plain matter of fact is, that when our Church presented itself to the Italians it was well-nigh unprovided with everything, and especially with places of worship. The Meetings were held in shops, warehouses, in the upper rooms of houses, and sometimes we were even driven to assemble in dark, prisonlike places, which made it easy for the priests to discredit the Gospel cause. We were also under constant threat of being turned out, and finding it next to impossible to secure any other place. The Clerical party was ever on the alert, creating immense difficulties for us. Even for these poorest of meeting-houses, we were obliged to pay large rents, which drained our small finances.

Then it was that our excellent friend MacDougall, to whom our Church is debtor for the immense services he has rendered, began to carry out his noble plan of purchasing properties for various Churches. From 1873 until to-day, thanks to the munificence of many friends, he has acquired buildings in Rome, Florence, Leghorn, Milan, Bassignana, Venice (two), Bergamo, Udine, Fara Novarese, and Pisa. He has also to-day in hand for the purchase of other places of worship the following sums: 8000 fr. for Bari, 8000 fr. for Savona, and 7000 fr. for Sassari. We earnestly hope in a few years to see suitable buildings provided in the towns where we have large congregations and Schools, such as Genoa, Bologna, Naples, and Palermo.

This is but one part of the service rendered by our Honorary Treasurer. I say one part, for his activity is seen in all departments of the Evangelical Church of Italy. How he has been able in so short a time to overcome so many obstacles, it is difficult to understand. Asking himself, the only reply is: "Pray, always pray."

Schools. It was also the intention of the Evangelical Church of Italy, that alongside of each of the congregations there should be established elementary and night Schools, as well as Sabbath Schools, for the future of the evangelization of the country largely depends on the rising generation, if a truly Christian education is imparted to it. For this purpose the Committee of Evangelization set itself to the study of the problem of providing Teachers, who should feel in their innermost heart the importance of their noble profession, and be faithful and well-proved Christians, and so fitted to shed the sweet odour of Christ in the heart of the little children.

Sabbath Schools were at once begun in all the Churches through the earnest efforts of the Evangelists, aided by many brethren and sisters in Christ as Monitors.

In 1870, however, there were only two Day Schools, one founded by De Sanctis in Turin, and another by Ferretti in Florence. Since 1872 many other flourishing Schools have been established, in Rome, Leghorn, Naples, Fara Novarese, Bassignana, Venice, Carrara, Spezia, Palermo, and latterly at Forano Sabina and Montefiascone.

2. Now I come to *the present condition of the Evangelical Church in Italy.* Here it would be convenient to make a journey together, which would not occupy many minutes, and pass in review all our Churches, Stations, and Schools, from the North of Italy to Palermo. But time presses, and therefore to complete my statement I shall only add a few statistics.

The Evangelical Church of Italy at this date has—
- 1820 Members (Communicants);
- 450 Catechumens;
- 1295 Children in the Day Schools:
- 1210 Children and adherents, whom I baptize by the name of Nicodemus.

The Church is composed of—
- 31 Churches or Congregations;
- 24 Stations and 50 places regularly visited;
- 30 Sabbath Schools;
- 10 Day Schools and 5 Night Schools;
- 1 Industrial Institution;
- 3 Young Men's Christian Associations;
- 8 Committees of Beneficence and Societies for mutual help.

The Buildings purchased are 13, and 3 are in process of acquisition, of the value of ... Fr.	916,000
Furniture of Church and Schools ... ,,	75,850
Reserve Funds ... ,,	232,625
Making a total of ... Fr.	1,224,475

During the past year (1890) the Churches have collected—

For the work of Evangelization ... Fr.	4,891·63
For local purposes ... ,,	16,326·25
Making a total of ... Fr.	21,217·88

or an average of fr. 9·20 per member.

This is all made up of the pence of poor working men, given for the work of God in Italy, and it is not a small offering.

Now let me bring my address to a close with two observations—

1. A word of thanks to all those friends who have aided us with their prayers and sympathies, and who will not fail us, we trust, in the future. Our gratitude remains eternal towards all of them, and especially to our great friend, Rev. John R. MacDougall, who has

spared neither labours, nor sacrifices, nor health, for the work of God in Italy.

Praise, and honour, and glory, to God for His divine aid, and for all the blessings which He has showered down upon us to this very day. All our trust is placed in Him for the future, and all our care is cast on Him, knowing that He cares for us.

2. The Evangelical Church of Italy has for its basis the Union of the Churches. You will find this principle in the first pages of its history, as in the early days of its existence. Without such a principle, indeed, an Evangelical Church of Italy would not be possible.

Not only so, but we were among the first to make proposals of Union to all the Churches in the first instance, and to the Waldensian Church afterwards, as all in Italy can testify.

We have held Conferences and Special Assemblies for studying the way to effect this noble purpose.

Our efforts have failed. It is said that the time had not yet come for this. Has the time now come for this much-desired Union? God grant it may.

Notwithstanding the shipwreck of these noble aims, we still feel and desire the Union of all the Churches in Italy. We long to be, and to be seen to be, one body in Christ, called to a common effort, for the glory of Christ, in our fatherland.

This Union of the Churches is longed for by all our brethren. It is a voice which sounds in the Italian air from the Alps to Sicily. It is desired by our Italian fellow-citizens, as you heard from the authoritative words of Professor Mariano yesterday.

It is desired by our friends abroad, and, above all, it is desired by God. Let us respond nobly to this divine and universal call.

In one word, the Evangelical Church of Italy sincerely, earnestly, resolutely desires union with all the Sister Churches, and prays that this Great Conference may send forth the word of command, that such a project may be speedily consummated, in order that we may in one serried rank send up the unanimous cry: " We wish all Italy for Christ."

Possessed by this delightful expectation, the Evangelical Church of Italy, through me, offers you its fraternal regards.

ADDRESS BY THE REV. T. W. S. JONES, Wesleyan Methodist Church, NAPLES.

DEAR FRIENDS AND CO-WORKERS,

The first present ever made me in Italy was the gift of a beautiful photographic copy of a statue representing Italy rising from the dust in which she had lain. Underneath the lovely, queenly figure there was graven this motto: "*Dopo 12 anni*"—"After 12 years." Surely in this gathering of the representatives of Christian work and workers in the Ninth International Conference of the Evangelical Alliance it is well to take as our motto: "*Dopo trent' anni*"—"After thirty years." Thirty years of toil and disappointment, years of hope and of success. I would that, as I occupy the brief moments allotted me, I might strike a note of praise! As the review of the past comes up before us, our hearts and voices must blend in a hymn of praise to God, for what He has wrought out for Italy by those who are now in heaven, for what He has wrought in and by us, by you the Evangelical Churches, the Evangelical Church of Italy. We all are the Evangelical Church of Italy.

The Rev. Cav. Prochet has told the story of the Martyrs of the Valleys and of the Calabrias. We all of the common faith and hope of Jesus claim those martyrs as our own. Our heroes are your heroes too. "Ye are not your own." We all are Christ's. We may then sing loud our praise to God for these our martyrs.

It will do our friends here, gathered from the hundred cities of Italy, from the wide world, good to know and feel that amidst the calm enumeration of the difficulties of our work—the faithful survey of what we now are doing, even amidst the wise counselling as to more perfect service, there ought to be also the faithful and loving testimony of what God has done—praise for what God is doing.

Let it then go forth from this assembly to the Vatican itself, let it go round and through our Churches, from the Alps to the farthest sea, to England and America, through France, Germany, the Continent, let the hymn of blessing go the whole wide world round, that we, the Evangelical Churches, *the* Evangelical Church of Italy praise God for what He has done, for what He is doing—"God be praised."

"Blessed be the Lord God." Forgetful of the great things God has done, the hands fall helpless and the spirit faints and fails—when the memory of the wonders He has wrought comes freshly over the soul, then is there light and life!

It is right that we should review the *tendencies of public thought and feeling* as gauged by those without as well as those within the Evangelical Church of Italy, as has been done with master hand by Professor Mariano.

It is well that we should number, weigh and measure *the difficulties* with which we have to cope; and that we should search out and acknowledge the weaknesses, imperfections, and troubles that are ours;—and on account of these we humble ourselves before God:—but we must also remind our friends gathered here from England, America, the Continent, and the world, that these troubles are not other nor are they worse than are found in other Churches and in other lands.

It is right to measure the forces out-growing from the genius of the people, from the social and political condition of Italy, forces that may be drawn into association with and in favour of our work. That we should consider and attain the best methods and modes of working; but I cannot forget that all methods and modes of work are only potent as is the spirit and power with which they are wrought out.

The existence of the Evangelical Church of Italy is *the still continued existence of a Martyr-Church.* Witness the massacre at Barletta—the terrible attack on our work in Marsala, and the thousands breaking into our apartment there; the rising of the people in Pozzuoli, led on by priest and monk; and the life-martyrdom endured by many of our people from day to day.

"After thirty years!" "God be praised."

As we review our own little work in Southern Italy, as we hear the reports of the Churches, our souls are glad with praise. Our Churches, our Day Schools, Evening Schools, and Sunday Schools; our Y.M.C.A. Associations—a goodly array of loyal, earnest Christian workers,—what hath God wrought. We are glad, and thankful; we are not a vanquished band of Christian soldiers; we will not know defeat. The Lord be praised!

The Signs of the Times.—It is not only Signor Mariano, amidst the Professors of the University of Naples, who is bringing the religious question to the front. There is also Professor Chiappelli, who gave us his inaugural address before the University, on the "Millennium." He has promised to give a Lecture on "Christ" in our Church. Deputy and Professor Bovio, one of the leaders of naturalistic thought, publishes his "*Christ at Purim.*" Bonghi gives his "Life of Christ," and before an audience of priests and people of all classes, gives, on a Sunday afternoon, under the auspices of a Literary Society, his reasons why he, a layman, must make known the Life of Jesus. Oh, how many hopeful signs, did time permit, could we recount. We praise the Lord; and we say, Praise *ye* the Lord!

ADDRESS BY THE REV. G. B. TAYLOR, D.D., OF ROME.

I PROPOSE to name some of the advantages and disadvantages, some of the helps and hindrances, in the work of Evangelization in Italy.

I.

One of the advantages is that we have not, as Morrison in China, and Judson in India, to toil long years in making a translation of the Bible, but that one was ready to our hand in Diodati's version, published in 1603, a classic as to style, and at least so faithful that it anticipates many of the improvements of the English Revised Version. And if any object to Diodati's as a Protestant Bible, there is the version from the Vulgate, of Archbishop Martini, thousands of copies of which we are gradually putting into circulation. Yet a third translation by the lamented Professor Revel, at the high level of modern scholarship, is most precious for the student.

So also, for the Roman Catholic controversy, the works of Dr. de Sanctis, and others, furnished a well-stored arsenal from which every needed weapon may be drawn. And I have also noticed that not alone ecclesiastics, but others, who come to us from the Church of Rome, fight their way through so much of opposition, that they are thenceforth well able not only to give a reason for their faith, but also to confute an adversary if not win him to the truth.

We have almost perfect protection and freedom in our work. Petty annoyances and local persecutions are indeed encountered, but the former are overcome with patience, and for serious grievances the law provides ample redress. And the grossest outrages often turn out for the furtherance of the Gospel when met with a manly resistance unmixed with desire for retaliation. Our brethren in the tortures of cruel disease, and in the hour and article of death, "witness a good confession" before many witnesses. The burial of deceased brethren also is a valuable opportunity of Evangelization. Twice lately at the municipal cemetery of Rome, I have assisted in funeral services attended by many who would never enter one of our churches, yet who listened with rapt interest to the hymn, the Scripture, and the words spoken.

The generous kindness of Italian Christians towards their own poor brethren is very beautiful. In part it proceeds from that affectionateness of disposition which is a striking race trait. But it is also to-day, as in Apostolic times, one of the first manifestations of the outgoings in love and helpfulness of the heart which bears the image of Jesus.

I am happy to say in this connection that there exists a fairly good understanding among the various bodies at work in Italy, as among the workers themselves. While the lines dividing us are clearly defined, perhaps *because* they are, there prevails a general good will and fraternal love. We have practically demonstrated how we can be true to our respective convictions as to doctrine and ecclesiastical practice, and yet walk together as far as we are agreed, work together in various lines, and together meet for prayer and praise, not as Waldenses, or Free Church, or Methodists, or Baptists, but simply as the disciples and servants of our one Lord and Saviour. In the intercourse of life there is much of that mutual courtesy, and sympathy, and helpfulness, which greatly promote interdenominational comity, and often make us forget everything save that we are the sons of one Father, and the heirs of the same blessed, everlasting home. In a word, all candid people who know the facts must see the substantial unity which exists among us, in harmony with that diversity which is the necessary fruit of freedom. If many as the waves, we are yet one as the sea. The Evangelical Alliance has done much to promote the unity of Protestant Christians in Italy; and God grant that it may do yet more in the time to come!

II.

Jesus Christ and His Apostles preached in the open-air and in the Synagogues, and missionaries in various lands preach in the streets and market places. But not only are Catholic Churches closed to us, but the law very properly does not permit meetings save in our own *locali*. Hence any extension of our work—save by private labours like those of the humble but useful colporteur—requires the renting of preaching-places, which is attended with considerable difficulty and expense. Nor is house-to-house work done without great embarrassment and labour. Suppose you have wearily climbed several flights of stairs, then to obtain admission into a home into which you have not been previously introduced, and to make there a visit, is a matter of extreme delicacy, if it be not of doubtful advantage or impossibility, and this, too, even among the very poor. The circumstances are utterly different from those of England or America.

And in our conversations and preaching, words often fail of their due effect because of that superficial knowledge of the Bible which is generally possessed, and which makes our message less fresh, unless indeed to those who go deeper, to whom certainly the Gospel comes with the shock of a joyful surprise. But most Roman Catholics think of us as irreverent and irreligious, while the sceptical say that ours is only a different kind of *cottage* or shop.

An analogous difficulty is the weakening, aye the *degradation*, which religious language has undergone. Sin, Saint, Repentance, Confession, Holiness, and many other pivotal words, have been either emasculated or perverted from their true meaning.

Of disadvantages external, may be named the fact that in many parts of the Peninsula the plainer people, who are those usually most ready to hear the Gospel, are in such subjection to clerical landholders that they fear to take a step which may, at least temporarily, take the bread from their mouths and the roof from over their heads. In fact, Romanism has been for centuries so bound up with the institutions, the property, the commerce, the social customs and the whole life of the people, that it must long remain a mighty foe to the Gospel, even apart from its influence as a moral and religious entity.

A problem not easy of practical solution is that of helping the needy who are all around. To be blind and deaf to the cries of the hungry and naked and homeless, were inconsistent with the spirit of the Gospel. But to respond to them as might be done in a Protestant land, were to incur a double peril, as we should thereby repel the truth-seeker, and draw around us those who care most for the loaves and fishes, while we should, at the same time, cater to an eleemosynary spirit which has been fostered for ages.

Our converts are liable to err in opposite directions. On the one hand, they retain customs, which, if in themselves innocent, are yet intimately bound up with the errors they have left. For instance, many are careful to name their children after a saint, and they themselves celebrate not their first—nor their second—birthday, but that of their saint. It may be a convenient custom, but it tends to still further obscure the New Testament doctrine that all believers in Jesus are saints, while it promotes the disposition to have some other mediator than the "one mediator between God and man, the man Christ Jesus." On the other hand, it is easy in the recoil from a system which makes work the price of salvation, to go to the other extreme of not practically recognizing the true place of good works, and the absolute necessity of a holy life.

Possibly in part, on account of this, the sight is not so rare as might be desired, of Churches which have little of the expansive spirit of the Gospel, and little resemble the Thessalonian converts who were "an example to all," and "from whom sounded forth the Word of the Lord, so that the Apostles needed not to speak anything." Such Churches remain stationary, and sometimes worthy brethren have a tendency to preach to their handful of believers instead of going out into "the highways and hedges," with the importunity of those who believe in heaven and hell, and compelling men to come in and partake of the Gospel feast.

After all, religious indifference, the ground swell of Romanism, worse than Romanism itself, is our greatest obstacle, and only the Spirit of the living God can "make these dry bones live."

ADDRESS BY THE REV. JAMES WALL, OF ROME.

IN the brief space of time accorded to each on this occasion, the most one can attempt is to give an idea of some part of the work the Baptist Mission is doing in Italy. The Mission was commenced in Bologna in 1863, and in Rome in 1870. Rather, however, than commence a new mission in Italy, we desired to build on the ancient foundations which lie ruined in the catacombs and testify to the forgotten truth in so many parts of Italy. We recognize that evangelical work in Italy is of vital importance to all Protestants, and that the time has not yet come when the Protestant lamb may venture to lie down with the Catholic lion.

Our mission in Italy comprises three districts—North, Central, and South. At present, I speak of the latter, or at least, of work at its centre. Pardon me if I refuse to regard our Church or work in Rome as *foreign*. The presence of two or three foreigners in a Church of two or three hundred natives does not *un-romanize* a work now any more than when Paul was in Rome. Three of my colleagues deputed to present the salutation of our brethren in Rome to this Alliance are Roman citizens.

In Rome, then, we have *five* preaching stations, while in the neighbouring towns we have *four others*, which are visited from Rome. The principal hall is in the mission premises situated in Lucina, on the Corso, in the centre of the city. It is here that the missionary resides, that the Church meets, that the printing is carried on, and also many branches of city mission work.

In each of the halls we have preaching three times a week; in the Central Hall weekly communion, a meeting for prayer and one for the study of the Scripture. During Lent we have preaching every night except Saturdays. In four of the halls we have Sunday-schools and medical missions; in three, working meetings for mothers; in one, a shop for the sale of their work; in another, a meeting for the very poor, where, according to the need, Mrs. Wall gives bread or soup or seeks to find work for special cases.

The *Church* which meets in the Central Hall has its native ministry, composed of elder (just deceased), deacons and deaconesses, evangelists and helps. It manages its own affairs, has several small societies, and carries on several branches of work. The number of members is between two and three hundred, its form of Church government is free, communion is open, discipline maintained. Everyone is expected to give or receive, everyone is expected to work, either as help to the deacons, or the evangelists, and thus maintain the ministry; all are invited to take the place in the Church on earth, which they hope to occupy in the Church in Heaven. Our only code is the Bible; our Church ideal, Christ's Risen Body; our temporal model, the primitive Church; our mission to come out of Babylon, get back to Jerusalem and rebuild the House of God.

Our statistics of attendances in Rome for the first quarter of 1891 are as follows:—At the preaching, 11,516; Communion, 1,146; Bible Class and Prayer, 863; Sunday School, 3,411; Mothers, 696; Medical, 4,523; Poor, 3,756; Total, 25,910.

I am not discouraged by the strength of Popery, but by our own inability to comply with God's conditions of success. The Vatican is strong because we are divided. Rome is an amalgam of truth and error, both of which find the reason of their existence in the present state of Protestant truth, which must be kept until you receive it—error, which must remain as long as transgression of grace has to be punished. Israel went to Babylon to pay its debt of broken sabbaths, and unlearn the idolatrous lie: when this was accomplished, fingers of flame signed the destruction of the king. So now God's Sabbath is rest in Christ, and ritualistic and rationalistic rejection of this sends multitudes to the slime and willows of Popery. Return to primitive Christianity and Popery is exhausted.

When brought forth from Babylon there must be no stopping short of Jerusalem, and when again on primitive holy ground, instead of building private houses on private plans for private purposes, as the Israelites did, we must think of the House of God, of the plan beneath its ruins, and the worship He requires. This building of private houses has stopped the dew of Heaven. There is much talk of Pentecost, but who sees it? This building of private tabernacles has brought darkness down on the Mount of Transfiguration. Our programme in the Church must be JESUS ONLY.

This work of re-edification requires the heart and hands of all the people of God: not only the ministry, but all the people in mass, everyone in his place. Then, when the ancient lines have been retraced and the ruins restored, we may wait confidently for the glory of the cloud and the power of the *presence*. Thus real Church testimony would be rendered and all those glorious laws of power, now latent, be called into vigour, by which alone the kingdom of Satan can be overcome. Seek, then, the *old paths*. Wait not in Jericho, but in Jerusalem; build not sects, but *the* House of God; watch for deliverance, not from yourselves but from the shining forth of God, the Holy Spirit. If you prefer, however, to take your own ways and think your own thoughts you are free to do so; but, thank God, there is a law according to which you cannot divide for ever. You divide the Church, you may possibly carry your divisions into the congregation of your own soul; but in the Kingdom of God division has no place—*unity* is its law of gravitation. Meanwhile sin calls for chastisements—deep calleth unto deep. Rome has a mission to you; she says: *unite* a dozen little sects at your own door, even while preparing to subdivide tauntingly cry, "unite." The politician, the philosopher, the sociologist recoil before your division, and Italy, after its successful struggle for unity, forbids you to settle down into diminutive vaticans, with their relative primacies, inquisitions, and infallibilities. The Holy Spirit is not blessing denominations in Italy *as such*. He is recognizing individuals whenever He can do so, and is thus keeping the truth alive until His time has come for *resting bodily* upon believers who are of *one heart* and of *one mind*. In such a moment, "whereunto we have already attained," by that same rule let us walk. This is the present limit of our liability, to which, if we are faithful, light shall reach us as we meet the difficulties which successively arise—"*even this shall God reveal unto you.*" So shall our "path be as the dawn, shining more and more unto the perfect day," "till we attain unto the unity of the faith and of the knowledge of the Son of God."

ADDRESS BY THE REV. WILLIAM BURT, D.D., OF ROME.

THIS is not the time or place to sound the denominational trumpet, nor to boast of our personal work. Now it becomes us, it seems to me, to look over the whole Evangelical field, and in the light of our experience in that field ask what are the difficulties, and what are the means most efficient for accomplishing the work proposed.

The Christian world knows how important is the Evangelical work in Italy. Here we contend, not only for the cause of Christ and humanity in Italy, but in the entire world. We know, also, how great, powerful, astute, and implacable is our enemy, the Papacy. It is true that it has not all the worldly means that it once possessed, though it still has enough. Permit me, however, to say frankly that in spite of all these worldly means, all this power and cunning, the greatest obstacle to the Gospel in Italy is not so much the Papacy as the Evangelicals themselves. I cannot here give the history of Evangelization in Italy, though this would furnish the clearest proofs of my assertion, but I will simply and frankly say a few things which I have learned during five years of study in the field itself.

1. There is much that we could and should do together as Evangelical Churches, but there is a lack of the true spirit of union. There are those who speak of and apparently exert themselves to effect this union, but generally speaking these mean uniformity to their methods rather than unity, and they are intolerant of those who do not conform to their ideas. There is a spirit of egotism, of prestige, and of pretension, which wishes to rule over others instead of admitting them to fraternal equality. True unity begins with union of heart, of scope, and of principle, leaving to each the liberty to adopt those means which may seem to him the most effective, provided that they are not contrary to the Word of God. Here is the basis of a true union among the Evangelicals of Italy, and united we would be strong.

The history of Protestantism teaches us that union is possible, and of very great advantage; but that uniformity is impossible, and that the efforts to effectuate it are injurious to Evangelical work.

We have before us, in the Papacy, the Giant Goliath well armed from head to foot, who challenges the most valiant of the army of

Israel. Who will vanquish him? Perhaps some other giant among us? But where is this giant in the Evangelical camp? Behold a David called of God! The youngest of all, and somewhat small of stature, but he is full of courage and certain of victory, because full of faith in God. The giant despised David because he was young, and Saul and the others, seeing how small he was, tried to dissuade him from his intention to meet the giant. Finally, however, seeing the persistence of David, the king caused him to be armed with his own armour. But David said, I cannot walk with these because I have not tried them. And David chose from the brook five smooth stones, and, with his sling in hand, said to the Philistine, "I come to you in the name of the Lord." The giant fell with his face to the earth. From that moment began the popularity of David, and the consequent envy and hatred of Saul. Why could not the great and magnificent Saul do that which David did? Because the power of God was no longer with the proud and pretentious king, but with the humble and trusting shepherd lad. If the Lord should call into our camp a David, who among us would wish to take the position of Saul, and insist that the newly called David wear our armour?

Our success in this work is not a question of nationality, nor of denomination, nor of prestige, but of our fidelity to God. And if we truly love God we shall love each other, and be united at the Cross of Jesus, and there will be the consequent fraternal equality.

2. In my opinion we have sought too much to make the people Protestants rather than sincere and living Christians. In order to have numbers we have not always been sufficiently careful about the genuine character of those whom we have taken into the Evangelical Churches. And sometimes we have not respected as we should have done the rights of each other in the passage of members from one Church to another. The desire has been to make a good show to the committees in charge, and especially to the foreign committees, in order to stimulate the contributions. This has greatly damaged the work in two senses. We have lowered our ideal of the work, and we have inscribed as members of the Church those who are Christians only in name, and who have brought discredit to the cause. The statistics have been enlarged in order not to make a bad show, but in the end we have not only made a bad show, but have positively injured the work.

3. We have made a mistake in Italy by neglecting the lay-element in the work of Evangelization. In the Romish Church the priests do all, and are, in fact, the substitutes of the people. Sometimes I have thought that it was almost the same in some of our Evangelical Churches. The ministers preach, pray, and, in fact, do all, while the brothers and sisters of the Church are mute. Have they nothing to say? Has not Andrew found the Messiah? Why, then, does he not go and find his brother Simon? Must he first go and find a minister who has a diploma from some Theological School, and who has been regularly consecrated? If we have tasted of the grace of God we are all apostles and missionaries of Jesus Christ.

Last month I had the great privilege to be present in one of the popular Evangelistic services in the city of Geneva. How beautiful and cheering it was to see so many distinguished laymen zealously occupied in the work of the Lord!

Speaking with the distinguished president, Count St. George, he said, "I do not believe in ruts, but I do believe in rails." For many here in Italy the argument that closes all is, "*We have always done so*, and, therefore, no change in our methods of Evangelization can be approved."

Brethren, the Lord has wonderfully blessed in these last days the work of the laity, the men and women of the Church. But some one says, In Italy we have no laymen, or very few, capable of speaking in public. It is certain we shall never have them with the present system of exclusiveness.

4. To have perfect communion and co-operation there is too great a distance between minister and people. As ministers we are willing to be doctors, professors, directors, teachers, and I know not what else, while we forget that we are called to be shepherds, ministers, and servants of the flock of Christ, sent to save the lost and re-conduct to the right way the erring.

5. In conclusion, I must say that in the so-called Evangelical Work in Italy, we hear little or nothing about the Holy Ghost and His work in the conversion of souls. Here, probably, is the principal reason why there are so few spiritual conversions.

"That which is born of the flesh is flesh, and that which is born of the spirit is spirit. Marvel not that I said unto you, ye must be born again." In the presence of so many and so great difficulties, we are weak if we have not the Divine Spirit. We are often face to face with those possessed and tormented by the devil, and although disciples of Jesus, we are not able to cast him out. We have not the power. What can we do without the divine fire, the power of God? It is not enough that we are Protestants by birth, that we have been baptized by evangelical ministers, or that we have regularly completed all our studies as theologians. We have need of something else that comes alone from God.

May God pour upon us the Holy Spirit!

ADDRESS BY SIGNOR VARNIER, OF MESSINA.

ADDRESSING this august assembly, I feel I would rather abstain from referring in any way to my personal history, but for the development of the subject on which I am called upon to speak, I am obliged to touch on a few points in connection with it.

Brought up most rigidly in all the tenets, superstitions, and practices of the Church of Rome, and joining at an early age one of its religious Orders of the strictest discipline, I determined to devote my life to Missionary labours in heathen lands. Ordained a priest, and while yet in Rome finishing my theological and controversial studies, I was directed to learn the English language, with a view of working among the English Protestants for their conversion to the Church of Rome. At that time the many secessions from the Church of England to the Church of Rome, consequent on the Tractarian movement, had raised up the long-cherished hopes of the Papacy of re-conquering England to the Church of Rome; and all efforts were being made by the Jesuits to favour that movement, by setting at work all possible agencies, and multiplying Missions in Protestant England. Our English friends may not know that Rome attaches the highest importance to subduing and re-conquering England to the Papacy. Rightly or wrongly it is believed in Rome, that if Protestantism be *crushed* and *stamped out* in England, it will die away in every other country. England is considered as the great bulwark of the Protestant faith, and the mainstay of all Protestant Institutions, Missionary Societies, Bible Societies, and other Gospel agencies throughout all countries. If so much energy, activity, earnestness, zeal, devotion, and above all, wealth, which England devotes to the cause of Protestantism, could be taken hold of by, and made subservient to the cause of the Church of Rome, the Papacy would completely triumph over Protestantism, and stamp it out in all other countries.

Animated by zeal for the conversion of Hindoos and Mahomedans, but above all for the conversion of English Protestants to the Church of Rome, I left for India. There I set to work earnestly and *bonâ-fide*, having learnt the languages of the land indispensable for the work, but my chiefest charge was for English work. It is not here the place to say by what providential circumstances the Lord brought about my conversion to the Gospel of His dear Son, drawing and rescuing me from darkness to His marvellous light. I published a little book at the time of my conversion "Why I left the Church of Rome." Suffice it to say that it pleased God of His infinite mercy to draw me to the excellent knowledge of Christ Jesus and the power of His grace, by the very means I was employing to draw Protestants to the darkness and superstitions of Rome. Nor let it be supposed that I was ignorant of the Bible. I was acquainted indeed with its letter, and had studied it in its original languages, but I did not know its spirit. A Roman Catholic does not read the Bible to find therein the mind of God and the teachings of the Holy Spirit; but he reads it to find therein the *mind* and the *teachings* of his Church. Received into the Church of England, and Licensed by Bishop Cotton, of Calcutta, I was sent to open the Patna Mission for Hindoos and Mahomedans in connection with one of the Church of England's Missionary Societies.

But from the time of my conversion, I felt an ardent desire to return to this land of ours, and devote all my poor energies, all my life, in promoting a thorough Reformation of the Church in Italy. But alas! at that time our dear Italy was split into petty kingdoms, tyrannized over by petty princes in alliance with the Papacy. Sicily, my native island, was groaning under the oppression of the Bourbon Government, and in total spiritual darkness. No native of the land was allowed to profess the religion of the Gospel, much less to preach or to teach it to others. The Italian Bible was a proscribed book there, no less than it was here. The only bright spot in all Italy was little Piedmont. In this state of things I had but to pray, and wait the Lord's time if He would use me in His blessed Gospel cause in my native land.

This time, however, came. It pleased God to grant that the Italians should realize their long aspirations of political emancipation, freedom, and national unity. Constituted into one great, free, and united nation under the sway of the glorious house of Savoy, every citizen was free to return to his home, and profess whatever form of religion his conscience dictated. As soon as I could conveniently do so, I obtained leave from the Bishop and the Missionary Society I belonged to, and came to Europe. In England I made known my purposes and my plans to some kind Christian friends, who were interested in the spiritual restoration of Italy by a thorough Reformation of its Church, just as they had rejoiced at Italy's political regeneration. Helped by them, I left England for Italy, my ultimate destination being Sicily, where I had fixed the field of my operations, and from where, if blessed by the Lord, they would be extended to other places. With a view of ascertaining what prospects there were to effect a thorough Reformation of the Church of Italy, I visited some of its principal towns, exploring the views, ideas, tendencies, and dispositions of the clergy and laity to that effect, and their actual state of religious thought and religious aspirations.

The idea of Church Reformation I had cherished for Italy was that it should be effected from *within*, and not from *without;* that it should be a corporate Reformation brought about by a national impulse of a *want deeply felt* for a purer, higher, and spiritual Church life; a return to the primitive Gospel doctrine, faith, discipline, and Evangelical simplicity of worship, which distinguished the Church at Rome in Apostolic times, when the faith of the Roman Christians was spoken of throughout the world. Just as Italy had effected its political emancipation from *within*, inspired by the *deeply felt* want of being a great, free, and united people; so a similar felt want of a purer and more spiritual life should lead them to effect the Reformation of their Church.

But alas! I was very sadly disappointed in my expectations, and soon I perceived that such a Reformation, as I had designed in my mind, was impossible. In ascertaining the real state of religious thought, tendencies, and aspirations both of clergy and people in the different towns of Italy and Sicily, I found there was a desire indeed for a Reformation ; but their ideas of Church Reformation did not rise above simple *Ecclesiastical Reformation.* It was a *Reformation* of forms, a simplification of Ritual ; the performance of the Church Services in the language of the people ; the abolition of enforced celibacy, and restoration of the right of marriage to the clergy ; a limitation of Papal and Episcopal power over clergy and people ; the suppression of gross abuses in the Church, and such-like externals. But as for a *Spiritual Reformation*, a return of the Church to the *Spirit* and the *purposes* of the Gospel ; to a renovation of mind and heart in its members in accordance with the revealed Will of God, feeding in, and abiding by His Word ; to a higher spiritual and inner life hidden with Christ in God, seeking communion with Him in faith and acceptance through the blood of Christ,—of this *Reformation*, the *real, indispensable* and *needed Spiritual Reformation* of the Church in Italy, neither clergy nor laity seemed to think of it or have any conception of it. In fact, all the attempts made, and the religious movements set on foot, by good and well-meaning men, in several towns of Italy, both enlightened and liberal priests and laymen, did not go beyond the limits of *Ecclesiastical Reformation.* In my interviews with some of them, I was told that for the present it was not safe to touch Dogma ; neither clergy nor laity were prepared to go thus far in Italy ; but they thought that *Ecclesiastical Reformation* would lead, in time, to Spiritual Reformation. I frankly expressed my own convictions to them that I thought they were beginning at the wrong end. Spiritual Reformation would *surely* carry with it *Ecclesiastical Reformation ;* but the past has shown that *Ecclesiastical Reformation* has seldom, if ever, led to a pure Gospel and Spiritual Reformation.

It was on these lines that the work was initiated by me at Messina, in the year 1863. At first, a few personal friends gathered round me, anxious to know what reasons had induced me to leave the Communion of the Church of Rome. This I told in a series of addresses or lectures, affording me the opportunity of contrasting the Church of the Gospel with the present Church of Rome, and thus of preaching to them the grand vital truths of eternal life.

My house was open at all hours to inquirers after the truth, amongst whom there were not a few Priests, and I was ready, by God's help, to answer questions, to solve doubts, to evangelize, and to witness for Christ. Thus a nucleus of believers was formed, and the work began to assume a shape. At this time, by God's providence, the Rev. Signor Scuderi was called by the Lord to see the errors of the Church of Rome and to believe the Gospel. And he, faithful to the Divine call, renouncing his living and benefice in the Church of Rome, joined me in the work of evangelization among our countrymen. From this time our plans assumed a definite shape, and our method of evangelization a definite form.

Our work is undenominational, our aim not that of organizing Churches. This we leave to those Evangelical bodies and Churches already in the land, who will follow on our wake, and gather in those that have believed through our preaching. Our aim is to draw people to Christ, to realize His Divine power as a personal Saviour. To do this we go among the people and try to make friends of them. We have found by experience that it is not by preaching in buildings and halls that the masses can be reached. We must go to them, as the Apostles did. We avoid controversy as far as possible, and when it is forced upon us, we conduct it in a calm and friendly spirit. We have found by experience that preaching the Word in faith, "Christ, the power of God;" "repentance and remission of sins in His Name," and reconciliation with God through His blood, walking henceforth in newness of life—these are the grand truths that have power of converting the hearts and winning the day.

It is thus that by preaching the Gospel through good report and evil report, by scattering broadcast the Divine seed of the Word everywhere, in open-air places, in house-to-house visitations, in railway waiting-rooms and carriages when travelling, in places of public resort, in conversation rooms, in hospitals, in factories, and wherever we can get opportunities of reaching individuals or a body of people with the Gospel message, by endeavouring to use all such influences and means in our power to enlighten the masses, we contribute our mite towards preparing the materials for the building of God's spiritual temple, a pure Gospel Church in our dear land.

ADDRESS BY THE REV. GORDON GRAY, D.D., OF ROME.

THE Presbyterian Church in Italy differs in one respect from all the other Churches, whose representatives have just spoken. While its special work lies among English-speaking residents and visitors, it has always abstained from setting up any mission of its own. The wise founder of its various stations very early in his experience of Evangelical work in Italy, came to the conclusion that "the Italians would do the work best themselves." His life work, so admirably summed up in "The Italian Campaign," was nought but the consistent application of that principle. In this respect the late Dr. Stewart was thoroughly supported, not only by his own branch of the Church in Scotland but by the Presbyterian Churches of the world.

I must refer to the share which the Presbyterian Church has thus far borne in the great movement. Its stations in Italy are five in number. Leghorn was established as far back as 1845, Florence followed in 1849, Genoa in 1854, Rome in 1859, and Naples in 1861. Not one of these stations has been without its work among Italians, though the principle has been steadfastly adhered to that they "can do best for themselves."

I do not now allude to the work done among English seamen at the ports of Genoa, Leghorn, and Naples. A special place has been assigned on the programme for reference to that important work, which after all belongs to and benefits foreign nationalities. Our Church has given itself largely to educational work. Dr. Stewart, in addition to his many labours on behalf of the Waldensian Church, established in Leghorn elementary schools, through which hundreds of young people have passed and have obtained an acquaintance with Evangelical truth. Naples station has been even more remarkable for the numbers of young people that have been brought under Evangelical influences by the same means. Though the actual additions to the membership of the churches have not been numerous through these schools, a wide field has been prepared for the colporteur and the evangelist. Prejudices have been dissipated. It has been made far easier for many to profess the Evangelical faith and identify themselves with one of the Evangelical Churches. I do not mention Florence in connection with school work because our station here is an illustration of what another of our ministers has been able to do for another Italian Church. The labours of Mr. MacDougall on behalf of the Evangelical Church of Italy (better known as the Free Italian Church) have laid that Church under the deepest obligations. He has been very largely instrumental in making it what it is. There is not a school nor congregation connected with it that does not owe much to his energy and zeal. All the influence which he has gained during these many years as minister of the Scotch Church here he has without stint devoted to the Free Church of Italy. What Dr. Stewart has been to the Waldensian Church Mr. MacDougall has become to the Free Italian Church. The two Churches of the country, most thoroughly Italian in their origin and direction, are thus generally acknowledged to have become what they are in large measure through the self-denying and most devoted labours of two Presbyterian ministers. And so the special function which our Church believes has been assigned to her has been doubly fulfilled, while manifest proof has been given of the liberty which she allows to her sons who serve her, always within the limitation that has been already more than once alluded to.

This sketch would be still imperfect if I did not allude to what our Church has been honoured to do in connection with the education of girls of the better classes. In Naples and Rome there exist schools of this character. As our minister from Naples will speak on this subject, I do not enter into detail. It may suffice to say that some 270 girls are receiving an education based on evangelical principles at these two schools, of whom by far the larger number are in the Naples schools. Among these girls are to be found daughters of noblemen, senators, deputies, officers of the army and navy. One of the special benefits that cannot fail to flow from such work, is the bringing of an element into the Churches which will tend to make them self-supporting. We are gathering the elements on which the Churches are to work, and we shall be only too glad to pass them on to those who can utilise them.

In regard to the work of the Evangelical Churches in Italy, as hitherto carried out, there has always seemed to me to be a very great want, one, too, which could be so easily supplied. Local branches of this Alliance in all the leading cities would be of great service in the direction which I am to indicate; and I trust that one of the fruits of this General Conference will be the thorough establishment of such branches, each with its monthly united prayer-meeting connected with it, and with its joint evangelistic efforts as well, because prayer and work should go together.

COUNT CAMPELLO, who hoped to have been able to attend all the meetings of the Alliance, and to take a prominent part in them, was, to the deep regret of all, seized with illness, and was only able to be present at one meeting—that held on the evening of Tuesday, the 7th of April. On that occasion he was too ill to say more than a very few words. He was followed by one of his young evangelists and preachers, the Rev. Ugo Jani, from San Remo. The Rev. Alexander Robertson, of Venice, introduced Count Campello to the meeting. Time only permitted him to give a much curtailed address. We asked him, however, to write out his notes, which he consented to do, and we here give them in full, as they tell in a succinct form the story of the Count's life and labours.

COUNT CAMPELLO'S CATHOLIC REFORM MOVEMENT,

BY THE REV. ALEXANDER ROBERTSON.

CONTE Enrico di Campello is well known throughout Italy and beyond the bounds of the Peninsula as an able preacher and evangelist, a courageous reformer, and a patient sufferer for the cause of liberty, truth and righteousness. To him it has been given, as it was to Paul and to the Philippians of old, "in the behalf of Christ, not only to believe on Him, but also to suffer for His sake." Count Campello was brought up in the Church of Rome. About forty years ago, when he was a young man of twenty, he was constrained, much against his will, to enter the ranks of the Roman Priesthood, under that unwritten, but then almost universally obeyed, law by which every family was expected to give a son to the Church.

Whilst never reconciled to his position, he determined from the first to make the most of it, and to lead an active, useful life. This determination, coupled with his great natural abilities, his scholarship, his earnest Christian character, and his frank and sympathetic disposition, opened for him a clerical career of great promise.

In 1861 he was made a Canon in the Church of Santa Maria Maggiore, a position which he held for six years. During that time he founded evening schools in Rome for young apprentices, and did missionary work amongst the boatmen of the Tiber, in addition to discharging all the offices of his canonry. Indeed, his activities in an educational and evangelistic direction outside his official duties rendered him obnoxious to his brother Canons, who, in contempt, called him the "black canon." But the "black canon" soon left them all behind, for in 1867 Pio Nono bestowed upon him a canonry in St. Peter's. Count Campello was then thirty-six years old, and was the first ever appointed to such an honourable position at so young an age. It was whilst holding this canonry that he began his work as a reformer. The difference between the Catholic Church of Italy of early centuries, and the Roman Catholic Church of the nineteeth, painfully pressed itself upon his mind. In those early times the Church was free. The people elected their priests, and the priests and people elected their bishops, and there was no Pope, and no curia of ambitious worldly-minded cardinals to lord it over God's heritage. Then the Church was pure. The monstrous claims and irrational doctrines of the Church of Rome, which make her to-day the enemy of education, of liberty, of righteousness, of almost every principle that is essential to human progress, were unknown. The idea of a return to the Church of primitive times took possession of the Count. He talked to others of this. He found many at one with him. And so a Reformation Society was started inside the walls of the Vatican itself. But Count Campello soon discovered that it is an impossibility to effect reform inside the pale of the Church of Rome. Those whose interest it is to keep things as they are will listen to no argument in that direction, and will scruple at the adoption of no means to crush those who do. Why, even the Pope himself is only a puppet in the hands of the curia, and dare not cross their will. He is free within a certain circle, if he oversteps that he gets a cup of poison. The *Reformation Society* was destroyed. Some of its members were coaxed into acquiescence in the existing state of things, others were driven into submission, and others were buried alive in obscure parishes where they could exercise no influence. Count Campello was examined, and threatened, and flattered. At last the prospect of a cardinal's hat was held out to him. Nothing, however, could move him from the cause of reform. But now, having for a long time been convinced that inside the pale of the Church of Rome he could never accomplish much, he nobly resolved to sacrifice everything, to resign his canonry, to turn his back on his brilliant ecclesiastical career, to separate himself from all his old friends and associations, and, shaking himself free of all trammels and obligations, to stand forth, though he should do so singly and alone, before his countrymen as the champion of Italian Catholic Reform. On the 13th September, 1881, he broke with the Papacy, and went forth from the Vatican, with all its pomp and luxury, never again to enter it.

During the past ten years Count Campello has laboured in Italy in the cause of Reform, that is to say, he is seeking to bring about in his native land a reformation such as was brought about in England in the sixteenth century. Briefly stated, the chief things in his programme are these—the rejection of Papal supremacy, of Mariolatry, of Saint worship, of Purgatory, of the Mass, of compulsory auricular confession, of celibacy in the clergy, and of Latin in the Church Service. He holds the leading doctrines of Protestantism, and the Episcopal order of Sacraments and Government. He demands that all Church Services be conducted in the mother tongue, and that the bible should form the subject of public and private reading and study. Like Wycliffe, he believes "that every man's guide should be in every man's hand." Count Campello is therefore virtually one with all of us now present, and with the different Churches we represent, in all that is essential in our faith, whilst differing from some of us as to the secondary matters of policy and ceremony. There is one feature in his mode of working to which I especially want to draw attention. He conducts services on Church lines and on Evangelistic lines, but whilst doing so he keeps them strictly apart. There is no confounding of the one with the other. The Church Services are held in his chapels, when robes and liturgy are used, and the worshippers are, for the most part, enrolled members. His Evangelistic Services are held in schoolrooms, barns, private houses, and in the open air. At them robes, liturgy, and all the formalities of a Church Service are laid aside. By means of an Italian flag, or a hand-bell, or hand bills, the passer-by is invited to attend. Sankey's hymns are sung, and short pithy Gospel Addresses are delivered by several speakers. By means of these services the Gospel is carried to the people, and thousands are made to hear the good news for the first time. I think the distinction here drawn by Count Campello between Church and Evangelistic Services is one to a great extent lost sight of in Italy. In Presbyterian and kindred Churches the so-called Sunday or Week-night Evangelistic Service generally differs in no particular from the Sunday morning one. It is conducted in the Church, by the Pastor alone, who preaches a sermon, and observes in other particulars his usual Church order. The result often is that the attendance is simply his Sunday one reduced in numbers. Members and adherents of his congregation are there, but outsiders are not reached nor brought in. I think, then, it would be well if many of us in Italy learned a lesson from Count Campello as to the way of conducting Evangelistic Services, and if we could hold many such in every quarter of the land.

The adaptation of Count Campello's Catholic Reform Work to meet the present needs of Italy is very apparent. Wherever he plants a cause success attends it. It was so in the Valnerina, where his headquarters are, at Terni, at San Remo. It could not be otherwise. Although Italy is the centre and shrine of the Papacy, it is no longer a Papal country. Secondly, for *intellectual* reasons. The unprofitableness of a service of ceremony conducted in a tongue known neither to priest nor worshipper, which is often the case, is apparent. The young intellect of the land denounces it as a mockery. Thirdly, for *moral* reasons. No class in Italy, as the records of police courts and parish registers testify, surpasses the priests in looseness of morals. The great fact of marriage having been taken out of the hands of the Church and made a civil rite; of education being now national and secular, and entirely outside the control of the priests, who are no longer employed as teachers; the fact of public charities being now removed from the control of the Church, and being administered by lay government commissions, on which it is illegal for a priest to hold a seat; the passing of those clauses in the new penal code which threaten with fine, imprisonment, and dismissal from office, any minister of religion who talks against the unity of Italy and its constitution; all show the attitude of bitter hostility that exists between the king and Pope, the Quirinal and the Vatican, the State and the Church in Italy, and also show that the people are masters of the situation, and have chosen their king and country, and have repudiated the Pope and the Papal Church. But whilst they have thus thrown off Popery, they have not thrown off religion. Their religious instincts are strong as ever. This is seen in the fact that they are printing the Bible for themselves, and that its circulation is every year increasing. Nor have they thrown off Catholicism. They have ceased to be *Roman* Catholics, they have not ceased to be *Catholics*. And so it is just here that Count Campello's Reformed Catholicism comes in to meet and to satisfy what is fast becoming a national demand.

Again, the Ecclesiastical Property Law of Italy favours a Reformation on Count Campello's lines. All Church property belongs to the State. The Papacy as a Church owns not a stone in the land. The State lends that property to the people for religious purposes. It rests with the people to say of what nature these services shall be. The moment they demand a Reformed worship the Churches are theirs in which to conduct it. At Mount Orfano, near the Lake of Maggiore, this law was lately put in force, and a Protestant service is now being conducted in the Parish Church. At present there is a widespread state of callousness and indifference. There is nothing to move the nation as a whole religiously. But things cannot continue as they are. The State cannot for ever recognize and support in its midst a Church which is its most bitter and most dangerous foe. The Papal guarantee clauses in the Constitution of 1870 cannot always remain in force. They have long been denounced by the Italian nation as "infamous." And so, should a national crisis arise, should Italy be involved in war, she will then turn fiercely upon her internal foe. Roman Catholicism will no longer be the national Church of the land, but if the State continues to recognize a Church at all it must be one on the lines of Count Campello's movement—

a Reformed Italian Catholic Church. Should such a crisis arise soon, Count Campello's present labours are preparing the people for it. Should it not come, his labours themselves are bringing about this Church Reformation, only slowly and peacefully. Men flock to his standard wherever he can plant it. At present his resources are very limited, and utterly inadequate to the necessities of the case. Italy needs to be evangelized, to be Christianized. But a fraction of the twenty millions at present outside Roman Catholicism has been gathered within the pale of any other Church.

Not a few Evangelical Churches and Societies, strong in numbers, and in resources, and in the sympathies of Christians in England and America, are at work in Italy. Count Campello, I know, rejoices in that fact. His presence here this evening is a proof of it, and of his desire to recognize and to co-operate with all who, though they wear different uniforms and carry different ensigns, are yet fighting for the same cause, under the same great Captain; and I trust that all here regard Count Campello in the same way. Let us seek to put in this way into practice everywhere and always the spirit of the Evangelical Alliance, under whose auspices we are here met. Let us seek to embody in our lives the spirit Paul manifested when he said, " Christ is preached, and I therein do rejoice; yea, and will rejoice," and so hasten on the day when this land of Italy, so long sunk in ignorance, and superstition, and idolatry, shall be brought back to its primitive state of Christian knowledge and of Christian worship, in which its early inhabitants rejoiced; and which made them blessed, and a blessing to many nations around.

WEDNESDAY, APRIL 8, 1891.

FIRST SECTION.

THE REV. BP. WALDEN, D.D. (UNITED STATES) PRESIDED.

The Divine Authority of Holy Scripture.

PAPER BY THE REV. PROFESSOR R. A. REDFORD, M.A., LL.B., OF LONDON.

ALL Evangelical Christians will unite in recognizing the Divine authority of Holy Scripture. They will differ very considerably from one another when they make the attempt to formulate the grounds of that authority. Our Lord Jesus Christ in discoursing with the Jews employed language which must have been clearly understood by them to mean that there was a Divine authority in the written word which forced them to receive it as a statute or commandment, to be obeyed not discussed, when once the voice was distinctly heard. "*The Scripture cannot be broken*," said the Saviour (οὐ δύναται λυθῆναι ἡ γραφή). That is to say, there is no possibility, in consistency with the position of a true Israelite, a true child of God, a true citizen of the Divine Commonwealth, of escaping the obligation to accept as true what God says in the Scripture, and to submit to the written Word as a final court of appeal.

We take it for granted that in some or other meaning of the words there is a divine authority in Holy Scripture. In claiming for the collection of writings which we call the Bible, divine authority, we wish to escape at the same time the "*Scylla*" of a *rationalistic Individualism* and the "*Charybdis*" of mere *ecclesiastical dogmatism*.

We think it is not necessary to be drawn in by either to the destruction of our Faith and of our Freedom. We cannot satisfy ourselves with a definition of authority which seems to exclude the main fact that God has given to us a special and positive revelation in the Scriptures.

To say, as many are saying, the authority of the Bible is the authority of Truth itself, Truth recognized as truth, and therefore binding upon the reason and conscience, the authority of Scripture in its commanding power over me—is not enough. That is only one side of the matter. The subjective must have an objective corresponding to it.

Nor are we much helped to define authority when we are told that the Word of God is in Scripture, but the Word of God is not identical with Scripture. The Bible makes no claim to be the sole and exclusive means of divine communication with mankind. God speaks to His creatures in many ways and with many voices. There is no single sentence in the Scriptures which can be rightly interpreted to mean that there is no other source of divine light than the pages of the Bible, nor is there any possibility of defining the exact limits of Scripture by the words of Scripture. Moreover, when we speak of divine authority, it must be clearly understood that verbal infallibility is not meant, nor are we bound to acknowledge the seal of a canonical imprimatur put upon a certain collection of writings. We may rightly and reverently enquire, What is Scripture? In answering such a question we entirely disclaim all ecclesiastical authority as such. We may agree with the Canon, but divine authority is to us something far higher than decrees of councils.

Another preliminary point is this—divine authority of Holy Scripture does not mean the absolutely uniform value of every book of Scripture, and of every portion of every book. There was a distinction preserved among the ancient Jews between the Law and the Prophets, and between the Prophets and the Holy Writings or Hagiographa. All had divine authority, but all did not stand upon the same level. The Pentateuch lay at the foundation, the Prophets were built upon it, and the Hagiographa was a kind of supplement, confirming and filling up the grand outlines. The divine authority of the Apostle Paul's epistles is not destroyed by the admission that an argument, or an analogy, or an allegory, or form of speech, is peculiarly Pauline. The divine authority of the Mosaic writings is not destroyed by the admission that a superseded theory of the physical universe appears in their language. We cannot identify divine authority with mere details of external form. Holy men of God spake and wrote as they were moved (φερομενοι) impelled and guided, by the Holy Ghost. The men were inspired, and the people to whom they spake were inspired; the authority was both in the messenger and the message, and as preserved and handed down to us, it was both in those who ministered in God's name and those who testified to their message. Unless we believe in a providential superintendence by which the Scriptures have been preserved to us, we shall find ourselves compelled to be satisfied with an external argument very far from complete. And the form of that principle of providential care of the Scriptures, if it is not to fall into a mere blind acquiescence in tradition, must spring from the Bible itself. The *internal* authority and the *external* authority mutually confirm and support each other.

Our position, then, is this—the Divine authority of Holy Scripture is the authority of the Spirit of God, the authority of divine facts, the authority of special divine grace, the authority of a divine testimony in the Church, and lastly, the authority of manifest superiority and supreme success in the world.

I. *The divine authority of Holy Scripture is the authority of the Spirit of God.* No one will deny the fact of Inspiration. No one will refuse to admit that some of God's servants have been lifted above others in knowledge and enlightenment. If such men, inspired men, have written books, it is no unreasonable demand that we should place such books above other books. If you find that there are books, now included in the Bible, which have been made books of final appeal in matters of faith and practice by believers, distinctly on the ground that they are given by Inspiration of God, that to the Jews before the time of Christ they were the books of "*the Oracles of God*" committed to them, and to the Christians after the time of Christ, they were set apart from all other writings as the Law of Christ for His people on the same ground, that they were given by inspiration;—then such writings certainly come to us with the seal of the Spirit upon them. If we have any doubt as to any individual writing, we shall appeal to the same Spirit of God to guide us to a decision respecting it, asking to be led into the truth in deepest humility and reverence. It is not necessary, however, to dwell upon this part of the subject. As a general principle it is sufficient to state it. All Scripture that is given by Inspiration of God has divine authority. The divine authority of the Bible claims inspiration for a particular collection of sacred books. Therefore, the stress of proof must lie on the evidence which attaches to the books.

II. *The divine authority of Holy Scripture is the authority of divine facts on which they rest, and which are the substance of them.* Christianity is a body of facts, it is a kingdom of God on the earth. As such there must be an authoritative history on which it rests, and that history is in the Bible; there must be an authoritative institution of the kingdom, an authoritative exposition of its nature and laws,— the Bible comes to us as such. It is emphatically the *Book of the Kingdom*, published in the name of the King. Every one of the sacred writers professes to speak with authority, and those to whom he spake and who gave his writing the place it holds in the sacred volume acknowledged that authority. The Bible comes to us as a State Book, with the stamp of the Divine Government upon it. If any portion of it is challenged, it must be on the distinct ground that it is not genuinely that which it is said to be, and which its place in the volume asserts for it. We hear a great deal in these days about evolution. The Law of Continuity is much in men's thoughts. No one can deny that there is a close connection of continuity between Christianity and the antecedent Judaism. There is a line of facts which culminated in Jesus Christ and in the Christian Church. Looking back over the fifteen centuries which preceded the appearance of our Lord in Palestine, if we take the books of the Old Testament as representing those centuries, and coming out of them at different intervals, it is easy to recognize in the succession of books a marvellous unity, a continuity, and a manifest fulfilment in the Gospel. The Old Testament and the New are mutually interpretative. Each is the complement of the other. Christians with the New Testament in their hands still find the Old Testament full of divine teaching, and see in it an authority which clothes itself afresh with the Spirit of Christ, in the Gospels and Epistles, but is substantially the same.

And the Bible as the Book of our Religion stands quite apart from all other religious books identified with religious life. In the Eastern world there are religions and religious books, but there is nothing like the Bible. In the cases of Hinduism, Buddhism, Confucianism, Parseeism, Taouism, or any other heathen religion, the religion has grown out of the books or out of the teaching of an individual, but there is no divine history on which the books themselves are founded at all comparable to what we find in Holy Scripture. There is a wonderful course of facts in Scripture, and they form the substance of the Book, and they culminate in the one supreme and pre-eminently Divine fact, the sum of all previous facts and the beginning of the New world, the manifestation of Jesus Christ. The books of the East are not at all like the Bible: they are prayers, songs, ritual, in their earliest form simple, devout, elementary, religious teaching and worship. But most of the sacred books of Eastern Religions are commentaries upon other sacred books, books of complicated ritual, developments, philosophical treatises, remains of great religious sages, rules of common life.

There is no parallel anywhere to what we find in Holy Scripture, that is, an historical germ traced from its beginning to its full growth and firm establishment in the earth, the Kingdom of God shadowed forth on the first pages of Genesis, described in its development in connexion with the history of God's ancient people, and then at last, in fulfilment of distinct predictions of Old Testament Prophets, set up as an everlasting kingdom in the person of the Lord Jesus Christ. Can we compare with this, for one moment, the story of Gautama, the dreamy conversations of Kreeshna and Arjoon in the Bagavad Gita on the mysteries of human life, or the philosophical meditations of Lao-Tse? Admit there is legendary matter in the Bible, will that destroy the continuity of the great line of facts in the record? There is no people of whose national life we can say what we must say of the people of Israel, it had a distinctly divine commencement and divine direction. The books written by its great men declare and expound that divine character and destiny of the nation. It was built upon the hope of a personal Messiah. As soon as the kingdom, which was prophetically embodied in the Jewish people, became, visibly, an accomplished fact in the Lord Jesus Christ, the nation, simply as a kingdom of this world, was swept away in the destruction of Jerusalem, and a spiritual kingdom took its place, of which the New Testament is the statute book as well as the historical foundation. The authority of Scripture is the authority of *the Tree of Life*, which is seen more or less clearly in every book of it, which stands out in the Gospels deeply rooted in humanity, and claiming the whole earth as its sphere. Is there any book in the world which contains in it facts at all comparable in greatness and gloriousness with those of the New Testament? If such facts are accepted at all, they must be accepted as more closely identified with the Divine Author and Ruler of the Universe than anything else in human history. If Jesus Christ really lived and worked and taught and set up His Kingdom on earth, as the New Testament says He did, then in some supreme sense He must have come forth from God, and His Book, the book which we call "the New Testament of our Lord and Saviour Jesus Christ" has divine authority amongst men. The New Testament carries the Old Testament with it. As the Apostle Peter said at Cæsarea, "to Him give all the prophets witness," and as our Lord Himself said to the Jews, "Ye search the Scriptures, for in them ye think ye have eternal life, and they are they which testify of Me." We may be tempted sometimes, in our desire to find Christ in all the Scriptures, to read Christian meanings into particular words and phrases and facts, which they will scarcely justify; but whether we say the Old Testament is full of types and foreshadowings or not, it cannot be denied there is a progressive development in it, a Messianic development, and it is only a very uncandid mind that will hesitate to admit, now that we can place the two volumes side by side, that they stand to one another, as the Epistle to the Hebrews declares, in the relation of shadow and substance. The grandeur of Christ gives divine authority to the whole Bible. It is full of Him from beginning to end. Every page has a watermark in it. Hold it up to the light of the Christian consciousness and you will see that it is the watermark of the divine government, and the sign manual of the King of kings can be recognized in the midst of it. Criticism, with its hard, narrow, and often presumptuous dogmatism, may compel us to change our views or to doubt our old positions, as to the authorship or date of particular books of Scripture, but criticism cannot overturn the main facts. No one can read such a book as the book of Psalms and not believe that it came from a people very much higher in their religious character than any other, and that behind those sacred songs there is a Law and a history at the root of the national life substantially the same as that described in the Pentateuch. Such facts are divine, and give divine authority to the Bible.

III. *The Scriptures are authorized by Divine grace.*

The books which are collected together in Holy Scripture are not, as some have represented them, mere remains of Jewish literature, they are not an anthology, they are not writings of great literary men or sages, which by their inherent merit have overcome oblivion, and been preserved by the universal reverence of a whole people. They are the religious books of a nation, but they came forth from a portion of the people, a remnant according to the election of grace, whose position was that of steadfast adherence to the Law of God, while the great majority of the nation went astray, walking in their own ways, not daring, it is true, to disown the authority of the Scriptures, but contributing nothing to them, and neglecting the institutions which grew out of them. This was very strikingly seen at the period of the restoration of the Jewish state and religion on the return of the Jews from captivity. There must have been a very much larger number of the people who preferred to remain in the provinces of Persia and mingled themselves with the heathen, than the comparatively small number who were re-settled in Palestine. It was the select few, called out by the grace of God, who started afresh the Jewish nation, and they did so on the basis of the Law of Moses. The fact that the Samaritans claimed to have a Pentateuch of their own, shows that the Mosaic writings were still acknowledged to be the fundamental Scriptures of the nation. No Jews in Persia set up a different religious authority and standard, while at the same time they were more in numbers, richer and more powerful than the small remnant in Jerusalem. Through eighteen hundred years the Christian Church has been inviting the descendants of those people, scattered over the earth, persecuted and oppressed, to accept Jesus as the true Messiah who fulfilled the Law and the Prophets; unwilling as they are to occupy the Christian standpoint, they still read and reverence the same Scriptures which predicted their ruin, and to which their own history is a solemn testimony. How could prophets have ministered to such a people; how could such men as led the work of restoration; how could Haggai and Jeremiah and Malachi, have secured a hearing and been the voice of God to the whole nation, while in fact surrounded by so small a minority, unless the grace of God had clothed them with a spiritual power which was supreme and indisputable? The seal of conscience is upon the books. Their place in the Bible is a witness to the divine authority which they not only claimed but exercised.

The Bible stands on holy ground. Even those who are condemned by its message, and whose sufferings fulfil its predictions, put off their shoes from their feet when they approach it. Afflicted Jews stand and wail against this sacred wall of divine Scripture as they do against the ruins of their Temple at Jerusalem. How different it would be if the Jews had simply gathered together a number of ancient books and said, These are the remains of our literature which flourished through fifteen hundred years—these are the writings of our greatest men. In that case we should place such books in the one vast library of human thought and progress, and should see in them no more than contributions of various value and significance to the providential education of the race. But we have only to glance at the Bible to see that it bears no analogy to such a national literature. Not only are all the books deeply imbued with the same religious spirit, but in several instances, particularly among the prophets, there would seem no reason for the preservation of the writing, save that it was the fruit of special grace bestowed on the writer. Unto the Jews were committed these "*oracles of truth*" as the Apostle Paul has called them. They have come from a small minority who were the Church in the world, the Church in the nation, yea, more, the Church in the Church; they were spoken to ears divinely opened to hearken, they were uttered by lips touched with a live coal from off the altar of God. Various as they are, both in character and value, they carry with them the authority of that special grace of God which called out the individual writer, and which surrounded him with the few select souls who heard and read and kept the words of his prophecy, and were blessed of God in doing so. And this leads us to another statement of the divine authority of Holy Scripture. We may say,

IV. *The Divine authority of the Scriptures is the Divine authority of the Church of God.* It does not seem possible to maintain the authority of a positive revelation in sacred writings unless we admit that there is a true Church of God, and has been a true Church from the beginning, to which and by which the revelation is given to the world. God may reveal Himself to a great poet, and his poetry is in a sense a revelation of God to the world, but we cannot attach to the works of a great poet special divine authority. There is an admixture of truth and error in his writings which deprives them of any claim to be a universal and authoritative standard. But the Bible is the Book of the Church. The authority of Scripture is the authority of the true Church holding forth the Word of Life to the world. Are we, then, in the position of subjection to fellow men, and are we compelled to define where the true Church of God begins and ends, and who are its representative leaders? In the midst of modern ecclesiastical controversies it is absolutely necessary that we understand what we mean by the authority of the Church. There is a Canon of Scripture, but there is no divinely-given Canon. There is an imprimatur on the books which we receive, but there is no obligation on true believers, because they are members of the body of Christ, to recognize the imprimatur of a particular ecclesiastical organization. We have no evidence in the case of the Old Testament writings that any Jewish assembly or council prescribed the exact limits of Scripture. After the time of Moses for many centuries there was no attempt made by the Jewish people to put together their Scriptures. It is true that at the time of the Restoration, under the personal guidance of such men as Ezra and Nehemiah and their companions of what is called the great Synagogue or assembly, there seems to have been something like the formation of a Canon of the Old Testament, but it is impossible to say when it was closed. It was certainly left open for the addition of other writings for a considerable period, and what was gathered together was not stamped by any formal decree as neither to be added to nor taken from on pain of exclusion from the Religious Commonwealth. We have a large collection of writings in the Old Testament which are simply called "*The Writings*," and that title was probably given to them ages after they were published, simply because they were preserved and regarded as sacred writings by the

Jews, though not placed on the same level with the writings of Moses and the Prophets. For three hundred years the books of the Old Testament were exposed to the trial of being preserved among a fallen, corrupted people, and through great political convulsions. A number of books, chiefly written in the Greek language, came into existence through these centuries. The fact that the Jews of Palestine never mingled them with the books of Scripture, proves that there was all along the ages a "remnant according to the election of grace," who kept the Word of God pure, and to whose influence it was owing that the Bible was not destroyed by the corruptions of the nation. At the time of our Lord's appearance, there was no confusion of the Apocrypha with the Old Testament. Jesus never quoted the Apocryphal books and never referred to them. Degraded as the people were in many respects, they still honoured, outwardly at least, the ancient Scriptures.

To some extent the writings of the New Testament may be said to have gone through the same kind of trial. There was a period which may be called the period of formation; then there was a distribution of the writings through the communities of Christians, and a general acknowledgment of their authority; and after the Churches received them, they were exposed to a very severe test of circumstances, the fiery trial of persecution, the attack of heathen opponents and heretics, and great apologists rose up who defended not only the Truth itself, but the writings in which the Truth was set forth. From the fifth century onwards, there was a universal acceptance of the books in the great ecclesiastical organization which called itself by the name of the Church. Division there still was even in the Western world, but it was not over those books which now form the New Testament, but on the question of the Apocrypha. The Council of Trent settled that controversy as far as the Roman Catholic Church was concerned, and bound that Church to a false view of Scripture. But in doing so, the distinction was clearly put before the world, between the voice of the true Church of Christ and the voice of ecclesiastical Councils. Decisions of Councils have not been the work of the Divine Spirit, they have frequently been obtained by unworthy means and by the suppression of religious liberty. No Canonical decree is binding on Christians generally. No Canon of

Scripture is of any importance except as evidence by which we may judge what has been the prevailing view of Christendom. For some centuries, as there was no recognition of the necessity for dividing and separating the books of Scripture from all other books, some of the writings of early fathers of the Church were read in the public assemblies of Christians, and sometimes bound up with the books of the Bible. But the very writings which were so honoured witnessed to the authority of the Scriptures. The voice of the early Church was not the voice of accurate scholars and critics, but it was the voice of faithful and devoted Christians, and it always set the words of Apostles and Evangelists above all others. We are bound to respect the judgment of those who lived during the first four centuries as to what books were Apostolic.

As an external argument nothing can outweigh the evidence of men who represent the great leading currents of opinion among the Churches. The books were not only read as the Word of God, but they became more and more identified with Christian life. The Spirit of God set His Divine seal upon them. He kept them in the hearts of God's people; He maintained their superiority over all other books. Nothing short of a spiritual miracle could have preserved the New Testament from corruption, during ages of ignorance, persecution and strife. The thousand years which preceded the Great Reformation, though they were full of spiritual darkness and superstition, still bore a continuous testimony to the Word of God. Great men in the Roman Catholic Church wrote their commentaries on the books of Scripture and elaborated their systems of Theology. Tradition was set up side by side with Scripture as an authority, but the New Testament itself was never dethroned as the highest record of the Divine Mind and Will. When the light broke forth over Europe from a German Monastery, and the true people of God were summoned by the voice of Christ's faithful witnesses to a work of Reformation, the Bible was subject again to a very severe trial. The sacred writings had to be brought out into the light from the holes and corners where they were hidden. Criticism began its work as never before. The new life of the Church had to be distinctly based upon the Word of God. The spiritual revolution tried the Word just as the Word tried the Reformers. And the New Testament came forth from that trial with undiminished divine authority. The Roman Catholic Church condemned itself as unfaithful to Truth. Attempting to hold up what was supposed to be a falling ark, it put forth its hand upon the Scriptures, and by its Canon corrupted them, and so brought the curse of God upon itself. The real Bible is not the Bible of any Church Canon, it is the Bible of God's own people, the Bible of His Spirit, the Bible of Christian life and experience. Whatever changes criticism may necessitate, the ultimate appeal must always be not to scholarship or intellectual judgment, but to the Spirit of God in the Church of Christ. The *"onus probandi"* must fall upon those who deny the authority of that which comes to us with the seal of Time and Truth upon it. Looking at the present position of the Bible in the midst of a stormy sea of critical controversy, surely it becomes us to be patient, and at the same time watchful and prayerful. The dogmatism of the so-called scientific school of Germany has imposed upon some, but new and startling facts and discoveries are continually reminding us that Time will often do for us what argument fails to do; we shall keep hold of our divine assurance, and therefore we shall not be "tossed to and fro, and carried about with every wind of doctrine, by the sleight of men, in craftiness after the wiles of error," we shall "prove (or try) all things, and hold fast to that which is good."

V. Lastly. *The authority of Holy Scripture is the authority of its own manifest superiority and divine success in the world.*

We do not maintain the divine authority of any Ecclesiastical Canon, of any traditional names, titles, dates, or critical readings, manuscripts, or editions. We cannot prove with absolute certainty that the words as written are in every case Holy Scripture. But there is what Jerome called *the Divine Library*, the collection of books written by men who were inspired by the Holy Ghost. And we can appeal to the testimony of experience when we place these books above all others. The facts of the last fifty years have been wonderfully confirming the truth of Scripture. Biblical literature is now the commanding feature of the age. The greatest powers of mankind are being occupied with the Bible. Heathen nations are being provided with the light of God's Word. The throne of the world will be given up to that which manifestly is taking captive the thoughts and sympathies of men. We stand upon what one of our greatest Englishmen has called "*The Impregnable Rock of Holy Scripture.*" There have been other lights shining in the world. Sir Edwin Arnold has described in his beautiful poetry, "*The Light of Asia,*" but he has shown us in his recent poem, "*The Light of the World,*" that before the "Sun of Righteousness" all other lights grow pale—that He was "*the Great Consummation.*" What can we put above the Bible?

And this internal superiority, this manifest miracle in the Book itself, is confirmed by the divine success which attends it. The Bible is practically master of the world. It is practically proved divine by what it is accomplishing. Who is there that will venture to deny the facts? Is it not indisputable that the Bible has been and still is casting out the superstition of the human race, that it has wonderfully promoted and stimulated the civil freedom and advancement of the world, that it has fed and nourished the human intellect, that many of the greatest minds have done homage to its commanding power, and that it has kept alive in the hearts of millions, and is at this present time waking up afresh in the midst of all the confusions of modern society, a grand social ideal of universal brotherhood, "the parliament of man, the federation of the world," that it is filled with a sublime optimism which lays hold by faith of "*that divine far-off event to which the whole creation moves.*" The Bible is the Book of Christ, and that gives it divine authority; for the personal character, and history, and teachings of Jesus Christ are the greatest motive power of the modern world. We may say of Holy Scripture what Bishop Butler said of conscience—Universal authority is in it, universal dominion is its right, and our hearts say, let it have *might* as it has *right*. The Divine authority of Holy Scripture is the proposition of faith, the demonstration of history, the testimony of a countless multitude of redeemed and rejoicing souls. Like the Incarnate Word Himself, when on earth—men may crucify it, they may apparently break it in pieces, they may pierce it through and through, and lay it in the sepulchre, but it proves itself divine by a resurrection and ascension to the right hand of God. And, like the glorified Son of Man, the Written Word shall yet reign over all its enemies, it shall judge the world, it shall be translated from the language of human lips to the language of human life, and remain an everlasting kingdom of truth and love, into which all kingdoms shall be lifted up, in which God and man shall be united in perfect fellowship, in which the Water of Life never ceases to flow in the pure river, and the fruits of the Tree of Life are yielded all the year round, and the Rest of God is the rest of His people for ever.

The Word of God the Source of Spiritual Life.

OUTLINE OF PAPER BY THE VENERABLE JOHN RICHARDSON, D.D., ARCHDEACON OF SOUTHWARK, LONDON.

Electric light will not ripen a harvest field. Phosphorescent light will not illumine heaven. The sparks from a man's own anvil will not suffice to show the path by which he may safely travel towards the home above. The illumination upon things divine comes down in mercy, and lifts thought upward, a heavenly direction about heaven. And all Churches need light by which to see, and shine, and grow; and be it error, or sorrow, or sin, or doubt, or opposition, the believer can say, "The entrance of Thy word giveth light." And the revelation covers the whole area of saving and sanctifying knowledge, for the written Word "is profitable for doctrine, for reproof, for correction, for instruction in righteousness." Shield and sword, helmet and breastplate, girdle and sandals, weapons for all warfare, protection against the fiery darts of the wicked—"the whole armour of God"—come out of the provision which God has made. And "all the Churches." What are they, and how do they differ from all the Church? The Church, in its universal and perfected comprehension, catholic in its fullest idea, is the "multitude whom no man can number," the aggregate people of God when all shall be gathered under the great King. And the Church, in its present constitution and development, as visible to the eye of God, is "the multitude of them that believe."

But the Churches—whether "in the house," as in Philemon's case; or local, as the "Church of the Laodiceans"; or aggregate, as "the Churches of Galatia"—larger or smaller communities, in their fuller or narrower organizations, are those on whom we endeavour to bring the statement of our subject now to bear.

And we take the Word of God to mean God's Word written; and we say, "All Scripture is given by inspiration of God," the only source from which the light has come. Christ is the true light as God manifest, and the Scriptures are the true light by which the Holy Ghost has made known Christ.

The Word of God has raised man's ideas of moral beauty by its grand portraiture of the Lord Jesus. It has widened the scope and purified the principle of love's holy labour for the glory of God and the good of man. The river of the water of life may be traced through the ages by the fringe of beauty and fruitfulness which its holy stream has fertilized.

Now we claim that this source of light is to be opened to all the Churches. Oral tradition may be, and has been, corrupted. Historical transmission, in passing through the hands of many generations, may not have been conveyed without taint of party spirit and bias of ecclesiastical mistake. But God's special providence has protected God's written Word; and quotation by enemies, or encomiums by friends, assure us that "the Word of God is true;" and "to the law and to the testimony" is each man's reasonable appeal. The Churches are the keepers of Holy Writ, but not so as to hide it. The Father's will, not merely an extract, or an explanation of it, belongs to the family; and free access by all the members at all times is part of the family compact. And the Churches that keep nearest to the Bible, opening, spreading, explaining, and recommending that, are the Churches in which we find power, and love, and a sound mind. Superstitions wither, bitterness ceases, sloth shrivels, when the healthy and bracing air of God's holy breath is kept in circulation by honest and trustful love.

And the Word of the living God is not only truth, but power. It is "mighty through God" to pull down and to build up, to instruct and persuade, to empty and to fill, to strengthen the muscles of character, sharpen the appetite of faith, and to tighten the grasp of hope. Therefore, to put the barrier of authority, or leave the hindrance of ignorance, between the humblest soul and the Holy Book, is an injury to the individual, and a mistake in the community, out of which mischief is sure to come. All the Churches are bound by the most solemn obligation to leave nothing between the eye of the soul and the light of God. There is nothing to conceal, for God's love is as free and as fresh as the air, and deep as the unfailing fountain. There is nothing to be afraid of, for after all the divergences of Christian opinion, and all the wilfulness of anti-Christian opposition, the whole race of men stand higher, cling closer, and live happier, when the controlling and consecrating truths of revelation are left to do their work.

Besides, there is an inner and an outer sparkle, because it is a jewel that gets its beauty and its brilliancy from God Himself. The Word of God, in fact, fathers itself; and we look up from the holy page to its Heavenly Author, and feel how real, how good, how suitable the message proves. Thus the heart is first enlightened, and then the home is cheered, and the community is cleansed, and the Churches are strengthened and enlarged, and so the world is fettered, and the devil is checked, and the Saviour is honoured, and the Holy Ghost is trusted, and the great God over all is loved, served, and worshipped in the beauty of holiness and from hearts that are attuned by grace.

But we do not worship the Book, when we plead for a reverent handling of it, because it is our Father's gift from heaven. Bibles may be made cheap in money value, because poverty should not place any man beyond the reach of this pearl of great price. But they must never be made too cheap in the estimate to be made of this great treasure of holy truth.

And we do not disparage the Book when we call to mind the fact that it has been inspired, and must be explained and applied by the power of the Holy Ghost. No Church has a sound or a safe theology in which the Comforter has not a conspicuous place and honour. No heart has a true beat about holiness and consecrated power if the Spirit's regenerating, strengthening, and sanctifying grace is not known, obeyed, enjoyed, under the new life which is in Christ Jesus, and no work will ever get to the bottom of its labour upon souls, or rise to the height of its happy achievements in the Church of God, if this witness and seal of power of the Holy Ghost be not both acknowledged and enforced.

When Ezra, the scribe, stood upon his pulpit of wood, the man was above the people. And when he opened the book of the law, the book was above the man. But "Ezra blessed the Lord, the Great God, and all the people answered Amen, Amen." And there above the people, and the scribe, and the book, there was enthroned the High and Lofty One." And here, before all the Churches, and in the presence of all the nations that our faith can gather round us by its mysterious power of peopling desolate places and giving substance to things not seen, we put forward our resolve, our testimony, our honourable distinction that "we are not ashamed of the Gospel of Christ," we are not alarmed about the final outcome upon the darkest nations or the most unbelieving age, that the Word of God must have free course and be glorified; for though "all men have not faith," yet "the Lord is faithful," and "His word shall not return void."

The Position of the Bible with reference to Science.

BY PRINCIPAL SIR J. W. DAWSON, K.C.M.G., F.R.S., OF MONTREAL.

I PROPOSE to refer in the following notes not to mere speculation or to literary or historical criticism, but to the relation of facts and inductions of Science, and especially of Natural Science, to the cosmogony and history of the Bible, in so far as these can be fairly brought into comparison with each other.

It will be necessary in the first place to refer to certain popular misconceptions on this subject. These have been well summed up by Mr. Gladstone in a recent work,* and may be stated as follows:—

1. It is taken for granted and affirmed that modern scientific discoveries have contradicted the statements respecting creation and nature in the Old Testament, and show these to be errors of an ill-informed age. Along with this is mixed up the curious misconception that when any effect is referred to natural law it loses thereby all dependence on a personal God or lawgiver.

2. It is also maintained in connection with hypotheses of evolution that man must, as a descendant of lower animals, have begun his existence in a low or semi-brutal condition, and that all his improvement is the result of his own action and the interaction of his environment, thus leaving no room for revelation.

3. That science leaves no room for the miraculous or supernatural, an assumption which goes far beyond any basis of fact, inasmuch as we know that beyond the limits of man's knowledge and power there must lie a practically illimitable region of the unknown, which may yet be well-known and capable of being used by higher intelligences or by God Himself.

4. That certain historical and critical evidence has been found to prove that the older books of the Bible were written long after the dates which they claim and to which they have been ascribed, and that they consequently have no authority as to matters of fact.

---

* "Impregnable Rock of Holy Scripture."

5. That the ideas of the older biblical writers are of a low and even immoral tone, and unworthy of an enlightened age.

It is not too much to say that these conclusions are merely loose impressions, floating in a confused manner in the minds of men, and that when they are traced to their sources they have no foundation in science properly so called. This however we can inquire into in the sequel.

I.—Necessity of the Narrative of Creation.

The geological chronology has always suggested comparisons with the narrative of creation. These have often been unfavourable to the latter; but this state of things is passing away as our knowledge extends. Few men now doubt that there is in many respects a marked coincidence between the six creative days and the history which has been found in the rocky strata of the earth. There are, it is true, some apparent discrepancies respecting details, but these can be at least conjecturally explained, and recent discoveries have been diminishing their extent, while men are beginning to see more clearly the necessary difficulties of comparing a very short historical statement with the results of investigation of monumental details.

A primary question here is as to the use of any revelation of creation. As to this, I have in a previous work* gone very fully into the question, and have shown that it was in the highest degree necessary that such statements as those in the first chapter of Genesis should be prefixed to a divine revelation, even at the risk of being afterwards placed in comparison with the records preserved in the crust of the earth itself.

1. The grand fundamental doctrine of a beginning of the universe and of its divine origin forms the substratum of all religion properly so-called. This doctrine also is and must always be in perfect accord with natural science. We have traced everything organic and inorganic in the present machinery and inhabitants of the world to a beginning, and we cannot imagine an eternal procession of finite things, therefore there must have been a beginning of all. In this beginning it is impossible that the universe can have been self-created or a product of chance, therefore there must have been a Creator. Science and

---

* " The Origin of the World."

philosophy can rationally reach no other conclusion than that embodied in the first verse of Genesis.

2. If there is an omnipotent and all-wise Creator there must have been a divine order and method in nature, leading up to its culmination in man, and indicating to him his duty and interest as a worker and enjoyer of rest under God. Hence an order of creation, conveyed most naturally under the figure of working days and a day of rest of the Creator, and bringing out in the most general way the leading points of the work, more especially as related to man.

3. In connection with this the idea of one God must be maintained, and no room left for the supposition of good and evil beings contending with each other. Hence all nature, whether apparently helpful or harmful to man, the tempests of the atmosphere and the ferocious beasts as well as the things pleasant to us, must be ascribed to the one infinite Creator.

4. Men had from a very early period ascribed divine power and attributes to heavenly bodies, to streams, to trees, to animals, to heroes and demigods of old tradition, and all these materials of idolatry must be bound together within the doctrine of monotheism. This is most effectually done in the creation narrative and the subsequent statements as to early human history.

These great objects were served in the time of the Hebrew lawgiver and in our own time by the cosmogony and history of the early chapters of Genesis.

II.—Character of the Narrative of Creation.

It may next be proper to enquire as to the resemblances or differences of the order and nature of the process of building up the world as we would infer it from the record of the rocks and that of Genesis. This may be best understood by noting the points in which they agree.

1. In both we are struck by the evidence of an orderly process in which inorganic arrangements are first perfected and then the organic world of plants and animals culminating in man himself. In both we read the unity of nature and a grand uniformity of development and progression from the beginning onward.

2. Though geology carries us only a part of the way to the genesis of the earth itself, yet when it joins its facts and conclusions to those of physical astronomy we reach a formless and void condition, a nebulous mixture of all materials, chaotic and undifferentiated, as the beginning of our planet and our system. Physical astronomy is also making plain to us the fact that the first stage in the conversion of dead and cold matter into worlds consists in the development of those vibrations which cause light, heat and electricity. The only physical idea of a nascent planetary system is that of a self-luminous and condensing nebula. Light is the first demand of science, but such light can at first only be diffused. The next stage is its concentration around a central luminary, and then comes the distinction between light and darkness, day and night. This is clearly the conception of the writer of Genesis i. as much as of modern physicists.

3. After the first formation of a crust on our nascent earth, the geologist postulates an ocean, and he finds that all the stratified rocks composing our continents bear evidence of having been deposited in the waters and elevated therefrom to constitute land. This also is the conception of Genesis. The fiat, "Let the dry land appear," implies its emergence from the ocean.

4. Now, however, we find two apparent points of difference between Genesis and modern science. In Genesis the introduction of vegetation immediately follows the production of the continents, and precedes the creation of animals. In Genesis also the perfection of the arrangements of the Solar system follows this early vegetation, constituting the work of the fourth creative day. Of all this geology professes to know nothing, yet it has some dim perception that the old historian must after all be right. Why should land have existed a long time without any vegetable clothing? Would it not be natural and even necessary that the plant should precede the animal? May not the great beds of carbon and iron ore in the oldest rocks of the earth's crust be the residence of an exuberant vegetation otherwise unknown to us? Again, may not the final gathering of the luminous atmosphere around the sun, and the final regulation of the distance of our satellite, the moon, have been of later date than the origin of the first dry land? There is nothing to contradict this and some things to make it probable. We know that in all the millions of

years since the first crust formed on the earth, the sun must have undergone great contraction, and reasons of at least a very plausible character have been assigned for the belief that in those early ages the moon may have been greatly nearer the earth than at present. Thus, while as astronomers and geologists we may consider these statements as yet unproven by science, we cannot condemn them as untrue or even improbable.

5. When we come to the introduction of animal life, the parallelism becomes obvious. The great incoming of the *sheretz* or swarmer in the seas corresponds with those early Palaeozoic ages which have been emphatically called the Ages of Marine Invertebrates. Not that land animals had not appeared, but they were altogether insignificant in numbers and importance.

In no respect has the author of Genesis been more unfairly treated than in his reference to the *Tanninim* of the fifth day. The word has been translated "whales," and still more absurdly, "monsters." As used elsewhere in the Bible the word Tannim seems invariably to denote a reptile, either serpent or crocodile. It first occurs as the name of Moses' rod when turned into a serpent. It is used afterward for a large predaceous animal inhabiting large rivers, armed with scales, and used as an emblem of Egypt and Babylon.* Evidently it is a generic name applied by the Hebrews to the larger serpents and to the crocodile. If then great Tanninim and flying creatures are represented as immediately succeeding the marine invertebrates, the writer means to picture an age in which reptiles and flyers, which may be either birds or flying reptiles, were dominant. He has before his eyes a picture exactly similar to that represented in the sketches of the Age of Reptiles, by the late Mr. Waterhouse Hawkins. The quadrupeds of the land obviously come into their proper place on the sixth day, as immediate predecessors and contemporaries of man.

6. The comparative recency of man is one of the best-established geological facts, and while, as in the second chapter of Genesis, man may be said to have made his appearance in the latest Tertiary or Quaternary period, along with a group of land animals suited to him and to the condition of the earth when he appeared, on the other

---

* See the Author's "Origin of the World," p. 405.

hand his place in the general chronology of the animal kingdom is that of its latest member. Farther, even since the appearance and wide diffusion of man, there has been a great continental depression which is connected with the extinction of certain early tribes of men, and also of a great number of the quadrupeds of the land. It is, therefore, undeniable that we have in the geological history an equivalent of the biblical deluge.

III.—Antediluvians and the Deluge.

The biblical history of the antediluvian period is apparently mainly intended to inform us of the fall and its moral effects, and to reduce to the level of ordinary humanity certain heroes and inventors who had in a very early age become the objects of mythical stories and idolatrous worship. The deluge itself is presented to us rather in its moral than its physical aspects; and the narrative of it is with much literary skill put into or left in the form of the testimony of a witness— a form which of course relieves it from all the difficulties as to universality, and at the same time enables a graphic delineation of facts to be given in a condensed manner.

I have elsewhere discussed somewhat fully the questions concerning the deluge,* and may here content myself with some questions recently raised respecting its "universality" and the conditions it implied.

It is obvious that there are four senses in which a catastrophe like the deluge of Noah may be affirmed or denied to have been universal.

1. It may have been universal in the sense of being a deep stratum of water covering the whole globe, both land and sea. Such universality could not have been in the mind of the writer, and probably has been claimed knowingly by no writer in modern times. Halley in the last century understood the conditions of such universality, though he seems to have supposed that the impact of a comet might supply the necessary water. Owen has directed attention to the fact that such a deluge might be as fatal to the inhabitants of the waters as to those of the land. In any case, such universality would demand an enormous supply of water from some extra terrestrial source.

2. The deluge may have been universal in the sense of being a

---

* "Origin of the World." "Modern Science in Bible Lands."

submersion of the whole of the land, either by subsidence or by elevation of the ocean bed. Such a state of things may have existed in primitive geological ages before our continents were elevated, but we have no scientific evidence of its recurrence at any later time, though large portions of the continents have been again and again submerged. The writers of Genesis (chapter i.) and of Psalm civ. seem to have known of no such total submergence since the elevation of the first dry land, and nothing of this kind is expressed or certainly implied in the deluge story.

3. The deluge may have been universal in so far as man, its chief object, and certain animals useful or necessary to him, are concerned. This kind of universality would seem to have been before the mind of the writer, when he says that "Noah only" and they who were with him in the ark remained alive.*

4. The deluge may have been universal in so far as the area of observation and information of the narrator extended. The story is evidently told in the form of a narrative derived from eye-witnesses, and this form, as I have already observed, seems to have been chosen or retained purposely to avoid any question of universality of the first and second kinds referred to above. The same form of narrative is preserved in the Chaldean legend. This fact is not affected by the doctrine held by some of the schools of disintegrators, that the narrative is divisible into two documents, respectively "Jahvistic" and "Elohistic." I have elsewhere † shown that there is a very different reason for the use of these two names of God. But if there were two original witnesses whose statements were put together by an editor, this surely does not invalidate their testimony or deprive them of the right to have it understood as they intended.

It is thus evident that the whole question of "universality" is little more than a mere useless logomachy, having no direct relation to the facts or to the credibility of the narrative.

There are also in connection with this question of universality certain scientific and historical facts which should be clearly stated in any discussion of the subject. Nothing is more certainly known in geology than that at the close of the later Tertiary or Pleistocene

---

* Genesis vii. 23.   † "Modern Science in Bible Lands," chap. iv.

age the continents of the Northern Hemisphere stood higher and spread their borders more widely than at present. In this period also, they were tenanted by a very grand and varied mammalian fauna, and it is in this continental age of the later Pleistocene or early modern time that we find the first unequivocal evidence of man as existing on various parts of the continents. At the close of this period occurred changes, whether sudden or gradual we do not know, though they could not have occupied a very long time, which led to the extinction of the earliest races of men and many contemporaneous animals. That these changes were in part, at least, of the nature of submergence we know from the fact that our present continents are more sunken or less elevated out of the water, than those which preceded them, and also from the deposit of superficial gravels and other detritus more recent than the Pleistocene over their surfaces. The human period of geology is thus separated into two portions by a submergence which must have been fearfully destructive of human and animal life, and vastly more extensive than that portion of the Noachian deluge which came under the observation of the author or authors of the narrative in Genesis. If, therefore, we suppose that existing men are the descendants of survivors of this event, there can be no reason to doubt that a catastrophe so terrible might remain in remembrance, and might be the same with the historical deluge recorded in the traditions and early history of so many races of men. Further, since large tracts of land in the Mediterranean, in the Persian Gulf and its vicinity, and on the coasts of Western Europe, which are known to have been above water in the antediluvian period are still submerged, it is possible that as yet we know nothing of the arts or literature of the greater and more civilized peoples of the antediluvian world, except from historical records. If we could ascertain all the facts of this kind, it is possible that fewer difficulties would attend our speculations as to the origin and extent of civilization both before and after the deluge. At one time, indeed, it was supposed that the geological deluge was a much more ancient event than that of Noah, but recent discoveries have tended greatly to strengthen the probability of their identity as to date. Thus geology and archæology have no alternative but to believe in a deluge of wider range geographically than we could have inferred with any certainty from the narrative in Genesis.

One other objection to the deluge narrative perhaps deserves a word of comment—that urged against the statement of the gradual disappearance of the waters. The extraordinary difficulty is raised respecting this, that the water must have rushed seaward in a furious torrent. The objection is based apparently on the idea that the foundation for the original narrative was a river inundation in the Mesopotamian plain. This cannot be admitted; but, if it were, the objection would not apply. River inundations, whether of the Nile or Euphrates, subside inch by inch, not after the manner of mountain torrents. Thus this objection is another instance of difficulties gratuitously imported into the history.

In point of fact the narrator represents the deluge as prevailing for a whole year, which would be impossible in the case of a river inundation. He attributes it in part, at least, to the "great deep"—that is, the ocean; and he represents the ark as drifting inland or toward the north. Such conditions can be satisfied only by the supposition of a subsidence of the land, similar, in kind, at least, to the great post-glacial flood of geology. Partial subsidences of this kind, local but very extreme, have occurred even in later times, as, for instance, in the Run of Cutch, the delta of the Mississippi, and the delta of the Nile; and if the objectors are determined to make the deluge of Noah very local and more recent than the post-glacial flood, it would be more rational to refer to subsidences like those just mentioned, and of which they will find examples in Lyell's "Principles," and other geological books. It is, however, decidedly more probable that Noah's flood is identical with that which destroyed the men of the Mammoth age, the palæocosmic or "palæolithic" men;[*] and in that case the recession of the waters would probably be gradual, but intermittent, "going and returning," as our ancient narrator has it; but there need not have been any violent debacle.

I may add that the importance and authority of the Déluge narration are supplemented and enhanced by the invaluable table of the early affiliations of nations in Genesis x., which all scientific investigation confirms.

IV.—Scientific Work relating to Hebrew History.

There can be no doubt that within recent years a large amount of

---

[*] "Modern Science in Bible Lands," chaps. iii. and iv.

work on the part of surveyors, excavators, and archæologists has been throwing light on the older Hebrew books, and remarkably vindicating their historical truth.

The signal confirmation of the topographical accuracy of the books of Exodus and Numbers by the Ordnance Survey of Sinai is one of these, though its force is scarcely yet appreciated by theologians and linguistic scholars. The late Professor Palmer has extended this evidence to the north, and I have myself ascertained the geological and topographical accuracy of the part of the narrative relating to Egypt. My own studies of the region of the Dead Sea have also enabled me to vindicate the accuracy of the narrative of the destruction of the cities of the Plain, and recent discoveries in Chaldea have unearthed corroborative evidence of the battle of Abraham with the Euphratean kings.

The excavations of Tanis, Taphanes, Rameses and Pithom, the Tel el Amama tablets and multitudes of other Egyptian facts have all tended in the same direction. The excavations of Lachish, the ruins of the ancient Minean cities of South Arabia, the monuments of the Hittites, and the extension of the evidence of literary work and education to times long antecedent to Moses in Egypt, in Arabia, in Syria, and in Chaldea, all tend in the same direction. These are subjects on which others who have given them special attention may dwell; but I may be pardoned for saying that as archæological evidence they can be fully appreciated by the geological student.

While, therefore, certain lines of literary criticism and philosophical speculation have been reaching conclusions adverse to the Bible, and even to Theism and natural religion, the testimony of nature and ancient art as disclosed and interpreted by actual original workers has been tending altogether in the other direction. Thus the practical work of science is placing itself in antagonism to evolutionary dogmas and refined textual criticism. In other words, nature itself is coming forward to testify to revelation as an emanation from the author of nature. In an enlightened age like ours, it is scarcely possible that fact will not ultimately overcome conjecture, however able and plausible, while on the other hand, the intensely practical character of Christianity and its reflex action as a spiritual life on all ordinary work and research, cannot fail to promote the scientific pursuit of truth, and to discountenance vicious, superstitious and degenerate tendencies. The present outlook for both religion and natural science is therefore hopeful; and we may expect that they may more and more work together as allies, and that the triumphs of the Word of God in the immediate future will surpass those of the past.

In so far as present difficulties relate to science they seem to depend mainly on two features of our time.

1. The prevalence of systems of Philosophy which have arrived at the absurd conclusion that the Kosmos shows no indications of divine wisdom and power, but is a result of mere mechanical reactions or of chance. By such systems scientific men are naturally easily misled.

2. The exclusive pursuit of specialties in which men bury themselves so deeply in pursuit of particular veins of truth, that they lose sight both of the landscape around and of the heaven above. In reference to these errors it is necessary that we should revert to the teaching of God as the Creator of Heaven and Earth, a doctrine as essential in our time as in the dawn of revelation.

SECOND SECTION.

M. LE PASTEUR RECOLIN (PARIS) PRESIDED.

Christ, the Foundation of the Authority of Scripture.

OUTLINE OF ADDRESS BY THE REV. PROF. G. GODET, OF NEUCHATEL.

THE differences which divide theologians are too great to allow of any theory of inspiration. Our ideas on the subject proceed from our inmost experience, and from our individual development, intellectually and theologically.

I. There is great disturbance among Christians, even among those who believe in the great evangelical facts, by the assaults of modern criticism. The problem is how to settle the question of the authority of Scripture so as to preserve the faith of our contemporaries. There are many proofs that the Bible is divine. Its unique beauty, its superior teaching, the presence of the Holy Spirit in it, its power to regenerate, the prophecies included in it. Many are satisfied with such proofs, but others think them too vague, and while they appear conclusive for portions of Scripture, they do not remove objections to other portions. We might reason *a priori*, Christianity is a revelation from God, God must therefore have provided for its preservation, therefore an infallible inspiration is necessary, and a canon formed providentially and indisputable. But this will not serve to answer the questions of criticism, which historical proof alone can meet. We cannot take each book separately and prove its authority, and there is no guarantee that the tradition of the Church is trustworthy.

II. There is a simpler and safer road to reach the same end. The authority of the Bible can be established on a ground where it is safe. The central point in the Scriptures is the Person of the Lord Jesus, announced and prepared for in the Old Testament, proclaimed and set before us in the New. He who is the centre of the Scriptures is also the centre of History. His existence is universally acknowledged, even by unbelievers themselves.

Of Jesus and His work we have records contemporary or almost so, and our question is, are these records to be trusted?

Now when the Apostles tell us that Jesus claimed divine authority, we cannot doubt that He did so. Others, however, have done the same, as Mohammed, Joseph Smith, and all who have founded religions. Had Jesus more claim than they to be received as divine? The facts answer. The perfect holiness of Jesus Himself. The Apostles could not be deceived as to this. The Saviour's own consciousness of perfection shines through the whole narrative. Such a consciousness is itself sufficient testimony to the fact; otherwise we must suppose an inconceivable pride and fanaticism in Jesus. Again, the perfect holiness of the Saviour springs from His perfect love of God; it is a relation of free dependence, of absolute confidence, of perfect fellowship between the Son and the Father. This it is which exalts Him in holiness infinitely above the most virtuous of Jews or heathen. And the evidence of the Gospels proves that Jesus believed Himself to be the Son of God in a higher sense, by an essential relation to God the Father. This we find not only in the fourth Gospel, but in the synoptists as well. The pre-existence of the Son of God, the essential deity of the Christ, that is the key to a full understanding of the personality of Jesus. When we come to the Apostolic Epistles and the Acts we find the Master, twenty or thirty years, yea, even a few days after His departure from this world, addressed and invoked as "*The Lord.*" The whole Church is fully persuaded that He is divine, not on metaphysical grounds but on the evidence of facts. He appeared as a man, humbled Himself to the form of a servant, being obedient unto death, even the death of the Cross. (Phil. ii. 6, 7.) And this perfect holiness and essential deity of the Saviour are confirmed by a third fact, *His Resurrection*, attested by the twelve, by S. Paul, and by the whole primitive Church. We can only escape the force of such a fact by accusing the early Church of illusion, which a sound criticism, free from rationalistic prejudice, will never do.

III. We may pass, then, from the personal authority of Jesus to the infallibility of His teaching. On the question of His authority in matters outside the domain of religion it is not necessary to enter. Being perfectly holy, He could not err in religious matters. His filial relation to God lies at the foundation of His moral and religious life. His words are the words of God. His Resurrection demonstrated His divine authority, for if He had died in sin He would not have risen again; He was not a blasphemer, as the Jews said, but truly the Son of God.

IV. On this authority of Jesus we can found that of His Apostles, and that of the Old Testament. As to the Apostles we must distinguish the Apostle Paul from the twelve. The Apostles were not merely witnesses of facts, they were trained by Jesus, they assimilated His thoughts, they lived His life. And Jesus promised them His Holy Spirit to lead them into all truth. The fourth Gospel especially gives evidence of this spiritual guidance of the Spirit. It is as one of the Fathers has called it, the " Pneumatic Gospel." The epistles of John and the Apocalypse reveal the same special inspiration. But the Apostle Paul holds a somewhat different position. If we believe in his miraculous conversion we must believe in his authority as at least equal to that of the other Apostles. This is proved by the conformity of his teaching with theirs, together with an absolute independence towards them, and the special relation of his teaching with that of Christ, the inmost thoughts and perfect spirituality of which he alone unfolds.

As to the Old Testament. Its authority rests on that of Jesus Christ, just as in the case of the New Testament. *First*, He used the Old Testament. He recognized it as a divine revelation. If He was infallible in religious matters He could not be deceived in this. *Again*, the revelation in Christ presupposes a preparatory revelation, of which the Old Testament is the record. It may not have for the believers under the New Dispensation the same weight as the New Testament, but it is still indispensable, for without it we should be unable to understand the perfect revelation in Jesus.

Thus the whole authority of Scripture rests on that of Jesus Christ. The problems of Biblical criticism still remain. But we can study them calmly. However they may be settled they can never rob us of Christ Himself, Whose word, life and work are the immoveable foundation of our salvation.

Our time needs authority in regard to religion. Give it the authority of Christ. All false authority will disappear, when the conscience recognizes Him. We must establish that authority not by a visible theocracy, as in the middle ages, but spiritually by the reign of the word of Christ in human souls.

The Waldensian Bible in Germany before Luther.

ADDRESS BY PASTOR BAUMANN, OF BERLIN.

In my earliest infancy, I heard from my pious mother about the valiant and faithful inhabitants among the Alps, who for centuries held their own tenaciously, against the persecutions of the Church of Rome, but it was not until 1857, when the Evangelical Alliance met in Berlin, that I became aware that these heroes were the Waldenses.

It has fallen to my lot, dear friends, to say a few words to you about the version of the Bible which was prepared by Peter Waldo, and taken by the Waldenses into Germany. It is a matter of controversy whether this version has been preserved, and whether it was made use of by Luther. This question is, at the present moment, very warmly discussed in Germany and elsewhere.

It is certain that the Waldenses of Savoy came very early into Germany. These people were scattered about Austria, Bohemia, and Silesia, going as far northward as Berlin and the borders of the Baltic. They were devout students of the Bible, and led a pious and truly Christian life, although remaining still within the pale of the Papal Church. They were regarded by that Church as true believers, as they did not deny or openly repudiate the doctrines, usages, and forms of the Church, such as the Mass, Confession, the veneration of the Saints, and the recognition of the Priesthood. They probably hoped that they would be as the salt of the earth, and purify the Church by remaining in it.

The priests, however, showed themselves but little disposed to tolerate the proceedings of the Waldenses, who succeeded in occupying fresh ground in various parts of Germany. Princes, and nobles, and priests viewed them with dislike. Whole villages, provinces, and countries felt their influence. In 1395 there were forty villages in Steietmark entirely peopled by them, and they had their own spiritual directors.

It appears that both people, nobility, and priests massacred the peaceful inhabitants who were living a quiet and virtuous life, offering up daily prayer at the family altar, who were good citizens, and obedient to the laws, refusing only to take an oath and to serve in the army.

These Waldenses distributed pious writings wherever the people were able to read. They also sent deacons, and popular preachers, and consecrated assistants into the houses to hear confessions, and to read portions of the Scriptures, parts of sermons, and short tractates, by Chrysostom and Augustine, two fathers of the Church, who warmly recommend family worship. Alas! of all these writings scarcely any remain.

It is surprising that no trace is to be found of a German translation of the Waldensian Bible. The Waldensians used the translation which was already in Germany. The persecution which the Inquisition carried on against them was so violent that all trace of their Bible, even if it were translated, has disappeared, destroyed either by the flames at the stake or in the cells where the torture was applied.

What a history theirs is! By hundreds and by thousands they were tortured and burnt. Among their martyrs was the celebrated and learned Reiser, of Nürnberg, called Frederigo, by the grace of God bishop of the faithful, who tried in vain to organize his brethren against the enemy. He was burnt alive in 1458 at Strasburg. Unfortunately his followers mixed themselves up with some Hussite fanatics, who fell victims to their democratic and socialistic excesses. All lovers of peace—people, nobles, and princes—withdrew themselves from them, and repudiated their extravagance, calling those who, up to that time had been looked upon as the light shining in the darkness ("Lux lucis in tenebris"), "Luciferi," *i.e.*, "The servants of Satan."

The Waldenses disappear in Germany with the Hussites. Before the time of Luther all trace of them is lost.

Towards the end of the fifteenth century the art of printing occupied much the attention of the public, and it was made use of first for the Bible. Nineteen German editions were published before the great Reformer set his mark upon the age, and of each of these we still possess a large number of copies. None of them agree with the provençal Bibles of the Waldensians. The Waldensian Bible, therefore, never fell into Luther's hands; it had disappeared from the scene.

We have, however, discovered a book which was undoubtedly Waldensian. It was in the possession of some of the martyrs, who appended to it comments probably made in public worship. It had evidently escaped the eye of the Inquisition, as it was carried by its owner into the torture chamber, and retained there until he sealed his confession with his blood.

This book is the "Codex Teplensis." It is an extremely old manuscript of the New Testament in the German tongue, discovered a few years ago in the convent of the Premonstrants, at Tepel, in Bohemia. The margins are covered with glosses, and some additional matter is added, manifestly Waldensian.

The text of this Codex is very old, being of the time when a dialect was spoken in Germany which has become almost entirely extinct. The writing is minute, the size of the book being so small that it could be carried in the pocket, and, therefore, easily concealed.

Comparing the text with the Waldensian MS. in Dublin, it is believed that they are quite separate. The Dublin MS. being written in the Provençal.

But how are we led to believe that this MS. was in the possession of a Waldensian if the text itself is not in his language?

It is proved, we think, by the marginal notes, and also by the additions. No Roman Catholic would have made such comments. The person to whom it belonged was evidently a victim of the persecution. By the remarks which he makes, he is in danger of being found out, and is a faithful and loyal believer, as well as a man of science and culture, as many of the Waldenses were. He objects to be judged by the authorities, because he does not believe in their enlightenment, and knowledge of the truth. Only at the Last Day, when the great white throne is set, will he submit to have his motives and conduct laid open before them. But for the time being it is his duty to proclaim the Word of God.

There is but *one* God, Christ alone is the Saviour of men, and no man ought to take an oath.

Added to the MS. there is, first: "*The seven articles of Faith*," which coincide with the formula used in ordination by the Waldenses, and which are perfectly orthodox; next, "*The seven Holy Things*," i.e. "*The seven Sacraments*," which evidently were formally accepted, but which were not necessarily practised by the Waldenses.

Then there is likewise a short list of the Saints' Days, which were observed by the Waldenses, but in no wise superstitiously. Also the days when mass was said on behalf of the souls of the departed, at which they occasionally assisted.

Finally, there is a lectionary, and a list of sentences (pericopi) such as was in use among the Waldenses only.

At the end of the Gospel of St. Matthew, there is inserted an extract from the writings of Hugo of St. Victor, who was held in high esteem by the Waldenses.

The most striking evidence, however, is that frequent quotations are made from Chrysostom and Augustine in relation to the Bible and family worship; for example: "*A layman is a bishop in his own family, and has the charge and the care of the souls of those who belong to his household.*" One who thus writes could not possibly belong to the Papal Church of the fifteenth century.

The subject however is still subjudice. However it may be decided, this much remains certain, that the Waldenses, long before the time of Luther, exercised a powerful influence in Germany, and were always the depositaries of truth, and as such a continual danger to Rome, at a time when all was enveloped in the clouds of error, superstition, and hierarchical tyranny.

The blood of the Waldenses flowed in torrents throughout Germany. Their preaching awoke the sleeping conscience of the people, and their adherents were faithful unto death.

And now with gratitude on our part and merit on theirs, we offer our fraternal greetings to the descendants of those heroes who have handed down to the present time a true German manhood.

God bless the Alliance which has been the means of bringing us together; blessed be the holy bonds of that faith which knows no obstacle either of distance or of race. Blessed be God for this word of joyful congratulation.

"*Lux lucet in Tenebris.*"

[An Excursion was made, Wednesday afternoon, to the Piazza di Michael Angelo, a beautiful open space above the city.]

WEDNESDAY EVENING.

M. VISCHER-SARASIN, OF BASLE, PRESIDED.

Evangelistic Addresses were given, with one exception, in the Italian language, by M. MEYHOFFER, Pastor at Brussels, SIGNOR BERUATTO, of Venice, the Rev. WALKER KING, of England, the Rev. Dr. MURRAY MITCHELL, of Nice, and the Rev. Dr. STACKPOLE, of Florence.

THURSDAY, APRIL 9, 1891.

MORNING MEETING.

DR. EDOUARD NAVILLE, OF GENEVA, PRESIDED.

CHRISTIANITY AND SOCIAL QUESTIONS.

Poverty and Riches, from the Gospel point of View.

BY THE REV. DR. STÖCKER, COURT PREACHER, BERLIN.

ALL the world is moved and agitated by the Social Question. Many, even profound thinkers, believe that a crisis is at hand; no one is safe from anxiety. Socialistic movements, all history shows, have always preceded great popular agitations. So it was in ancient Greece and Rome, and so it was at the conclusion of the middle ages. The peasant war, wrongly attributed to the Reformation, yet preceded it, and reached its climax in Luther's time. The fanatics of Münster were still more cruel; and a hundred years ago, the French Revolution was more a socialistic than a political outbreak. We are passing from an old world to a new—by a kind of international earthquake.

Formerly, however, the agitation commenced in one part of society and spread itself to others, now Socialism is not confined to the social democracy in so far as it is sound and practical, it is shared and accepted by all classes and ranks. Princes desire social reforms; governments help them; national economical science has prepared the way for the work, and takes an active part in it. All classes of society have bid farewell to the old traditions, and unite together to bring about the inevitable reform in a peaceable manner. With the exception of a few narrow-minded believers, we all desire that that which is good in the aims of the social democracy should be accomplished; but no reasonable person approves of the evil objects among them, anarchy, unbelief, annihilation of personal liberty and the destruction of family life.

A change in men's thoughts has plainly come about. The Manchester school is no longer followed. The reign of Socialism has begun. Fundamentally it is a Christian law which is reorganized, the royal law of love, which for eighteen centuries all believers have obeyed in thought, if not in practice. The Manchester school of political economy has done a good work in its time, especially in the direction of personal liberty and development of human energy and talent in connection with natural forces, thus giving an immense impulse to economic life; but the principle of it was *individualism*. We see now the insufficiency of it, and all society is filled with the *social* spirit. The abstract humanity of Rousseau with its idea of individual contract at the root of the State is gone. The Church which Voltaire attacked with his sarcasm, and Lessing with his rationalism, is no longer a citadel of truth but a ruin. Economical science in those days had for its motto, "*Laissez faire;*" "*laisser aller.*" The optimism which came from the school of Leibnitz, and believed that the best of all possible worlds would come out of forces left entirely to themselves, is passed away as a dream. The result of such a development of individual power has been seen to be egoism and mammonism, a materialism which, while it gathered the fruits of men's labour, neglected their personal and family life. Hence the terrible war of classes and interests which has ensued. In Germany, science has renounced the old theories, and the consequence is that they have been abandoned in practice. Economic individualism has proved itself an utter failure.

Socialism, which has risen on the ruins of individualism, condemns everything which is against the demands of the Christian conscience. The Manchester school despised the unskilled labourer, and injured family life, the rest of the Lord's day, and the highest interests of man. Socialism has vindicated the claims of humanity. And in so far as it does so we are not worthy of the name of Christians if we do not sympathize with it. But socialism and democracy are very far from being the same. The latter is the sworn enemy of the best interests of man, an anarchic and unpractical movement. This may be seen in such cases as Lassalle, in 1848, with his unpracticable scheme of national workshops. Democratic socialism is a mere Utopia. *Bebel*, the leader of the Geneva democracy, and *Mort*, the chief of the anarchists, have entirely failed, their economical ideas are worthless, and their social theories low. They both reduce the marriage bond to a mere bestial union, and human society to a zoological garden. Besides, the working out of the ideas of social democracy would be the destruction of the old world without the substitution of any real improvement in the place of it. It would be the ruin of the labouring classes while feeding them on these dreams. It allies itself with a revolutionary internationalism, and with enmity against religion and the Church. One who has no love for his country makes a great void in his heart which nothing can fill up. And the honest socialist must look upon Christ with love and adoration, for He left the riches of Heaven for the poverty of earth to suffer and die for man. No book ought to be so dear to socialism as the Bible, which teaches us in every page that the right of property is not human caprice, but a divine ordinance, for the observance of which everyone must give account; which warns the rich not to hide their treasures in the earth, but to give themselves to good works; which bids us care for our neighbours, and which makes the love of our neighbour the highest rule of ethical life. Social democracy makes war against the Bible, against the Church, against God, and against Christ. Its motto is the struggle for existence. Christianity denounces violence, revolution. Christ transforms the world within and without, just as He has transformed the family life and destroyed slavery. Social democracy, therefore, is against Christianity. The Gospel does not proclaim a universal equality in human life, and sets before men not earthly enjoyment as their goal but eternal life.

"*Heaven, let us leave it to angels and sparrows*:" so they sing among the democratic socialists, but they are not altogether responsible for their views, they have learned them from others, from the middle classes, and from the radicals; but notwithstanding the errors of the democracy there is a socialism which all religious socialists will favour, because it finds its root in Christianity itself, in Christ's own teaching of brotherhood, and in the Church's embodiment of it. Christianity only gradually substituted its own views for those of Paganism. Slavery was slowly but eventually destroyed. The Reformation proclaimed the equality of clergy and laity, and became the doctrine of moral liberty; and the French Revolution carried out the same idea to the legal and civil equality of men, which in several countries has led to political equality and universal suffrage. Modern socialism is the same movement carried into economics. But communism would destroy the real equality of man by suppressing personal liberty. All that the State and law can do to assimilate the condition of the rich and the poor should be done. We should not make the mere possession of terrestrial goods and their production the chief thing, but the personal welfare of the labourer and his employer.

To the State itself a new career is open. We have paid too much attention to "culture," that is, the intellectual instincts of man. Now, in Germany, we believe in "social Monarchy," in which a sound socialism prevails, not discordant with the present order, but aiming at the peaceable satisfaction, in every class, of their legitimate demands. If the Monarchy is disposed to give all that the working classes can properly wish for, we may hope that revolution will find no place for itself. What we require is to eradicate egoism from our hearts. And for this there is no power sufficient, but a living Christianity, that is, God Himself as Liberator and Peacemaker, acting on society, impelling and encouraging that which is good. It is one of the worst errors of social democracy that it believes that new laws and regulations can create a new social world, or that a wretched revolution will produce a nobler humanity. It is not from violence that a better life will arise, but from the power of ideas. The Kingdom of God as the Scriptures depict it, only too little realized in our official ecclesiasticisms, is a social kingdom, it is a kingdom not of the other world, but of this: invisible and eternal, but still with its power and greatness here. True, nothing can altogether remove unhappiness. The citizens of the Kingdom of God must believe in a better world—but social democracy would destroy such a faith. As prince and people, state and church, co-operate, every force will be brought into active operation, national culture will be developed, the relations between different classes will become more and more peaceful, and so more and more the Christian ideal of citizenship will be realized.

There are different kinds of prophets all round us. Some are pusillanimous, others are indifferent, and some think that a great catastrophe will be the only remedy. The best disposed will leave the future in God's hands, and work while it is still day for the present time. There is no doubt a great gulf opened in our time, but there are always bridges across it. In Germany, more than elsewhere, the separating crevasses are seen. The want of religious union affects the solidarity of citizens, and socialistic dreams are promoted by an imaginative and speculative disposition. And yet there is a possibility of conciliation. Our emperor, our leaders and governors, stretch out the hand and there are many who take it. The social democrats have changed their line, because they have recognized the change in the state of things. They must show us what they mean, how they are intending to carry out their programme. But we hear the voice of a new era coming to us. Let us trust in God, and hope that the Evangelical Church will unite all the peoples of the earth.

ADDRESS BY PASTOR BABUT, OF NISMES.

THE method of dealing with the social question and its aspect as found in Holy Scripture was pointed out with singular accuracy. Although the ground had already been gone over by the preceding speaker, yet there remained fresh fields for exploration. "God the Creator, is the rightful proprietor of all things," said Mons. Babut; and in making man an intelligent and active agent, he made him capable of, and a participant in, that right of proprietorship. Adam was rich; but becoming a rebel, he was compelled to gain his bread by the sweat of his brow. Here, then, is the root, or first principle of poverty. However, the fall and its consequences has not blasted wholly the prospects of humanity. The sons of Cain were wealthy though impious. The patriarchs were God-fearing and God-honouring men; they, too, were wealthy and increased in goods. Isaac recalls to us the divine beatitude: "Blessed are the peacemakers." Jacob united with the faults of the Jew the virtues of the Israelite. Jewish legislation was formulated with a view to temporal retribution alone. The priests were those who came into the closest communication with God, and yet they were the least wealthy. The laws of the Jewish Commonwealth tended to prevent the monopoly of wealth. Destitution was virtually "prohibited" (see Deut. xv.). If such existed, it was the fault of man, not of God. The laws of the Hebrew Commonwealth, as far as we can see, are the most efficacious with regard to the difficulty of dealing with the social question that have ever been promulgated. Look with what indignation the prophets denounce the oppression of the poor! None more than Isaiah and Amos. According to Ezekiel, the great crime of Sodom was not having pity on the poor. It must be confessed that, generally, the poor man is almost synonymous with the righteous man, as may be seen in the Psalms and Ecclesiastes. The poverty of the Lord Jesus is a feature of His dignity and of His terrestrial existence; and it should be observed in what light He regards the poor man.

Let us come to the New Testament as a witness.

The Magnificat shows forth the divine compassion for the poor. The disciples of Christ were poor men. The rich always hold an inferior place. Look how much is made of the widow's mite, though small it be. What solemn admonitions were addressed to rich men by the Saviour Himself, He even on one occasion counselling the selling of all that the man had, and giving it to the poor. What care the Church of Jerusalem had of their poor is only too well known. The special arrangements suited to the wants of the moment necessarily passed away; but the normal condition—the root—ever remains, and crops up perennially: the care of the poor it was which originated the diaconate, and the offerings for the poor were things inspired by charity. This may be seen in the case of St. Paul in his dealings with the Corinthians. He desired that their abundance should be a supply for the want of those who needed help (see 2 Cor. viii. 14). And is it not true that the stirring words of St. James against the rich are a fitting following up of our Lord's Sermon on the Mount, and of the warnings and denunciations of the prophets?

It is evident, from the whole teaching of the New Testament, that riches ought to promote the good of one's neighbour, and advance the interests of the Kingdom of Christ on the earth. Let us here ask ourselves one thing: "What has our Lord added to that which had been already taught in the Scriptures of the Old Testament regarding this question?"

Firstly, His teaching is to bring to the fore the perfection of spirituality. He always brings to the front the value of the immortal soul (see Luke xvi.). Material riches are only, so to speak, apparent: not solid good. Spiritual riches are, really and truly, precious: they are the true riches. Material wealth is only an apparent good, if one may so speak. The first are only really and truly ours; the latter but too often cause much evil and suffering, and cannot, in fact, be looked upon as truly and actually our own.

In the second place, the present is brought into contrast with the future. The things of the present are not worthy to be compared with the glory which shall be revealed. We are told, "Make to yourselves friends of the mammon of unrighteousness; that when ye fail, they may receive you into everlasting habitations."

In the third place—charity or love. Its source is in God Himself; it is shown forth in Christ, and from Christ is passed on to His disciples. Those who are filled with His love will give willingly and lovingly.

To conclude. It cannot be denied that inequality has its root in the nature of things. God wills that it should be so; and for that reason it would seem to be futile to do away with it. But on the other hand, it cannot be denied that pauperism is the fault of man and a consequence of the fall. Christians, above all others, are called upon to effect all those reforms which will tend to make honest work yield a fair and just return to those performing it. They should co-operate zealously and actively in all efforts to that end. The Mosaic laws suggested certain remedies to the evil under contemplation. But now, we who seek for the establishment of Christ's kingdom should do our utmost to place the honest workman in that position which is his due; we should give him back all that is his due, all that is consonant with his self-respect—with his true dignity. In our Lord's time the poor occupied the highest rank in His kingdom;

in the present day it is the well-to-do and the wealthy who receive the applause and homage and the esteem of the multitude. This is a very humiliating fact for us. Is it a thing to be wondered at, therefore, that Christianity has become a religion of compromise and a thing of luxury and fashion? There is a very grave state of things between the classes: There is much bad feeling. The solution of the difficulty may be found in a judicious application of the admonition given to the rich young man in the gospels: "Go, sell all that thou hast, and give to the poor." There is need of self-denial; a conscientious rectitude in dealing with wealth, in the handling of money matters. We must make war upon the love of money. There is also a grave misapprehension among the poor with regard to the Gospel. We are not of the people as was our Divine Master. We do not take them by the hand and be as one of them as He was. We prefer to give them alms or a morsel of bread, instead of looking upon them as bone of our bone and flesh of our flesh—all of us members of one great brotherhood. Oh that there were a little of the zeal of Savonarola, and of the Spirit of Him whom he longed to see king of this city!

ADDRESS BY THE REV. DR. WILLIAM NICHOLAS, OF DUBLIN.

THE Bible stands alone, differing from all other sacred books in that it never commits itself to false geology, false chronology, false astronomy, or to the teaching of anything that is scientifically untrue. The false science which is maintained in the sacred books of other religions invalidates their claim to be regarded as "the oracles divine."

Not only does the Bible not commit itself to false teaching in matters of science, but it also steers clear of false teaching in matters of political economy.

In its pages the faults and failings of good men are impartially recorded; nor are the mistakes of collective bodies of good men, of communities or churches omitted. St. Paul in writing to the Church at Corinth does not forget to make mention of the party spirit, the numerous schisms, and multiplied divisions which were deserving of blame.

And shortly after the marvels of Pentecost, when those of the early Church who had lands or houses sold them and laid the money at the Apostles' feet, " neither said any that aught he possessed was his own, but they had all things common," so that they had practically a community of goods, yet the sacred writer utters no word of approval, no command that others were to go and do likewise, but merely records the historical fact.

From this incident we have no right to infer that the Bible is in favour of the communistic, or socialistic reconstruction of society.

It may be well for us to consider—What were the peculiar circumstances under which those early Christians established this community of goods? There had just been a great outpouring of the Holy Spirit, which resulted in the conversion of multitudes of sinners. Many renounced Judaism and embraced Christianity. In consequence of this a fierce persecution arose, and many who had recently become converted to the faith were unable to obtain employment, many of the poor were refused the relief formerly afforded, so that large numbers of the early Christians were in a condition of extreme destitution. Then, to meet the pressure of this necessity, those who had lands and houses sold them, and brought the proceeds to the Apostles, and distribution was made to every man according to his needs. Acting on at least part of the Communistic formula—" From every man according to his powers : to every man according to his needs."

It was thus only a temporary expedient, resorted to for the purpose of meeting a passing want.

If any persons tell us that it is the duty of Christians to do so now, that the rich Christians should divide their property with the poor ones, it is enough to say that not only is no command on the subject given, but that the early Church did not long continue to have " all things in common." Not very long after we read that St. Paul made a collection for the poor saints at Jerusalem, plainly implying that the distinction between poor and rich again obtained. But, supposing it were carried out in our day, suppose all Christians having property sold it and the proceeds were divided, how long would it be till the capital would be consumed, and then what would they do?

It is clear that the abolition of private property would be equivalent to killing the goose with the golden egg.

In order that there may be a supply for the necessary wants of a community, there must be the productive employment of capital, and if this is not done the result must be poverty, for if a community lives on its capital, the capital will soon be exhausted, and then hopeless want must come. It is a matter of absolute necessity.

There is no more possibility of evading it than there would be of preventing a cistern from which water was daily taken, and to which no fresh supply was imported, from soon becoming empty. It is, however, only the thoughtless Socialists who dream of living on a division of accumulated capital.

The Socialists who have thought the matter out give as the very basis of the Socialistic reconstruction of society the dictum that the means of production and the means of distribution of wealth should be nationalized. That means that land, mills, factories, docks, railways, sailing vessels, steamers, &c., should be no longer held as private property either by individuals or by companies, but should belong to the nation. A great writer has said "the Alpha and Omega of Socialism is the transformation of private and competing capitals into a united collective capital."

This collective or common ownership of the means of producing wealth, along with the public organization of labour, as opposed to the competitive anarchism of to-day, forms a compact and imposing plan, which according to its supporters would do away with extreme poverty on the one hand and great wealth on the other, and all our other ills. It is a scheme worthy of our careful consideration. Suppose it were agreed to adopt this scheme, then the question at once arises;—how is all this property, mills, factories, railways, &c., to be obtained from the present owners?

It must be either by purchase or by force.

Now, if by purchase, the amount required would be so enormous that the nation which raised it would be burdened with such a fearful national debt that prosperity would be impossible. A man may incur such an amount of debt that ultimately he must become bankrupt. If, however, the purchase were made on very favourable terms, so that a margin of profit would exist after the payment of interest to the bondholders, and suppose this were done in England, the workers in all these States in which workers lived under less favourable conditions than in England would come over, when either there would have to be laws against immigration, which would lead to prohibitive tariff against English goods, or the wages of the operative would have to be considerably lowered. So that Socialism to be of real use to the proleteriat would require to be established all the world over. Less than this would not do away with *international competition*.

But there is another expedient proposed by some Socialists, who do not advocate purchase but confiscation. We are told of a few enormous capitalists on the one side, and an immense proleteriat on the other: That the many could easily take the property of the few. If that were so, the State would not be safe. But it is not true. There are only a few enormous capitalists; but those who possess some capital—if only a few shares in a limited liability company—would range themselves on the side of the capitalist; so that to attempt confiscation would involve us in one of the most dreadful civil wars that ever occurred in the history of the world, and blood would run in the streets of our cities as it did in the streets of Jerusalem in the days of Manasseh.

I must ask,—suppose that it were practicable to have collective capital and the public organization of labour:—would it be desirable?

Socialists are never weary of telling us in the words of Prudhon, that, "Property is robbery." That private property has "its source in cupidity, and its end in confusion." Now, I am not going to deny that there is a great deal of property which *is* robbery. It is not to be supposed that the Church should always take the side of the rich man against the poor.

Property is robbery when it is acquired by the oppression of the poor: when a man acquires property by paying starvation wages to his employees, it is not for us to palliate it. We are not to come to terms with what the prophet calls "grinding the faces of the poor." We may well say to many in our day, "Behold the hire of the labourers who have reaped down your fields which is of you kept back by fraud crieth out: and the cries of them that reaped have entered into the ears of the Lord of Sabaoth." Then, there is property which is acquired by distinct robbery, though it keeps inside the letter of the law. The property of the directors of the numerous swindling companies which are constantly being started is "robbery" without a doubt. If a hungry man steals a loaf of bread, he is imprisoned for it; but a man may by unscrupulous company-promoting take the spoil of orphans wronged, and widows who have none to plead their right, or he may by bearing on the Stock Exchange ruin thousands; and yet hold a high position, and be received with honour by the magnates of society.

The Bible gives an answer to the question:—Should there be private property or not? The command "Thou shalt not steal," evidently implies that private property honestly obtained may be lawfully held: Else it could not be wrong to steal.

In connection with the incident in the early Church already referred to, St. Peter said to Ananias, "While it remained, was it not thine own? and after it was sold, was it not in thine own power?" Thus, there was no compulsion to yield one's private property up to the Apostles. There would have been no sin in retaining the proceeds of the property after it was sold. Ananias was punished, not for keeping back part of the price; but for saying that the part was the whole. He was punished for lying, not to man but to God. Consequently, the holding of private property is sanctioned by the sacred Scriptures. The Bible does not teach Socialism. The principles it does lay down on social questions will be found in practical operation in the highest degree conducive to mutual prosperity.

To hold private property is for the advantage of the nation in many respects:—

It is an incentive to industry: Every man has an instinctive desire to have something that shall be his "peculium." You see this desire even in a child: how he longs to possess something which shall be his "very own"; free from the control of father or mother. Take that incentive away, and what would be the result to the community?

An immediate and immense diminution of industry. Under a socialistic regime a large number would try to do as little as ever they could. Even at present with the incentive of gain on the one hand, and the spur of starvation on the other, many shirk work as much as possible; so that it is reasonable to conclude that under socialistic conditions their number would be largely increased—to the great detriment of the producing power of society. So that doing away with the right to hold private property would vastly diminish the total wealth of the community.

Socialism would have the public organization of labour, and it would pay equally for all kinds of labour in proportion to the time spent in the service of the community : the payment would be in the means of sustentation or enjoyment. Socialism would pay in kind. Hence accumulation would be practically impossible. So that the thrifty and the thriftless, the intemperate and the abstemious would be very much on a par. A dull, uninteresting uniformity would prevail.

In order to avoid the difficulty resulting from the numbers who would try to shirk their work under the public organization of labour, Socialism would provide a rigid system of inspection, and the prompt employment of force. It is evident that no strikes could be permitted, and that all must be kept to their work, or else the entire system would break down. The necessary tendency of organized labour is to create a large class who would devote themselves to work at minute portions of manufacturing, and a small class who would control and organize. Few are possessed of the faculties requisite for organization on a large scale, and those who devote their powers to, say, making pin heads, filing the points of needles, or some other department in the almost infinite division of labour would be incapable of organizing. Immense power would be thus placed in the hands of the few organizers. Let us see what they would have to do.

1. Settle what work each child should be trained up for doing, so that there might be the "direct adaptation" of the individual for his work.

2. Determine what shall be produced, and in what quantities.

3. Determine how long each man shall work.

4. Determine what amount of the common product each shall receive.

5. Determine what means shall be used to compel unwilling or indolent workers to do their due proportion of work.

These organizers, "omniarchs" as they have been called, would have power greater than any that has ever been possessed by the most absolute governments that have ever existed. Socialism that would train every man for a certain work, that would appoint every man his place, that would apportion his wages, and measure out his pleasures, would thus absolutely destroy individual liberty. So that those who now cry out against centralization and despotism, would establish a monster centralization, and a gigantic despotism, beyond anything that does now, or ever did, exist.

We have hitherto supposed that these "omniarchs" were fair conscientious men; but from what history teaches us of human nature, no small body of men possessed of such enormous powers, and not subject to the criticism of a free and enlightened public opinion would long continue pure. Soon they would become corrupt and tyrannical; and a more odious form of government would have been established than that of the "wicked ten" in Venice, or of the worst oligarchies of the ancient States of Greece.

Let those who favour Socialism remember that it can only be established by stamping out individual liberty. Freedom of demand is a first essential of freedom in general. If the means of life and of culture were somehow allotted to each from without, and according to an officially drawn up scheme, no one could live out his own individuality, or develop himself according to his own ideas; the material basis of freedom would be lost. The right to hold private property and individual liberty stand and fall together.

It is an essential part of the Socialistic scheme that the right of inheritance and the right of bequest should cease. There is no doubt that the "power of the dead hand," as it is called, ought to be modified. No man has a right to bind future generations to do that which is against their belief or their interests, and hence the living may lawfully exercise a very great control over the testamentary dispositions of the dead. This power is being exercised, and we believe rightly, more and more every year. At the same time we must believe that a man who has acquired property should be able to transmit it to his children, or to other persons whom he may select, or for certain definite purposes; as, for instance, the teaching of religion, or of science, or the relief of the poor and the sick. To determine that no man could have more than a life interest in anything that he might accumulate would cause a great and unjust depreciation of property; and would be injurious to society by being a direct incentive to extravagance. For, a man knowing that he could not leave his property to whomsoever he would, would naturally try and spend all he could during his life-time. A wisely controlled right of bequest is undoubtedly for the interest of society as a whole; and is evidently in accordance with the views of Scripture, which teaches that "the parents should lay up for the children," and that a man should provide for his own; and surely that includes as far as he can to make provision for them in the event of his decease.

But it may be asked, Has Christianity nothing to say to the present unsatisfactory condition of affairs, to the glaring inequalities that exist; to some living in squalor, ill-fed, ill-clad, ill-housed; not only without comfort, but without decency; living under conditions which render health impossible, and virtue almost impossible?

Does Christianity approve of multitudes of men, and women, and children living in dark, damp, fetid, unsightly slums, and tenement houses?

Does Christianity approve of those frightful "sweaters" shops?

Does Christianity simply urge men to save their souls, and not to take the slightest interest in the social condition of their poorer neighbours? Before answering these questions, it is well for us to remember that much of the misery complained of is brought upon men by their refusal to order their lives in obedience to the commands of Christ. A large part, we shall not attempt to fix the exact proportion, but a very large part of the suffering of degraded humanity is avoidable, and would be avoided if those persons who suffer had acted in obedience to the command of the Bible. Families are plunged in extreme poverty, and if you enquire into the family history you will find that dishonesty, extravagance, drunkenness, and similar causes have wrought their ruin. They suffer because they have sinned. They have been tried, and have been found unfaithful and unworthy citizens; and hence they are now amongst the "lapsed masses," or the "submerged tenth." Loafers and idlers abound who will not work but are ready to beg or to steal. Of many who are in want it may be said, "O Israel, thou hast destroyed thyself."

But whilst we cannot ignore the fact that much of the suffering is self inflicted, yet we assert that society is not free from blame; and we also assert that Christianity has much to say on the subject.

I am quite willing to admit that there are Christians who misrepresent Christianity on this matter. Christians, who are so bent on saving souls that they never think of saving men and women: Christians, whose religion is narrow and selfish, who are a strange compound of devotion and worldliness: who can sing and talk and pray, but who feel little for the woes around them; and make no honest, earnest, effort to benefit their fellow men. These are some, and all the desire they seem to have is to get men to adopt certain forms, and perform certain ceremonies; and there are others who are so extra spiritual that their only wish seems to be to get men to have certain experiences, or to have certain experiences of their own. All these misrepresent Christianity. Our Lord's teaching should be embraced in its fulness, and Christians should never forget the teaching of the parable of the Good Samaritan; or of the second great commandment:—"Thou shalt love thy neighbour as thyself." My contention is, that the principles of Christianity practically carried out would solve all our social problems; and remove all the evils of which we now complain.

Socialism would neither solve our problems nor remove our evils.

Let us see how practical Christianity would work in the settlement of a trade dispute. How would we settle a dispute between a capitalist, and his labourers who want more wages, on Christian principles? Christianity would not at once take sides, and say the capitalist must be right and the labourers wrong; nor would it say the labourers must be right, and the capitalist wrong; it would impartially listen to both, and would have a message for each, but would identify itself with neither. The workers acting on Christian principles would show all good fidelity; and would do their work, not with eye service, as men pleasers, but with singleness of heart unto the Lord, and they would be reasonable in their demands. The capitalist would be willing to do justly, thinking that the labourer is worthy of his hire. Both parties would recognize the fact that if the price of labour were raised above a certain point, the trade would be driven from the country, or would become so unattractive to capitalists that no one would embark in it.

And now, instead of what John Stuart Mill—a great authority—says is generally the case; the worker trying to get as much and do as little as possible, and the capitalist trying to give as little and get as much as possible; the capitalist would be willing to give as much as possible, having regard to his obtaining a reasonable return for the capital employed, and reasonable remuneration for his enterprise, work, and skill.

Both the parties meeting in this spirit would, I am convinced, settle their disputes amicably, and would for the greater portion of their time work together in concord.

Mr. Bradlaugh expressed his faith in the efficacy of "conciliatory conferences." How much greater may our faith be in the efficacy of Conferences between capitalist and workers, pervaded by a Christian spirit of mutual respect and justice? But, it may be said, how would a reasonable return in the capital employed be determined? Of course the percentage would vary in different times, and in different trades according to the risk run, and the fluctuating, or permanent character of the business. But if the rate of interest satisfied the capitalist, and the rate of wages satisfied the workers, inasmuch as the diligent, sober, thrifty worker was enabled to live in comfort, then by mutual consent the dispute would be settled. What Matthew Arnold calls the "sweet reasonableness" of Christianity would triumph.

Suppose, however, the capitalist is not satisfied with the workers, and that they cannot come to a mutual understanding and agreement, Christianity would urge them not to resort to a "lock out," or to a "strike," but to arbitration, or to a system of profit sharing. A wise system of profit sharing seems eminently equitable, and wherever tried has been most successful. I am firmly convinced that the difficulty is not the *intellectual* one of how to make an arrangement, but the *moral* one arising from the selfishness and cupidity of both capitalist and worker. Let both parties feel as Christian men ought to feel towards each other, and the difficulties that present themselves will soon be overcome.

Farther, Christianity teaches us the worth of the individual, and the brotherhood of man. Human life is cheap in China. At one time in England a man could be bought for less than a hawk!

Christianity tells us to "honour all men," not merely the noble, mighty, rich, but all the poor, the despised, because they are men having immortal souls, and redeemed with the precious blood of Christ.

Christianity tells us of a brotherhood of Christians, bound together in sympathy and love, but it also presents us to a broader brotherhood of a common humanity. Now, let these two ideas permeate our souls, and we shall not leave our fallen, and degraded, and offensive brethren alone. As we would not leave a brother according to the flesh alone, because he had some loathsome disease, so we will not leave our morally diseased brethren alone to perish in their sins. We shall try to heal the moral leper. We shall try to raise the spiritually dead. Let the principles of Christianity prevail; and oppression, and fraud, and over-reaching, and squalid poverty, and foul slums, and sweating shops, and opium dens, and gambling hells, and the multiplied allurements to drunkenness, and unrighteous gains, and the envy of the poor towards the rich, and the pride of the rich scorning the poor, would cease. I would almost venture to say:—Let the principles of Christianity be operative in all who profess and call themselves Christians, and instead of a selfish spirituality, a putrescent cant, and a pompous formalism, let there be a true, enlarged, and enlightened spirituality, consisting of a sincere love to God and to man—a simple, honest, following of the teaching of Christ, and soon our social difficulties would vanish, our bitter feuds would end, righteousness would exalt us, "peace would be within our borders, and plenteousness within," not only "our palaces," but all our dwellings.

PAPER READ BY THE REV. DR. O. O. TIFFANY, OF NEW YORK.

WHEN one confronts Christianity with social questions, he brings the two great forces of life directly face to face. No power over men's souls or inner life can compare with the constraining love of Christ, and no outward influence so grasps and moulds the form and fashion of purpose and of action as that intangible and magnetic force called the tone and temper of society. I deem the bearing of Christianity on social questions as one of the greatest problems of our age—nay, as its very special task given it distinctly by God's providence to solve, and to solve in the interests of His Kingdom. I have no fear of the result if Christians are only awake to their task. Christ has conquered in other spheres and will conquer in this.

When social tumult is abroad—when questions affecting the status of society, the relation of workmen and employers, the tenure of property, the laws of taxation, co-operation, strikes, temperance legislation, the housing of the poor, the education of the people, and prison reform, the laws of divorce, and the thousand and one topics which are but the special evidence of the great social upheaval of our time; when these come forth, as they are coming forth, as they have already come forth, as the burning questions of our day and generation, I look to Christianity to solve them, and believe that it must boldly confront and grapple with them, and make such solution of them as shall turn them from aliens into allies, and win men to the worship of the Lord of their souls, when thus proved, in the beneficence of His Spirit, the Lord of the body also.

When the Master of us all spoke of His Kingdom, He spoke of it under the form of a twofold parable. The Kingdom of Heaven is like unto a mustard seed, which when it is sown is less than all the seeds that be in the earth. But when it is sown it groweth up and becometh greater than all herbs, and shooteth out great branches, so that the fowls of the air may lodge under the shadow of it. And, again, the Kingdom of Heaven is like unto leaven which a woman took and hid in three measures of meal, till the whole was leavened.

The first parable shews the structural fabric of the Kingdom—the second its persuasive influence. That Kingdom is meant to teach and transform all human society. Its work is not done till the whole be leavened.

Nor are these two aspects of the Kingdom opposites, they are counterparts. They mutually involve and require each other. The Church ecclesiastical, with its ministry and sacraments, is essential for the conserving and the application of the truth to the souls of men. It is the instrument in God's hands of conversion and nurture in the grace of God. In it souls are born anew into the spirit of the Master. Its ministry, its needs, its documents, its worship, and its discipline—these are the apt instruments of the Spirit in awaking and confirming the individual Christian life, out of which all true reforms must spring. To deride the Church and exalt secular Christianity, is like deriding the roots and praising the fruits of the tree. It is saying to the Sun, Begone from the heavens; we want no such great burning luminary in space, we want only light and heat on the earth. Like bidding the spring in the hills dry up, because we only require rivers by our cities and streams through our fields. Like destroying the atmosphere that we may breathe more freely. What is Christian society, but the life of Christ in the life of men. And how much of that life should we have were it not preached and worshipped and loved. No; the Church, even as an ecclesiastical body, set to testify the gospel of the grace of God, is the pillar and ground of the truth. But it is not therefore opposed to the Church militant against the evils of society. We should get rid of some hindering misapprehensions if we got rid of the false notion that the clergy constitute the Church. I am a clergyman, and I magnify my office; high, holy, important, essential are the functions of the ministry to the souls of men. But it is not their function to absorb the whole life of the body in themselves. The body is not for the hands, or the feet, or the eyes even; but the hands, the feet and the eyes are for the body. And when we turn to the Church as the learning power of society, it is the great body of the laity of which the clergy are in some respects leaders, and in all respects servants; it is to the Christian laity, the great body of the faithful, the royal priesthood, the peculiar people, that we are to look for efficient service. The ministry of the Word is to raise up ministries of the Word in all who hear it. In a very noble collect of the Church which I have the honour to serve, there occurs a petition that every member of the Church in his vocation and *ministry* may truly and godly serve His master. Every Christian soul touched by the grace of Christ is called to a ministry for Him. The object of Christianity is not merely to get men safely out of this world, but to make them useful factors in it. A converted man is not converted to supreme self-consideration even in his own salvation, not to look merely on his own things, but on the things of others—not simply to get rid of his own burden even at the cross, but to bear one another's burdens, and so fulfil the law of Christ. And of these burdens many a social burden presses most heavily: so heavily as to crush out manliness and womanliness, to blot out self-respect, and to render nugatory the appeal of the Gospel, because that to which it appeals has died out within the soul, crushed out by the hard strain of unchristian law and custom.

How can a man or woman live a decent Christian life amid the publicity and squalor of our crowded tenement houses, or bring their children up in decent modesty where all are promiscuously herded; father and mother, growing youths and maidens, in one common chamber. In view of such festering dens of vice, is not tenement house reform a Christian task? Is it not a social question, this housing of the poor, so that self-respect may be preserved and modesty may have a chance, a question which may well be confronted with Christianity?

Nor are we to expect hard-working men and women to be sober, set in comfortless homes, if homes they may be called, and living in neighbourhoods where dram shops and gin palaces crowd on each other in long shining rows, offering momentary distraction at least and something bright and gay, and a jovial companionship for an hour or two out of the squalor and misery of the grimy dens they herd in. And does not a social question concerning temperance legislation and the duty of establishing decent and sober places of amusement for the poor, come to be a Christian question? The same social craving which gathers us in refined assemblies draws these neglected souls to dancing dens and drunken orgies. Preaching is not their first need, but brotherly sympathy and Christian help. These are social questions which must find their solution in Christian effort. For the Kingdom of God is meant to be a kingdom of righteousness here, as well as a kingdom of glory yonder. Thy Kingdom come is the Church's constant prayer. And that Kingdom is to control the environment of life which shapes its nature, as well as to touch the inward springs of action. The Christian life could survive in the face of martyrdom. But martyrdom was not intended to be a permanent form of Christian society. And in and through the efforts of Christian men much that was rife in the community once has been done away for ever. When the great Flavian Amphitheatre we call the Colosseum was built in Rome, it would not have been thought possible that the spirit of the martyrs who suffered in it would have made at last such ghastly scenes impossible. But it did. It was not only strong to withstand the evil, but strong to overthrow it. It made impossible the cruelties and orgies which were once the favourite amusements of the best society. It converted the souls of men, and also transformed the environment of their circumstances, so that they were freed from the horrible tyrannies and hideous slaveries which once lorded it over them. That is, Christ's Kingdom came not only in the souls of men, but to some degree into the focus of social life. And so it is coming, and is destined to come still, until the future of society and the municipal and communal relations of men are Christian in their structure, fitted to give expression to Christian principle and furtherance to Christian life. Society is to be converted as well as the individual soul. And the Church is now called to help to make it so. It is the one great evidence of its divine authority to this age, which is quite tired of argument and wants efficient action. Men will believe in a Kingdom of God, which is not a mere ecclesiastical city of refuge from civic evils, but which rights the civic evil, so that no refuge is requisite.

Without a true view of the future and destiny of man, society cannot shape its institutions to the best furtherance of his legitimate development.

The truest civilization must root itself in a true conception of man's nature, must gain its impulse and its light from what the Gospel reveals concerning him. It must be Christian, or it cannot shape his surroundings here to the best furtherance of his end and aim.

Thus in the older pagan civilizations, amid much that was elevating and ennobling, as in the literature and art of Greece, as of the deference to law and duty to the state among the Romans, there were evils suffered and fostered and encouraged which were the direct outcome of their contracted view of man as a citizen of this world only—refinement, law, art,—these in measure so high that they have never been surpassed, would exist coeval with tyrannies, cruelties, sensualities, which deny and degrade the true life of man. Slaveries and slaughters could comport into a civilization based on the value of a citizen—not on the value of a soul. The benigner features of Christian civilization are all engendered of that truth revealed in Christ, of God's Fatherhood and Man's Brotherhood. All attempts of society to realize and embody in its institutions this brotherhood are attempts of a Christian civilization. But, although civilization to-day has caught a benigner atmosphere than the older world could comprehend, it will not do to leave social questions simply to the trend of things even in a Christian state. Civilization and Religion may in regard to social questions to-day both work for similar ends, but they work from different aims. The type of honesty which comes from a conviction of its policy for society is a different one from that which springs from a conviction of its duty to God. Civilization stands to Christianity in the realm of action, as Philosophy stands to Religion in the realm of thought and motive. They may both seek and work out similar ends, but the one lacks the divine impulse and energy of the other. A Christian civilization needs the direct effects of Christian men, of those who not only embrace the ideas, but who breathe the spirit of Christian truth.

Those only can establish society, and mould it in its true form, who are possessed in their souls of what was always part of the essence of Christianity, the determination not to let evil alone for its own sake. And thus it is that not as a feature of ecclesiastial regimen but as an outcome of Christian life, Christian men must be earnest to mould a Christian society.

While the especial form of this talk of ours is peculiar to to-day, its underlying principle is neither new nor peculiar. It is as old as Christianity; yes, as old as the revelation in the law of Moses. The religion of the decalogue is the religion which regards the family and the community as really as the unseen Father. It is as crowded with moral duties to the home and society as it is with the doctrine and worship of God. The one spirit which underlies all the ten laws finds as true and as inevitable expression in the Second Table as the First. In the general Hebrew legislation the law of sacrifices is not more distinct or expressive than the laws of exact justice to man and mercy to the beasts of the field. God cares for oxen. The germ of our modern society for the Prevention of Cruelty to Animals is found then in the command—"Thou shalt not muzzle the ox that treadeth out the corn."

Later on, the Prophets who kept the Priests in order were especially raised up of God to bring the truths of theology to bear upon the practical life of the community and the nation. Their inspiration was that of practical politics and social justice. To foretell events was only an incident of their great task, wherein it was given them to see and expound the eternal underlying principles of God's government of men upon earth, and the sure outcome of evil and of good to the state and to society, as well as to the individual life. One could not have wondered if the Apostles had been wholly occupied with the theology of Christ. But they held that theology not apart as the philosophy of another life, but as motive and guide of men in their social as well as their ecclesiastical relations. They laid deep the foundations of all future national liberty and social equality, where neither Jew nor Greek, bond or free, were to be regarded as anything but brethren of one household of the family of God.

The inspiration of St. Paul, which only a great genius like his could receive, stirred him not only to expound the profoundest truths concerning God and redemption, but also as the direct outcome of such truth—to shatter the narrowness of social prejudice, which would have kept Christianity from a Jewish sect, and to develop out of the truths which burned and flamed within his soul, the universal brotherhood of man in a Catholic Church. What practical work for society has ever been equal to that? He brought Christianity to bear on the one great social question of his time. His solution of it became the precursor of all future reforms, which seek to apply and embody it in the social institutions of men. But some will still reiterate the cry, a Kingdom not of this world, as though that meant that the Kingdom of the world must always be the Kingdom of Satan, as though God's Kingdom could not come on earth, as we pray, but only in Heaven. Truly Christ's Kingdom is not of the world, as rising from the world, or as subordinated to the world, as ruled by its policies, its maxims, its mere earthly aims. But still a Kingdom *in* the world to transform it into a Kingdom of God, to breathe the spirit of its king into all souls and all forms of life—to leaven it with a noble passion—with that enthusiasm for humanity which rises from the conviction of man's sonship in God, which therefore conceives nothing alien from the Master's watch and ward, because all human relations can be transformed and sanctified by the Spirit of the living God.

Of what, then, we have said this is the sum. Christianity is the life of Christ in the life of men—and in all their life, social and national, as well as individual. The Church, as an ecclesiastical institution, conserves and propagates the truth, and brings it to bear on the individual life and conscience. The Church as a society of believing men carries out that truth into all the relations and institutions of life. Not in its official, but in its substantial character, it is set to purify and invigorate, to reconstruct and ennoble society. The bearing of Christianity on Social Questions is thus direct and essential. It is the peculiar task and duty of our time. Much of the social disturbance of our age is the legitimate demand for the extension of Christian principles and the application of the Christian spirit to irrational injurious and unfair social customs and institutions. Fidelity to the Master demands their sober consideration and amelioration at the hands of Christian men. To be faithful to the wrongs of our fellow men is to be faithful to the rights of Christ and His Kingdom.

AFTERNOON—FIRST SECTION.

M. LE PAST. G. P. PONS (Moderator of the Waldensian Church) PRESIDED.

Christian Testimony in Presence of the Wants of the Day.

ADDRESS BY M. A. DE LOES, PASTOR AT LAUSANNE.

THE Gospel, said Vinet, is ever young, and always ready to make a fresh start. It is eternal, immutable Truth. It meets the universal and abiding necessities of the human soul with an unchangeableness which is its strength, and it ceaselessly proclaims before all and always, salvation through faith alone in Jesus Christ. Does it not follow from this fact that Christian testimony can only change by ceasing to be faithful? Is it not to set our foot on an inclined plane, to enquire how we can meet the wants of our time? Certainly, if the question were how to lessen, to attenuate our testimony, how to accommodate the Gospel to the taste of the day, and to sum it up in a shallow doctrine and a superficial morality. There are those who recommend such a mutilation, and say that the age will never be reconciled to faith without it. This is not our solution. It confuses the imaginary wants of the time with the real and deep wants. The gospel draught is sweet and bitter at the same time. To substitute for it a sleeping draught is not to heal the sicknesses of society. But the everlasting Gospel must be set before men in a real manner, and the work of the Christian apologist must vary from age to age. We must take account of contemporary movements. We ought to decide when the battle is fiercest, and at what points the Christian testimony is most essential. It is often said that we are passing through a crisis. It is less a doctrinal crisis than a moral one. Voltaireism is out of fashion. Now the point of resistance is when the intellect refuses to accept the truth of Christ. Anarchy is the cry that is heard: "Neither God, nor Master." Multitudes follow that flag.

The citizen disloyal to his country, the workman suspicious of his employer, and treating him as his enemy, the young rebelling against the paternal authority; these are revolts against the Eternal and against His Anointed, and they mean finishing up with the old prejudice which goes by the name of the Moral Law. Reverence, away with it. Yes, alas, it is gone. Only the blind do not see it so. Conscience and responsibility are disappearing. Surely, brethren, it is a sad thing if at such a time our testimony should fail for lack of point and power.

(The speaker then went on to show that idealism and materialism were two forms of evil influence in the present day, destroying faith in the personality of God and the responsibility of man, and that the corrupt principles which are embodied in works of fiction did much to promote laxity of morals, and the death of the conscience in overflowing worldliness.)

To guard ourselves against such dangers, and produce a salutary reaction, believers must unite their efforts. Nothing will succeed which is not based on faith. If we cannot set up a barrier against such a flood, we are lost. What is the kind of testimony we must give? The question is urgent, and we should consider it without partiality in a free spirit.

Now Catholicism cannot succeed in this work of awakening the conscience. It is content with dreams of territorial dominion and the calculations of ecclesiastical policy. Its religious influence on the masses decreases from day to day. In social questions its doctrine of good works weakens its strength because it hides the true doctrine of sin. How can evil be evil, if man can obliterate it by his own merits? Romanism destroys the power of the Gospel by its subtle distinctions between different kinds of sin, and its indulgences given to those who swallow all its doctrines and submit to all its rites. Is it not evident that we must look for a new Reformation, not less thorough than that of the fifteenth century? And, therefore, Catholicism will not supply us with what we require.

Spiritualism is reviving at the present time in an interesting manner, especially in France. The youth of that country are growing weary of materialism and pessimism. They feel the necessity of strength for the battle of life. In the loss of faith they feel that they have lost, as Melchiorde Vogüe says, "*the mother of action.*" "It is not liberty we want," says the great Swiss naturalist and lawyer, M. Chrest, "for great works (as a poet has said), the soul of great works is God."

But now let us come nearer home and look. What in our own Protestantism is the testimony needed for the times? We cannot answer such a question without remembering the diversities of opinion which on such a vital theme have revealed themselves in the Churches which sprang from the Reformation. We know how Liberalism looks at sin. It is a reality, but a defect inherent in man, a necessity in his development, thus casting the responsibility on God Himself. How can we enforce the duty of resisting evil with such a view of sin? How can we awaken the conscience to repentance and prayer for pardon? In Germany there is more seriousness in the treatment of such questions, but sin is still regarded as weakness, resulting from ignorance. There is no room for the vital proclamations of the Gospel, deliverance through the sacrifice of Christ.

What is wanted, then, is the simple and powerful publication of the two facts—Man the sinner, Christ the Saviour. "*Jesus Christ,*" said Vinet, "*is the conscience of the conscience.*" Then is the way opened to us. Sin made certain to the conscience. The Saviour Christ apprehended by the conscience. That is the whole matter. Such a testimony must find its echo in the human soul, and if it is made living by the Spirit of God, it will soon call forth an experience which is the first step to a religious and moral elevation.

Who, then, in our time, are the most successful workers? Temperance societies, popular evangelization societies, yea, the Salvation Army itself, which teaches us by example, though we may not approve its methods. Why do such endeavours succeed? Because they are face to face with evil itself, they look to the real source of it, to the heart. They have proclaimed, with undeniable power, the tragic reality of evil and the real happiness of salvation. They have had the courage and boldness to say to men who are living without God, they are lost. They have declared that there is no uplifting of man, no victory, no pardon possible without faith in Christ. This is the testimony which has moved consciences, which has given strength to failing wills, which has called forth the manly resolutions and the radical reformations. God has manifestly given His blessing.

But our testimony must not be a written or spoken testimony alone. Life originates by living contact. We must live so that the world can plainly see that we are "*no longer our own.*" But are we not degenerate? Does the blood of the Huguenots, whom they called "*God fearing,*" still flow in our veins? Brethren, we must act, not merely lament; we must pray, not despair; we must love, and not merely condemn; we must obey, yes, above all, *obey*—that is what He expects of us, who said to His disciples, "Ye are My witnesses."

The Religious and Social Necessity of the Observance of the Lord's Day.

BY M. T. EHNI, PASTOR AT GENEVA.

THIRTY years ago the movement for the observance of the Lord's Day was inaugurated by a remarkable paper by Professor F. Godet, of Neuchatel. It was vigorously taken up by M. Alexander Lombard, the banker, of Geneva, and since that time has been carried on by an international federation of societies. Now it is a wide-spread movement in which not only Christian ministers take part, but eminent medical men, great statesmen and legislators, even emperors, not to speak of socialist leaders. So true is it that the cause of the Lord's Day touches the vital interests of humanity.

The observance of the Sabbath is founded on the Divine Rest on the seventh day. God rested not because He was weary, but because He had finished and perfected creation by placing man at the head of it. The life of man, who was created in the image of God, ought not to be one of unceasing toil, which is slavery, nor one of barren idleness, which is degrading, but a wise union of toil and rest. As a divine institution, then, the seventh day rest is appointed by the God of Love for the physical, intellectual, and moral good of man. "The sabbath," as our Lord said, "was made for man, not man for the sabbath." Regarded physically, the rest of the seventh day is necessary for health. Nightly repose is not all that is required. The physical powers need more. Otherwise there is a general decline of bodily strength and premature decay. Saints' Days and Feast Days are not enough. Nor was the tenth day an improvement on the seventh, which the French Revolution attempted, but without success. In these times of swift travelling and intense activity in every department of life, it is absolutely necessary to maintain the rest of the Sunday, as an oasis in the desert, where we find calm and refreshment.

Children specially need rest from their school labours, that they may not lose their elasticity of body and mind. And it is the same with adults. Whatever our employment may be, we should seek rest that we may return to our work with new strength and fresh inspiration. It scarcely need be said how important it is to secure the Sabbath rest for domestic servants, shopmen, hotel waiters, and the myriads of labourers who earn their bread with the sweat of their brow. What temptation there is to those who are robbed of their necessary rest to fly to alcoholic drinks to relieve their weariness by a temporary excitement. It is overwork and intemperance which are ruining whole classes in our society. What else can be expected when men are shut up, as miners are, for eight or ten hours of the day in the bowels of the earth in exhausting labour, and when they return to the light and air pass their remaining time either sunk in heavy sleep or in a state of drunkenness? Surely the rest of the Sabbath is absolutely necessary for all such labourers. Economically, too, there is great advantage in the seventh day rest both to employers and employed. We all know what Saint Monday means, and how injurious it is to the workmen. Sunday labour is never of the same value with that of other days. And it is universally admitted that where the day of rest is most observed, as in England and the United States, there business is most prosperous. Family life is greatly benefitted and blessed by it. And the family makes the nation. How can the children be properly cared for, and how can family life be united and happy, when there is no day of rest? How delightful it is to see a whole household meeting together for family worship on the Sunday morning, or preparing for worship in the House of God. What enjoyment they have in their quiet walk in the fields, and contemplation of the divine wisdom and goodness in Nature, while intelligent conversation is kept up or the children innocently amused. "Ah, how lovely the Sunday is," said a little girl to her father, "it is the day when we love one another so much." Nor should we forget that the rest of the Sabbath has a great influence in calming the excitements of the social state, and solving the graver problems of our generation. Socialists themselves have admitted the necessity of such a day, and if we would be protected from the dangerous commotions among the labouring classes we must take care that their weekly rest is not sacrificed.

But admitting the necessity of Sunday observance, what should be the employment of the hours of rest? Idleness is the mother of vice. Many Sunday amusements are degrading, leading to debauchery, intemperance, and violent collisions. And yet the remedy is not in renouncing the rest and employing the hours of the day in toil. Nor should all enjoyment be interdicted. Let our relaxation be pure and innocent, and let us substitute for public games and excitements the simple, homely enjoyments of the family. "All things are yours," said the Apostle Paul, but he added, "ye are Christ's." There is the law both of liberty and restraint. The Christian conscience, enlightened by the Spirit of God, must decide in each particular case.

Christians observe Sunday as a day of commemoration of the Divine Works, the work of Creation and the work of Redemption. We remember our Creator on that day, and we commemorate the resurrection of our Lord Jesus Christ and the out-pouring of His Spirit on His disciples. It was our Saviour's consecration of the first day of the week which led the early Christians to substitute it for the day observed under the Old Testament. Our Sundays, too, are days of special intercourse with God, when we fix our thoughts on divine things in prayer and by meditation on the Word of God, whether in private or in the public assembly. And to worship we add the exercises of a holy life in works of charity and beneficence, in imitation of the Lord Himself, Who wrought His miracles of healing on that day, and as the Apostle Paul ordained in the churches that collections should be made for the poor—and thus as it has been said, "*Sunday makes the week.*" The streams of living waters flow from that fountain through all parts of human existence. Let us then ourselves be more careful in observing the day, and let us remember our fellow men around us and labour for their deliverance from their oppression and their enlightenment in the Gospel of Christ. Many are still deprived of their Sabbath rest. Let us use all the means we can find to restore it to them. We should try to influence legislatures to pass good Laws, and follow the example of the Swiss Federal Assembly, which has secured by law to Railway servants and all employed in transport service, fifty-two free days in the year, including seventeen Sundays. But it is the work of the Christian Church to awaken the consciences and sanctify the Sunday in the spirit of submission to the fatherly discipline of God, thus making it a foretaste of the Eternal Sabbath. This, at least, is common ground where all Evangelical Churches can meet. The Sabbath is dear to us all. Its advocacy will draw us closer together; and may beautiful Italy, where we now meet, receive abundantly the temporal and spiritual blessings of its observance.

ADDRESS BY M. E. DELUZ, OF GENEVA,

Secretary of the International Federation for the Observance of the Lord's Day.

THE Federation, of which both pastor Ehni and myself are representatives, is the offspring of the Evangelical Alliance. It had been growing in Switzerland for fifteen years, from 1861 to 1876, and during the last fifteen years it has extended its influence over many different countries of the Continent, and has led to the formation of many committees, of which that in Geneva may be said to be the central point. Some of the work which has been done may be here noted.

1. Special committees have been established at Strasburg, Christiania, Bergen, Stockholm, Copenhagen, and Debreczen in Hungary. That in Copenhagen arose out of the meetings of the Alliance there in 1884, and is honoured by the presidency of Count A. de Moltke.

2. We were very fortunate in obtaining a gold medal at the Universal Exhibition in Paris, an unexpected honour, especially as we had encountered only neglect hitherto in such quarters.

3. The Congress, which was held within the precincts of the Exhibition, under the sanction of the French Government, on the subject of a seventh day rest, had the happiest results. The religious part of the Congress could not meet in the Exhibition itself, but Conferences were held immediately after the hygienic and social parts of the subject were considered. Forty-eight resolutions were passed, which were sent by the French Government to a number of French and Foreign political journals, accompanied with the text of the two letters addressed to the Congress by Mr. Gladstone and the President of the United States, Mr. Harrison, who had been appointed honorary president of the Congress. The journals to which these communications were sent were thus led to notice our movement in

numerous articles on the observance of Sunday. The result has been the formation of mixed committees of Protestants and Catholics in several towns, as in Paris the Parisian League under the honorary presidency of M. Jules Simon, and with M. Leon Say as the executive chairman, in Tours, in Lyons, in Bordeaux, in Besançon, in Lille, in Marseilles, in Limoges, and in Calais. At Bordeaux, nearly a thousand merchants and clerks are set free on the Lord's day through the closing of a large number of business houses. In Paris, and in 1,670 provincial places, the distribution of letters and their collection has now been given up after midday. The observance of the Sunday is now the rule in the French army, and the Minister of Marine, M. Barbey, has, some months since, given orders that in military ports the French fleet shall be under the same regulation. A few days since it was decided that all goods stations in France shall be closed at ten o'clock on Sunday morning.

There are now five publications in France more or less periodical, which are specially devoted to the cause of Sunday observance. One is published at Marseilles, another at Lyons, two at Paris, and one at Lille. And there are echoes of this movement heard in other countries at a distance, as Spain, at Madrid; Italy, at Milan; at Bucharest, Cairo, and in the North of Europe.

In Belgium, where Sunday goods trains have been stopped, our cause has made progress of late. Thousands of post office servants have their Sundays, and the goods stations are closed on the State Railway all the day. Public State labour is stopped, notwithstanding the outcries of some of the journals. The Belgian workmen appreciate the benefit, and a representative of the Ministry connected with the Post Office and the Railway has recently said that if they wished they could not now go back to the old state of things. These are results of the Paris Congress.

4. The movement for Sabbath observance cannot overlook the fact that first the Swiss Government and then the Emperor of Germany have put the question in the first place in the programme of the International Congress for the protection of Labour, which is assembled at Berlin. This must advance the cause, and must promote sympathy, and especially with those Churches which have hitherto been slow to express it.

5. It is generally known that our Swiss Federal Assembly has passed a law which has given to all our railway servants, post office, and telegraph, and steamboat employees fifty-two days of rest in the year, including seventeen Sundays. The countries which border upon ours must be influenced by this, and the railway companies are already alarmed lest their servants should require the same privilege.

Courage, then, dear brethren of Italy, and unfurl the flag of this noble cause in your beautiful land. Your opportunity may be small, but God works with you. Do not leave it to Romanism and Socialism to save for the labourer his day of rest. Christianity is the true source of all the benefits which God has appointed for man, and we should show it both by our words and by our deeds. Our International Federation needs help. We are in the midst of the fight, and we mean to go forward, with the divine assistance. But Switzerland alone cannot do all the work. It is a missionary work. It cannot and must not be arrested by a financial deficit. Help us both by your prayers and by your liberal co-operation to go on with this effort, for the glory of God, and for the honour of the Christian Church, and for the blessing of our neighbours.

SECOND SECTION.

THE REV. DR. C. A. STODDARD, OF NEW YORK, PRESIDED.

Christianity a Faith for all Nations.

BY THE REV. DONALD FRASER, D.D., OF LONDON.

It was the ambition of ancient conquerors to establish one sway over all nations. The Babylonian Emperors, for instance, exulted in the vast range of their authority, and issued their pompous edicts to "peoples, nations, and languages." But how small a portion of the earth they had mastered, or even knew to exist, and how quickly, when the bands were loosed by reverses in war, their empire fell apart!

It was Italy that sent forth the greatest world-subduing force, setting one head of authority over many nations, and for centuries holding them together by iron bands. The organization of the Roman Empire is an historical prodigy. It broke down barriers between nations, without destroying the autonomy of each. It made international communication safe and easy, and without attacking traditional customs or religions, imposed its authority on the most diverse and distant races, and set up everywhere the effigy of the Emperor, the master of the world.

Without attacking local religions: for the imperial policy was in that respect one of tolerance. Tribes and nations might retain gods which were not the gods of Rome. And yet the unity of the Empire did suggest some efforts towards a religious as well as a political bond for all the nations. Let me mention three of them: the first a kind of Broad Churchism, the second, an extreme Erastianism; the third, a philosophic Rationalism. (1) One attempt was made by way of comprehension, when all the gods were brought into the Pantheon, to dwell together in peace, so that worshippers from all nations might go up to one temple, though, within the temple, each should repair to his favourite shrine. (2) Another attempt was made by way of deifying the Imperial Majesty itself. The image of the reigning Cæsar was set up in all the provinces, and his subjects, whatever their traditional faith, were required to pay religious homage to that Figure of Power. Such was the test applied to the Christians in the early persecutions. Would they, or would they not burn incense before the statue of the Emperor? And, though it cost them their lives, they would not worship the wild beast and his image. (3) Yet a third, and a nobler attempt at religious unity emanated from philosophical thinkers, like Seneca, Epictetus, and Aurelian, who sought and "felt after" one true God, Lord of Nature and of Providence, whom the enlightened in all nations might acknowledge and worship, when the old legends of Greek and Egyptian gods and goddesses had become incredible. They meant well, but could not succeed; "the world by wisdom knew not god."

All such attempts only indicated a want among the nations: could not meet or satisfy it. Not in any of these ways was a universal faith to be found. In practice, each nation clung to its own gods, and tried to believe that these were stronger than the gods of its neighbours.

But a new thing began to appear. In various cities of the Empire, men were heard to speak of a God and Saviour for all nations. They, who so spake, were neither priests nor philosophers, nor did they wear any badge of office or authority. They were Jews, or proselytes to the Jews' religion; yet it was not Mosaism or Judaism that they taught, and they seemed to be wonderfully free from that racial exclusiveness which was so characteristic of Jews.

Any one could see that the Hebrew religion, though acknowledging only one God of the whole earth, was not fitted for universality. Its intensely national character, its localization of sacred privilege, its law of meats and drinks, and its elaborate ritual, could not be adapted to all lands and all climates. Yet men trained in that religion, and full of reverence for Moses and the Prophets, instilled into the Gentiles a faith which was destined to banish all the traditional gods and goddesses of the Empire, and spread to "regions Cæsar never knew." They proclaimed a Name above every name, a King of kings and Lord of lords, before whom the Emperor was but a cipher, and the gods of the nations were dumb idols. They announced a Gospel to all nations, conveying a salvation which was "of the Jews," but for all mankind. They called for an "obedience of faith among all nations." This phrase occurs both in the beginning and at the end of St. Paul's Epistle to the Christians at Rome, the seat of the Empire. Imperialism insisted on an obedience of fear; the Church on an obedience of faith. The Empire gathered the nations into one vast civil and military combination, and gave to favoured persons the rights of Roman citizenship; the Church swallowed up racial discords in one spiritual commonwealth, and gave to all who believed the Gospel the rights of a citizenship in heaven.

1. How far has this early promise of Christianity been fulfilled? Has it shown an adaptation to all varieties of mankind? What has history to tell?

It ought not to be claimed for Christianity that it is the only religion which has overstepped national boundaries; the same may be affirmed, within limits, of Buddhism (which is atheistic) and of Mohammedanism (which is monotheistic). It is a notable fact that religions which grew up, like indigenous plants, and gradually evolved themselves in a tribe or nation, always continued to be ethnic. So with the old faiths of Egypt, Assyria, India, Greece, and Scandinavia. But religions which were propounded by a leader or prophet never confined themselves to one race or one region, but were spread abroad by missionary zeal. So Buddhism was carried from India to Ceylon, Burmah, Thibet, China, and Japan; so Mohammedanism spread from Arabia to Egypt, Syria, Turkey, Persia, India, Tunis, and Morocco.

One reason for this is that the moral element entered feebly, if at all, into the home-grown polytheism. The gods were feared, and therefore propitiated by gifts and sacrifices; but they did not love or require righteousness. On the other hand, the religions which prophets taught and missionaries diffused had a distinct moral purpose, and sought more or less successfully to assuage the pains of life and govern human conduct.

Nevertheless, it is quite plain that neither of the great religions which we have named, and which, so far as statistics go, compete with Christianity on not unequal terms, can ever become truly

Catholic. Buddhism is for Asia only (Central and Eastern Asia); it cannot be naturalized elsewhere. Mohammedanism is for Asia and Northern Africa, but cannot be assimilated by the Western mind.

Christianity, on the other hand, born in the East, is mighty in the West, and exhibits no less propagative force now than it did when it was young. It does not fall within my present scope to trace its history, nor shall I do more than touch upon the painful fact that the Christianity both of the East and of the West lost much of the original simplicity and purity of the Gospel. It received both accretions and secretions from the very Paganism which it displaced. Yet even in this condition its progress was an advantage for the human race; its dim religious light was better than gross darkness.

We are not disposed—we are not able—to disown all relation to the Western Church in the long centuries which preceded the Reformation, nor are we so uncandid as to ignore or to disparage the missionary zeal of the unreformed Church in Post-Reformation times, though our own highest and best hope for the nations is with the Reformed and Evangelical Christianity. The function so well and bravely performed by our fathers in the sixteenth century was not to found a new Church, but to cleanse, correct, and renovate the old Church according to the Scriptures. When a ship, after long voyages, is taken into dock, the bottom is scraped clean from barnacles and weeds that have stuck to it, but are not of it; unsound timbers are cut out, and replaced by sound; the copper sheathing is removed, new spars are fitted, and there is a fresh suit of canvas. Something like this was the change effected on historical Christianity wherever the Reformation prevailed; and wherever it prevailed a brighter light shone, souls gained liberty, and a new energy entered into the life of nations.

I do not pour any indiscriminate praise on Reformed and Protestant Churches, or their offshoots. Such of them as have become formalistic and rationalistic are withered, and can bring forth little fruit to God. They have as much need to be prayed for as the Latin Church, or the Greek. Let us be thankful that the propagative force of Reformed and Protestant Christianity is almost entirely with the fervent and evangelical types of such Christianity. Be thankful, also, that those types are strongest in the strongest races, helping to make and keep them strongest. From these the Gospel in our time goes out to the most various and distant regions of the globe. While holding its ground against all rivals in Christendom, it spreads its influence over heathen nations, and even over barbarous tribes. It overturns the idols in India, Africa, and the Islands of the South Pacific, makes successful inroads upon China, and seems to be on the point of winning Japan.

There is really nothing else in the field. We shall not waste our words on *Positivism*, with its grotesque displacement of the worship of God by a worship of humanity, or of the aggregate memory of great men, for which M. Comte was so good as to provide a calendar and ritual. And just as little need we occupy ourselves with that dream of a new universal church and religion of the future which floats through unsettled minds—a colourless theism, without dogma, without prayer, and, of course, without any fervour or fire of the Holy Ghost.

Our reading of history, both remote and recent, encourages the persuasion that the future is with Christianity, and most decidedly with the purer and more Biblical type of Christianity. And here in Italy, where was the seat of that Empire which bestrode the world, and where is the seat of that Papacy which enthralled the Western Church, here we do well to know and proclaim our confidence in that genuine Christianity, which proved stronger and more durable than the Empire, and now resists and holds in scorn the pretensions of the Pope; and pledge ourselves to the defence and diffusion of that evangelic faith which alone can overcome the world and bless the nations.

2. May we now look into the contents of this Christianity, and recognize the elements of its fitness for all nations? No historical accident can account for such an all-round adaptation and success. The reasons must be inherent in the contents and character of the Christian faith. Thus—

(1). *Its Conception of God.*—It does not confuse God with man; and yet, in distinguishing the Being who is worshipped from the being who worships, it does not fail to establish mutual arrangements between them. The feeling and expression of such relation on man's part constitutes religion.

Dr. Flint has truly said that "Christianity alone of religions gives a clear, self-consistent, adequate view of God .... It alone of religions discloses and promises to man a complete communion with God." The more we think of this, and examine the theistic conceptions which have burdened and darkened the human mind, the more clear it becomes that the Gospel is "worthy of all acceptation." It says that "God is light, and in Him is no darkness at all;" He is love, and loves the world; He is holy, He is just, He has no respect of persons; Himself remote from human passions, He knows the hearts of men, and rules in righteousness; Himself ever blessed, He blesses His creatures with good and perfect gifts. Such a God all nations have but to know in order to hold in reverence.

(2). *Its Doctrine of Sin and Salvation.*—Thus it goes to the root of the misery of all mankind. No religion has ever looked the moral facts of life so fully in the face, or revealed so complete a deliverance from evil. The alienation of man from God, the guilt on his conscience, and the disorder of his affections and will are seriously recognized. Then it is shown how he may be purged and released from sin. There is a propitiation for the whole world in the heart of the Lamb of God; and thus there is divine forgiveness for everyone in all nations who repents and believes the Gospel. And not only so, but the heart of the repentant sinner is cleansed and renewed by the Holy Spirit and the Word. Nature tells nothing of this. Religions, other than Judaism and Christianity, have had no salvation to proclaim—neither free pardon nor inward regeneration. The Gospel has both, and for all nations.

(3). *Its Bond of Fraternity.*—To the amazement of all who heard it, primitive Christianity united men of different origins and stations, and measures of civilization, in one family. Jews and Greeks called each other brothers, and not only so, but admitted to the same fraternity Barbarians and Scythians when they believed in Christ. Freemen and slaves sat at the same sacred table, drank from the same cup, knelt on the same floor. And such is the tendency, such the purpose of Christianity to-day. Nothing has such power to soften racial prejudice, to break down barriers of caste, compose differences, and make men conscious of a blessed unity enfolding them all, and a sublime affection penetrating and embracing all. We claim that this is a faith for all nations, because this only of all religions makes men of all countries regard one another as brethren.

(4). *Its Ethic Standard and Impetus.*—We have pointed out that religions which have been promulgated by a prophet have had more in them of the moral element than those which were the growth of superstitious fears. Especially in Confucianism and Buddhism, the moral element is strong, and in many respects excellent. Confucius is a great moral preceptor, and Buddha the lord of a holy law. But here again Christianity is above all. It has not only a higher preceptive morality, but presents in Christ Himself the pattern of a just, merciful, and pure humanity. And then it applies a motive-power for the following of the example such as is provided nowhere else. The grace of the Holy Spirit impels the Christian to follow Christ, and fires him with an enthusiasm for well-doing. Too true, that this is imperfectly illustrated in the life and demeanour of many who profess the faith of the Gospel; but their imperfection of character is not the fault of their religion. It comes of their lack of religion. In so far as men live "according to Christ Jesus," they evince a style and degree of goodness, which no other faith, and certainly no unfaith, has produced.

(5.) *Its inspiration of Hope.*—On the face of all nations there has lain for ages the gloom of pain, and grief, and death. And this has been but faintly and partially relieved by the futurism of the world's religions. Even the Hebrew, with, as we believe, a measure of divine revelation, thought vaguely and pensively of that realm of silence, the *sheol* after death. A man as devout as King Hezekiah, when warned that he was about to die, "wept sore." The ancient Egyptians took vast pains with the preservation of dead bodies, and thought more of their tombs than of their homes. Souls outlived death; and went to the dread judgment of Osiris, which they could pass only by establishing their own blameless righteousness. A grim and awful prospect!

Religions generally have maintained the continuance of souls after death. Under many of them, the living are haunted by the returning ghosts of their predecessors, to whom they ascribe malicious intent. Under others there is a belief in the transmigration of souls into the forms of higher or lower animals. The famous "Laws of Manu," so venerable to the Brahmin, gravely assert that if a man steal grain in the husk he shall become a rat; if he steal milk, a cow; if he steal clarified butter, a weasel. Buddhism set before the best men only a negation, the ultimate death of all desire—Nirvana. Mohammedanism promises to the believers—*i.e.*, Moslems and no others—a paradise of palaces, gardens, and fountains; but the Koran barely recognizes any such bliss even for Moslem women and children. Mohammed himself declared that when, in his vision, he looked down into hell, he saw the great majority of wretches confined there to be women.

How much more rational and how much more consolatory the futurism of Christianity! The Lord heals the broken-hearted, and binds up their wounds. The rest of the departed with Christ; the hope of His coming, and of the blessed resurrection, and His judgment of quick and dead at the last day! Life, eternal life, bestowed as the gift of God; yet judgment passed on all according to their works. What an absence of the triviality and cruelty which attach to the futurism of other religions! What good hope through grace! What incentive to duty! What consolation to mourners! What peace for departing spirits in the hope of the glory to be revealed, and the resurrection from the dead, and the life everlasting! The Gospel has brought to light life and incorruption; and here is another good ground for proclaiming it a faith for all nations.

Let a few words be added on the relation of Christianity to civilization and culture. That it is a relation of close alliance no one can fairly dispute. The early triumphs of our faith were won among races that deserved to be called civilized. It prevailed with Jews, Greeks, and Romans, rather than with Scythians and the Provincial Barbarians of the Empire. Thereafter, on the downfall of the Empire, it seized on the vigorous races that rose into independent nations, and, in course of time, gave them a new culture—both intellectual and moral. The same effect followed the Mediæval Missions to Germany and Scandinavia. It has been truly said that "our whole modern culture-development rests on the Christianity of Europe."

Who does not see that it is mainly, almost exclusively, within Christendom that modern culture exists, and is at home? The rest of the world lags far behind in knowledge, in letters, in the arts of refinement, and in the esteem of private and public honour. Too true that in the most advanced countries of Christendom, there is not a little scepticism; but no one has ever seen civilization built upon scepticism, and no one can show that there is any race-elevating power in unbelief. The fact is that the modern admirer of culture who seeks to dispense with religious belief is trying to sever in twain the branch on which he is sitting, and if he could succeed, would do nothing but bring himself, and all who think with him, to the ground. Culture cannot last without morals; and morals cannot sustain themselves without religion; and there is no religion fit to influence civilized nations but Christianity.

But let us end: not with Christianity—even Evangelical Christianity, but with Jesus Christ our Lord—the Saviour for all nations, and the Supreme Master of all real amelioration and civilization upon the earth. For us, He is the pattern, and, in us, He is the author of that manner of life which is both godly and manly. He is the Light of the World; He is the Just One; He is the Prince of Peace. From Him have issued streams of influence that make for knowledge, for righteousness, and for brotherhood. And culture, in its noblest meaning, comes through Him. To be true, to be patient, to be courteous, to be just, to be large-minded and large-hearted—it is Christ Who teaches this, it is His Spirit Who leads to this.

So let us go out with Christ to the ends of the earth. There is no region which He cannot bless. And let us go on with Christ into the years unborn, of which the American poet writes:—

> "Years of the modern! Years of the unperformed.
> I see tremendous entrances and exits—I see new
>   combinations—I see the solidarity of races.
> The earth restive confronts a new era."

The real new era will be the coming of Christ in His Kingdom.

Jesus Christ is the only Lord of the future; and according to His Word, "the meek shall inherit the earth."

The Relation of the Church to Modern Society.

BY THE REV. G. STRINGER ROWE, OF LEEDS.

This is a subject of the utmost practical interest and importance, and by no means of a speculative kind. It touches us all at many points, so that a Christian can hardly live one day's Christian life without having to decide some question which it raises. But it is so large, and includes such innumerable particulars, that we must deal with it here almost entirely in regard to its controlling principles.

There are two great words of our blessed Lord which, taken together, give the true centre of our thought, if we are to come to a right decision concerning the relation of His Church to society. The one is in His intercessory prayer on behalf of His people: "I pray not that Thou shouldest take them out of the world, but that Thou shouldest keep them from the evil." The other is addressed to the disciples: "Ye are the salt of the earth."

All I say, therefore, will move round the pivot thus formed; for I take the position, which no one will dispute, that the Church, in dealing with this matter, has no licence to go beyond the ground which the Lord's own authority has marked out. The marking out, moreover, is surely clear beyond all need of mistake. The Church of Christ, in contact with the world at all points, is to be "kept from the evil"—or, if you prefer the reading, "from the evil one," the representative head of that evil: and the life of the Church is to be a power actually at work to arrest the fatal corruption of the world. The Church in the world has this destiny and calling: first, to be kept pure; then, to make pure.

What, now, do we mean by Society? We certainly do not use the word in any highly artificial and specialized sense which may be given to it in certain circles. We understand by society the general social life of the world, with its recognized laws, customs, relations, pursuits, and pleasures. In the midst of this world-life the Lord ordains that His people should dwell, and should have intimately close relation to it at all points, being most really in the world, but, like their Lord, not *of* it. His example here, as everywhere, is the perfect guide. As it is expressly recorded of Him that He fulfilled all *filial* righteousness in the home sphere, so He certainly fulfilled all righteousness in all other relations of human life, as a man and a citizen, as a neighbour and a friend, and as earning His bread by honest work. We know of not a single word or act of His to warrant a belief of after times, and the practice which grew out of it, making the ideal of a religious life to consist in seclusion from the world, and the self-infliction of manifold austerities. The gross errors of monasticism and asceticism have been reached, not only through an entire disregard of our Lord's teaching and example, but in direct contradiction of them.

There is certainly no need here for me to expose those errors. We observe, however, a very curious example of the way in which people, starting away from each other in exactly opposite directions, may come at last to meet at nearly the same point. There are some who are thoroughly and earnestly evangelical in creed; but, laying all stress upon the evil of the world, as an organized opposition to the kingdom of God, they set up strict limits which seclude a Christian from taking part in certain departments of social activity and responsibility, especially in the work of forming and controlling the policy of the state—all that is usually classed under the broad term "politics." Now, why should the line of limit be drawn just here? If the active presence of evil in this particular sphere of human affairs be given as the reason, why not, on the same ground, shut out all trade and commerce? Is the world of trade and finance any more pure, or less distinctively worldly, than the world of politics? And is the business of politics less necessary to the well-being, to the very existence of the social commonwealth, than the business of trade?

Just here, it is necessary that we should lift our minds out of the reach of a grievous conventional abuse, which obscures the truth, and would warp our judgment. Am I wrong when I affirm that in the popular mind the word "politics" is degraded into the meaning of political partizanship, in which the strife itself is of far more moment than anything that may be striven for? It is on account of this that the way of a Christian, nay, the way of any honest man, along this path, is beset with the most embarrassing difficulties.

Unhappily, it is a fact which, I fear, cannot be gainsaid, that the very first question which many people ask concerning any political measure is, not whether it is for or against righteousness, but how far will it further the interests of their own party, and next, how it may be made to injure the party to which they are opposed. Most painfully does this embarrassment confront the Christian pulpit, insomuch that the preacher finds his truest wisdom in shunning matters of political debate, except when some question of national morality and righteousness demands his protest and testimony. At all times he will teach and enforce those great principles of the kingdom of God, which will keep men from doing every kind of wrong, and will shape their policy aright in every department of life.

How it may be in regard to this matter in other countries, I do not presume to say, but I am fully convinced that, in England, one of the most pressing duties of the Church in regard to modern society is, that Christian men should take hold upon state affairs, and deal with them, first of all, *as Christians ;* holding themselves, for Christ's sake, absolutely free to give their whole influence to promote every measure that would make for righteousness, and to resist with all their power every immoral policy, whatever party interests may be involved.

Let us see where this doctrine, that Christians must not meddle with political life, would lead us. The man who binds himself with this rule must, of course, believe that it is equally binding upon all other Christians. What is right for one must be right for all. Therefore, the policy of the state, including the whole work of legislature, is to be forsaken by the people of God, and deliberately handed over to the children of darkness. Can any Christian face this result, and insist upon taking the road which leads to it? Can he be loyal to the commission received from his Lord, and yet determine that the salt is to be withheld from so vast and so central a portion of the world-life?

And the end of the error is not here. The circle of state interests and duties is so wide that it includes all lesser circles whatsoever of secular relations and responsibilities. If you withdraw your active Christian service from the wider, how can you consistently exercise it in the less? Obey this doctrine of political abstention, and, by the force of logical necessity, your active Christian influence will be driven in and in, the sphere of your godly service made ever narrower, until it becomes shut within the strait bounds of a mere religious selfishness.

What is most urgently needed, I repeat, is that Christian men should claim the whole political sphere for Christ; and, in asserting His claim, should make it unmistakably clear that, with whatever party they may be united, they are, first of all, and most of all, Christians; and that they refuse to acknowledge any party ties or claims the moment they would hinder them in upholding the laws of the kingdom of God and the work of the Church; and in giving an untrammelled resistance to any policy whatever, and by whomsoever promoted, which would be contrary to those laws. Those members of the Church of Christ will deserve well at her hands, who, in the very head and centre of all social life, boldly and incorruptibly carry out the task, and bear all the opprobrium and reproach they will surely suffer therein, of maintaining the absolute sovereignty of Christ. Though, on the arena of bitter, and often unscrupulous, party strife, they will be assailed by the angry abuse of both sides, and will be hated of all men for His Name's sake, they will, in their Lord's smile, have their reward.

Let us turn to another aspect of our subject, in the description of which you will have noted one significant word: 'The relation of the Church of Christ to *Modern* Society.' This suggests that in modern society there are some features peculiarly its own, which demand to be specially noted and dealt with by the Church. As times pass on, changes will take place in society; and it is alike the wisdom and the duty of the Church to observe these changes, and to direct its ministry of work and witness accordingly, always, however, refusing to adopt any change of principle. What is wrong in one age, however it may alter its form, cannot be right in another. Christians can never admit that their obedience to the law of truth and purity and love, or the degree of that obedience, are to be made to depend upon circumstances.

Now, what is there in modern society that needs to be particularly recognized and treated by the Church of Christ? A full answer to this question would involve almost innumerable details. I must content myself with pointing out one general fact, and what it is that this fact has to say to the Church. It is a fact which is full of encouragement, and calls for devout thanksgiving, while—paradox as it may seem—it creates its own new embarrassments and perils, and calls for the most vigilant fidelity. This general fact is, that modern society has become largely influenced for good by the life and work of the Church.

This is not optimism. I do not hide from myself that there is in the society which surrounds us to-day a godlessness as defiantly rebellious as ever; nor do I forget that it holds within it a corruption as foul as ever, nor that it is pierced through and through with an immorality as degraded, begetting and fostering vice and crime as hideous as in any former age. But though the plague of evil comes again and again to the surface, and shocks and appals us by its flagrant evidence, it cannot parade itself with the shameless effrontery of the past. The world's evil has been compelled, at least, to put on something of a certain reserve, and constraint of decency and decorum. I do not say that evil men have any more fear of God before their eyes; but they have the fear of public opinion; and the tone of public opinion has been raised by the pervasive influence of Christian truth.

Modern society, in admitting a certain amount of religion into its programme, has made a great advance. It has forsaken its old position of hostile aloofness from the Church, and has come near and encamped on the Church's borders. In doing this, it regards itself as having made an important concession; and it looks to the Church to do the same. It even asks for admission; but it is on condition that room be made for it to bring in with it all it may choose. It is here that the peril becomes very real and very grave. On all sides we are met with a cry for a broadening of our principles, and for a larger liberalism in our position. We are continually told that, if we would not repel people, we must be prepared to make concessions to them, and thus gain, by an easy process, successes which otherwise must be long delayed. The tempter's proposal, in some form or another, continually recurs; and this is its modern and more specious way of saying to the Lord, through His Church: " All these things will I give Thee, if Thou will fall down and worship me." It claims, in effect, that the day for the strait gate and the narrow way is past, and that, in our modern progress, we have left the Lord Jesus and His strict teachings behind; that there are many waiting to enter on the way of life, but it must be on the condition that the gate is made wider, and the road broader. It means that the sovereign claim of Christ is to be modified, and, at some points, withdrawn. It means that the golden ideal of a spiritual kingdom, bringing into subjection to itself all other powers, is to be given up, and in its stead to be founded a mixed state, part of iron and part of miry clay. It means that the Church is to take counsel with the world as to the terms on which an alliance may be brought about between the two.

The destined mission of the Church is to *change* society, until the whole body and system of it shall be purged from its vices, delivered from its selfish greed, and recovered from its godless follies. In this high mission the Church will always fail so long as it yields any of its principles, or claims, or action to be shaped, or changed, or limited by the world's fashion or opinion. The prayer which the Lord has put into the lips of His Church is surely to be answered. God's kingdom is to come; His will is to be done in earth as it is in heaven. Then will society no longer represent a power and state separate from the Church, but be included in one perfect theocracy, in which all things in man's social life, all family and all civil relations, all business and merchandise, all learning and culture and art, all men's pursuits and all men's enjoyments, shall be in joyful harmony with the will of God. Towards the brightness of that day the Church evermore turns her face, and is called day by day to watch and to work to bring it to pass. Questions arising out of her relation to modern society, or society in any age, cease to be perplexing the moment they are fully placed in this light. The Church, if faithful, can have but one policy. However expediency may offer to make for her smooth and easy paths, she must go straight on in the way of the Master's calling, refusing to countenance anything that is not according to His will and for His glory; and loyally and patiently striving, in all her members, to show forth righteousness, and purity, and love in every relation and duty of the social life.

A New Departure in Evangelical Alliance Work.

BY THE REV. FRANK RUSSELL,

Field Secretary of the United States Evangelical Alliance.

THE purpose of this paper is to outline some methods of applying the Gospel to the treatment of problems which are rife in my own land, and to the study of which the United States Branch since the last general conference of the Alliance has seemed to be providentially called. This has been styled the new departure, an evangelistic work, a community work. It is an effort to arouse the Churches to bestow more activity in their own home field.

The redemption of the community depends on the forces of the Churches. Their condition must be understood in seeking co-operation, and it discloses elements of weakness. There are divisions among the Churches. A leading journal of a great hierarchy, not favourable to Protestant advancement, has recently argued that such advancement, notwithstanding prestige, wealth, learning, and all hope will surely fail because Protestants are a divided army, and therefore are not to be much feared. Different names there will be, different traditions and teachers and customs; differences of administration, but all these are to be held with the same spirit. Divisions that are of Paul, excluding Apollos, that do not recognize the one family in Christ, the one flock under one Shepherd, the one body, are unscriptural and weaken the power of the Lord's hosts. In an epistle dedicated "unto all that in every place call on the name of the Lord Jesus" the Apostle beseeches that there be no divisions.

The prevalent ill distribution of forces is a weakness. In many communities, under the force of these divisions, there are too many Churches whose function is plainly the maintenance of the name of a Church rather than the application of the Gospel to the inhabitants of the neighbourhood. In other places there are too few Churches and too few workers, and large portions of the field are untouched. With little apparent consciousness of the fact there is great weakness in the selfishness of Church life. The Gospel is considered as something to be maintained, as we speak of maintaining an army in time of peace. Its existence is rather for its own sake. The Church itself unhappily becomes the field in which its activity is to be led forth and for its own sake. The Church is not a field, it is a force. The field is the community round about the Church. An engine for extinguishing fires may well be very fine and costly with polished metal shining in the parade, and showing its power in the parade and practice out at the reservoir, but all this is not its function. The engine is made for use amidst the ravages of fires. It is not for a parade and a plaything, neither is the Church. The Church was instituted to develop the love for the Lord our God that shall be with all our heart and with all our soul and with all our mind. But this does not cover its functions. It is also to develop the love for our neighbour that is like our love for ourselves. Our neighbours who have fallen, and among thieves, and who are by the wayside, and are passed by of many, are numerous in every community. The Churches of Christ must be called the Churches of good Samaritans. It is anomalous that there shall be an infectious disease raging in a city with the commission, appointed for the purpose, not knowing specifically about it, and not directly busy with it. The Churches are a royal commission appointed by the Great King to carry healing and see it applied to all the infections of the community. The children of this world are wisely attending to the interests of schools, of insurance, of taxation, of elections, knowing the fields in detail and pouring out their energies to the accomplishment of specific functions. But we find the Churches so busy with other things that their function of saving men, not souls only, but saving men, souls and minds and bodies, restoring and uplifting that which is fallen—these functions are found relegated to various other agencies, such as lodges, brotherhoods, and societies.

Happily the Churches have elements of strength. They have prestige, glorious traditions, good repute and comely habits. They have the royal charter of whatsoever things are true, whatsoever things are honest. They have also large numbers, thirteen million members and over ninety two thousand preachers in the United States; these forces are also well organized; they have good leadership, trained activities, grateful facilities for the development of all good efforts of women and young people, and sufficient variety of denominations to suit the most erratic tastes; and there is a growing unity of action throughout all the hosts. The Churches have the preaching of divine truth, the administration of that love which is the "greatest of all" and which "abideth." No enumeration of the weakness of the Churches can discourage us when we remember that they are the pillar and ground of the truth, the Church of the living God, and when their purpose to redeem the world to righteousness is a divine purpose.

The co-operation of these forces under one divine purpose is the New Testament idea. Christians were to be of one mind; they are one bread and one body; the whole is to be fitly joined together, it is God's building, and twice over the Lord in His own prayer petitions that His followers might be one, and twice He pleads the reason, viz., that the world might believe.

Yet the Alliance for the United States will not be understood as striving for the organic unity of the various denominations. They are the different brigades, or legions of one great army under one great Captain. Each, as such, has grand traditions, histories, achievments, songs, sermons, theologies; leaders, teachers and saints. But sectarianism is fast becoming an anachronism. The pastors, or porters of the lodges deem it quite unimportant to keep bars and gates in defensive order when fences have been taken away. People may differ about the comparative size of the moon and yet walk on as friends in the light of it; or, they may dispute a little about the distance of the mountain and yet walk on peacefully to its ascent. The authors of "Rock of ages cleft for me," and of "Jesus, lover of my soul," for a time would not recognize each the other as a Christian, but they came, it is said, to trust each other's faith and to sing each other's hymns.

Co-operation among the Churches of the United States is rapidly increasing. The cry of the unreached portions of the communities is rallying them together in united effort to save the cities and the country by saving the individuals. Trusts and syndicates are becoming exceedingly popular and the Churches are forming gospel syndicates. Discussions in the public prints and in pamphlets and books upon the matter are multiplying very rapidly. An era of special activity of the Churches in efforts for the whole people is well opened. Consent has obtained that a parish belongs for tillage, not to one, but to the several Churches, and the several Churches must unite in the care of it, if it is to receive the proper care under the Gospel.

Adequate forces for the work which the Churches are beginning to understand that they should do in the community cannot be secured excepting by a united campaign. General Sherman, midway in the duration of the civil war, wrote in a letter from the midst of the conflict that the North did not yet know that there is a war. The Churches are perceiving that the conflict is commenced. Parade or strictly camp service, or book study are not to entirely absorb their energies, but inspired by the conditions and opportunities of the community they are gathering their forces for a united onslaught.

Never from a religious standpoint has the field been so well studied as now. It is clear that the method to be applied, hitherto much disused, is that of home visiting.

Home Visiting.

The cornfield standard is to be adopted. In some communities what is called the Local Alliance consists of a Conference meeting a number of times a year, constituted of several, sometimes of all the evangelical clergymen of the place, and generally also of a number of representative laymen with them, to study together the problems of their own neighbourhood with the purpose, when they are understood, of applying to the healing of ills a kindly personal acquaintance, and persuading all to a Christian and a Church life. This form of an Alliance will soon feel the need of accurate information to be secured by a special religious census. The community will then be canvassed once a year, partly to ascertain conditions and classes and partly that all households of non-church goers may be interviewed with regard to their Church preferences, and that their names may be sent to the appropriate pastors. It is expected that the pastors will then see to it that such homes shall soon share the acquaintance of Church members, and through such ripening and helpful acquaintance be led to connect themselves with some Church. This combination of the Churches of a neighbourhood for such an annual canvass is a second form of a Local Alliance. But this canvass is quite inaccurate, Church preferences are only measurably expressed, or are open to revision; acquaintance is often not realized, the inhabitants are many of them transient, and the best good is not accomplished. The need of a more thorough effort is apparent, and the want is supplied with such a combination of Church forces as shall put the community under a kindly home visiting every month. Significant precedents for this are not lacking. In New Testament times visitors were sent out two by two. They that had heard the Gospel went everywhere proclaiming it, and the Apostles broke bread from house to house. The Master sought individuals more than masses; His influence was more personal than institutional. He said the profoundest things to the woman at the well, alone, and to Nicodemus at night, alone. Our trades-people put much of personality into their work, sending an individual to our homes who will write down what we may desire, return to the business house and bring it personally to our door. Great houses send men all over the country to secure personal interviews with buyers over the samples which they carry. It is probable that since the time of Christ men have not been saved without the effort of some individual in their behalf.

The home visiting must be a continuous work. Many of the population are transient; their removal should be known, and some one in the new neighbourhood should be advised of their coming. An annual visit is of little effect. Acquaintance is the avenue of help and healing, and acquantance matures only with successive visits. Questions of saving interest, of real need, will often not be disclosed until acquaintance has matured.

The territory should be carefully prepared. The object is to cover all the inhabited territory with the kindness of Christian acquaintance. Each co-operating Church can have a district proportionate to its relative membership. It will undertake in its own way to see that a visit is made to each home every month. Meetings will be held of all the workers to collate results and plan future efforts. This Church district is carefully subdivided, so that each visitor has only such a number of homes under care as can be efficiently and regularly reached. The work proceeds with the least machinery, but with as thorough a system as that of any other business. One only of the Saviour's miracles is recorded by all the four gospel writers. The disciples were annoyed with the hungry multitude and begged Him that He would send them away. His command was, "Give ye them to eat," for He had compassion on them. They were systematically arranged in companies of fifty each, so that they could be individually reached. Sufficient members of the Church can be found who will delight to assist the Master in seeking the needy to help them, the lost to save them. Not all the troops need to be in the academy, or hospital, or are merely camp followers. Let him that heareth say, "Come." We are stewards of the manifold grace of God. We have the leaven, but it is to be put into the three measures of meal. Would God that all the Lord's people were prophets. There is some reluctance at the first; but it is soon overcome. The activity itself promotes consecration.

In some cases the enthusiasm for this activity suffers misdirection, becomes attenuated, and the work seems to die out. But sufficient number are found who have really grasped the principles and are thrilled with the crying demand, so that it is easily resumed. In some places new and self-supporting Churches have been gathered through the visiting, while at the same time all the Churches engaged have been greatly strengthened. Some communities, after three or four years of the work, are able to say that every home is touched with the continued acquaintances of Church forces; incoming families are at once met, and welcome those who are enough interested in them to seek them out, and removals to other towns are preceded with neighbourly communications interesting new friends, and from the right Churches in behalf of the new comers. With the continuance of such co-operation the grasp of the power of the Churches becomes very strong for good. Some pastors say that the community is really transformed into better life; a temperance sentiment that is operative, labourers improved and encouraged, homes of various sorts built and maintained, and the defective and dangerous classes changed to better and useful citizens, and large numbers walking newly with the people of God. The movement will not recede, but betokens the coming of a better hope, the uplifting of many thousands of homes, the apprehension of the mediatorial reign of Jesus, our King, Who is to come to the homes only in the person of those who love Him.

EVENING MEETING.

M. PUYROCHE, PASTOR AT LYONS, PRESIDED.

On the Observance of the Lord's Day.

ADDRESS BY M. W. MEILLE, PASTOR AT TURIN.

1. *What is the State of Things?*—The Government, as such, sets a very sad example of Sabbath desecration, keeping both the House of Commons and public offices open, and ordering reviews and festivals on such a day. Railway and post office traffic is increased rather than lessened, men getting on an average one day's rest out of eighteen, but very seldom a Sunday. The Lord's day is reckoned as a work day in the contracts with industrial and commercial firms; it is, also, in the morning, market and banking day, the afternoon being wholly devoted to worldly amusements and gaieties.

2. *What is the State of Opinion?*—Roman Catholicism, while professing to keep the Sabbath holy, gives much more importance to the *fêtes* of Madonnas and saints, and creates a distinction between *servile* and *lawful* works, allowing the latter to be attended to of a Sunday. Besides, that system which gets so easily rid of conscience does not train its followers to look upon Sabbath observance as upon a matter of duty, but of choice; and even were they enforcing that duty they would never allow such a work of reformation to be started by the Evangelical party. The Radicals disguise the question, and make it a matter of fun, because they are afraid of anything bearing a religious character, owing to the unbelief which is spreading widely in this country. There are some, however, who have taken up the matter at heart outside the Protestant circle. Political men, publishers of every description in Milan, have issued a paper advocating the interests of the observance of the day of rest. A society has been started and has succeeded in getting several shops and offices closed. We must, as *Evangelicals*, back such a movement,

without taking the lead, and endeavour, first of all, to bring men back to God; then all God's privileges and blessings will be appreciated by man.

ADDRESS BY THE REV. A. F. BUSCARLET, OF LAUSANNE.

THE importance of the Lord's day and of its being kept holy is far greater than many Christians think. Ever since the Reformation other days of human appointment have been far more carefully kept, so that a French pastor once said on seeing his Church, which was generally pretty empty—filled at Christmas and on Good Friday— " Ah! I expected you to-day, you who are Christians at Christmas and on Good Friday!" How can those who virtually do away with the Fourth Commandment complain of Romanists who burk the Second. This Fourth Commandment is a link, divinely appointed, between the first and second Table of the Law. It establishes parental authority, often so much weakened in the present day, and it establishes that of employers of labour also, and that on the firmest foundations. It links together the glory and honour due to God, our Redeemer, with what we owe to parents and to children, to servants, and to the stranger—our neighbour—whosoever he may be. It was never made for the Jews, for it existed long before they did. It was made for man, and is the touchstone whereby we may try our love to God and to our neighbour. It is not the seventh but the day of rest that God blesses and bids us remember, on anything but Jewish grounds. In the Old as in the New Testament he claims these days as peculiarly His own. No Christian, like some spoilt child, should say: "I won't be ordered to do this or that."

From the very first the Evangelical Alliance has taken the deepest interest in this matter. All Christians can heartily join in work connected with it. It was at one of its meetings in Geneva in 1861, after admirable papers read by the Rev. Dr. Andrew Thomson, of Edinburgh, and the Rev. Dr. and Professor F. Godet, of Neuchâtel, that Sir Culling Eardley urged a godly Genevese banker, Monsieur Alexander Lombard, who had just retired from business, to devote himself to this question on the Continent. For nearly thirty years

M. Lombard did so, sparing neither his time nor his money. The first Genevan Committee was founded in 1861. An International Committee in 1876, also at Geneva. Monsieur Lombard there manfully and pertinaciously maintained that it should be called not only *Comité du repos* (rest), but also *pour la Sanctification* (for keeping holy the Lord's Day!)

We may say that all the great progress which has been made on the Continent in this matter has been due to him and to his devoted secretary, Monsieur De Luz, still in harness. All have awakened to its importance in connection with the great social question of the day; Romanists and Socialists vie with each other in wishing to take the lead. Each sees what a boon it is to the working classes. The French and German Governments have shown the deepest interest in it. And a gold medal was awarded to the Genevan International Committee at the last Paris Exhibition, after the most important meetings held under the auspices of the French authorities. It is, then, now the bounden duty of our British and American Christians to come to the help of this Swiss International Committee. They asked them to take up this great work. Our brethren of this committee in Switzerland, urgently need means, not for their work in Switzerland, but for all they have to do in Europe, and if it is not forthcoming their financial position is such that they will soon cease to exist. It would be a disgrace to us were we to leave them to perish. Mr. Buscarlet also gave some very interesting details on the work of the Genevan International Committee.

ADDRESS BY THE REV. SIGNOR SCIARELLI, OF NAPLES.

Whence are we to expect that the true upholders of the Sunday observance in Italy, will arise? To answer this question we should keep in mind that in order to defend and uphold the Sunday observance, we must strive to secure both the rest from labour and the sanctification of it.

Can the true defenders of Sunday keeping be expected from the Government side? The Government, indeed, should interfere, as it interferes in securing the children's cessation from labour at night, in regulating the sale of poisons, of gunpowder, of hazardous play at cards. But the Government, on various occasions, has already shown that it does not consider it its concern to do so. And even if it were willing to do so, it could only secure the cessation from labour, the rest, not the sanctification, of Sunday. The true defenders, therefore, of Sunday keeping cannot be expected to come from the Government side.

Can they arise from among the working-men and the employed themselves? The mutual help associations among the working-men, should, in the interests of their own funds, do their best to remove all that causes illness among their members. But continuous labour, uninterrupted by a day of rest, weakens the constitution, and predisposes it to various illnesses. The associations of mutual help, therefore, should endeavour that labouring men, and those that hold employments, should obtain the necessary weekly rest. This thing has not hitherto been well understood; hence all attempts in this direction made by working-men in Naples, Palermo, and Milan, have failed. But admitting even that this could be understood, the associations of mutual help could only concern themselves to secure the rest, not the sanctification, of the Lord's Day. We cannot, therefore, look for the true defenders of Sunday keeping to arise from out of them.

Can we expect them from among the Roman Catholics? No, for they, concerning the Fourth Commandment, are deficient in three things: (1) They, to the Lord's Day, have added the festivals of the saints; (2) They believe that the ecclesiastical authorities have power to dispense, in whole or in part from the Sunday rest—that is, from the cessation of labour; and (3), That they consider it lawful to buy and to sell, and to give themselves up to all kinds of amusements in the day holy to the Lord. We cannot, therefore, expect that the true upholders of the Sunday keeping can come from them.

Are we to expect them to arise from out of the Evangelicals? Yes, decidedly, for it is the Evangelicals that understand the true meaning of the Fourth Commandment, in the real light and spirit of. the Gospel. Hence it is much to be deplored that some Evangelicals in Italy spend the Sunday as they do; and not only some Italian Evangelicals, but, what is worse, some of those that come from

Protestant lands, where, by the admission of the Roman Catholics themselves, the Fourth Commandment is faithfully observed.

The Evangelicals should uphold the Sunday keeping, not only within their own Churches, but also outside; and this by some special associations. They should be the very marrow and soul of such associations. But in order to arouse the public opinion, and to influence it in favour of the Sunday observance, they must not refuse the co-operation of the non-Evangelicals.

Let the Evangelicals of Italy, then, unfurl the holy, glorious, and triumphant banner of the Lord's Day Observance.

FRIDAY, APRIL 10, 1891.

THE CONFERENCE THIS MORNING MET IN TWO SECTIONS; THE FIRST PRESIDED OVER BY THE REV. H. W. WEBB-PEPLOE, OF LONDON, AND THE SECOND BY JOHN PATON, ESQ., OF NEW YORK.

Foreign Missions.

ADDRESS BY THE REV. DR. MURRAY MITCHELL, OF NICE.

AFTER a brief reference to the connection between the Evangelical Alliance and Foreign Missions, Dr. Mitchell said he hoped some degree of novelty might be imparted to the consideration of this great subject, if we were to survey the field of missions as a battle-field, in which the revealed truth of God contended against the forces of Pagan error. It was a contest extending over thousands of years, having commenced, we may say, when Abraham was commanded to leave idolatrous Chaldea. But six centuries before Christ, Jeremiah had still sorrowfully to exclaim, "Hath a nation changed its gods, which yet are no gods?" From that time onwards, individual cases of proselytism occurred; but, up to the birth of Christ, there was no case of national conversion to Judaism.

A new epoch dawned on the world when the great commission was given: "Go and teach all nations," accompanied by the magnificent promise, "Lo! I am with you always." The whole Church became truly militant. There was, indeed, no rush to victory; but there was a continuous battle; and step by step the enemy retreated—rallying once and again—but all in vain. Dr.

Mitchell here mentioned and characterized the great Pagan systems of faith that were flourishing at the Christian era, but which have since perished without hope of resurrection.

But there were other creeds then, which have not perished. They are powerful still. How have they survived? Because the Gospel hardly came in contact with them. These are Zoroastrianism, Hinduism, Buddhism, and Confucianism—all great systematised religions. There are also many vague unsystematised superstitions generally classed under the names of Animism—*i.e.*, spirit-worship and Fetishism. And what is sadder still—there is one religion which has arisen since the great commission was issued, and which, though not the most widely extended, is the most formidable foe with which the Gospel has to contend—viz., Mohammedanism.

Of the four great Pagan creeds now mentioned, Zoroastrianism alone came in conflict with the Gospel. It was the faith of the revived Persian empire. Under the influence of the Magi, some of the kings became sternly intolerant; and there was frightful persecution of the Christians. But in the seventh century Persia was crushed by the Arabs, and Zoroastrianism fell almost without a struggle. Only a poor remnant of its professors still exists in Persia. There, under the heel of the Moslem, this once haughty faith is being crushed to death. But refugees fled to India—they are the well-known Parsees—few, but intelligent, active, and influential. Consciously, or unconsciously, they are refining their creed into pure Monotheism. Their leading religious guide lately said that the attributes of Ahuramazda are the same as those ascribed to Jehovah in the Old Testament. That only shows that they are reading the doctrines of the Bible into their sacred book, the "Avesta." There have not been many Parsee converts; but all of them have been men of mark.

Dr. Mitchell next spoke of Hinduism. The beliefs included under that name range from a subtle pantheism to the grossest fetishism. The Gospel advances rapidly among the aboriginal races, and those which—so to speak—hang on to the Hindu community, but are no proper part of it. These races, when converted, steadily rise in character, influence, and position. Among the Hindus proper, conversions are much fewer; but admirable men have come out, and the number of such is increasing. Meantime, the Hindu community is shaken: and "Christianity is in the air." Societies are formed for the purification of Hinduism, some of which rise almost to the position of Unitarianism. These are zealous for reform, both social and religious. But the most noisy of all, the Arya Samaj, seems inflamed with hatred to the Gospel. It rejects three-fourths of Hindu Scripture in the hope of saving the remainder. But everywhere the truth advances. The work among women—in proportion to the efforts made—is still more successful than that among the men. A liberal and reformed Islam is arising in India, especially in connection with the Mohammedan College at Aligarh. We shall doubtless hear much of this in time to come.

Buddhism was next referred to. Under that name are included forms of thought that are fundamentally distinct. The southern school—that of Ceylon, Burmah, and Siam—keeps nearer to original Buddhism; the faith of Tibet, China, Mongolia, and Japan is really another religion. Especially the Shin-shiu sect in Japan, while retaining the name of Buddhism, has rejected its essential principles, approximating in a remarkable degree to Christianity. Tibet is still closed against Missions. Buddhism gives way, though slowly, in Ceylon, Burmah, and Siam. So in China. In Japan it fights earnestly, but in vain. Among even the upper classes the Gospel is steadily supplanting it. A Christian—an elder of the Presbyterian Church—is President of the House of Representatives; and eleven avowed Christians are members of it.

Dr. Mitchell then said that time allowed him to do little more than mention Confucianism and Mohammedanism. The former was a fully-developed ethical system; but it ignored pressing questions regarding God and the other world which Christianity alone could solve. As to Mohammedanism, Turkey continues its fixed hostility to Missions. The Scriptures circulate largely in Persia. There is progress in Egypt—still more in India. Quite of late, conversions from Mohammedanism have been numerous in Dutch India—*i.e.*, Java and the neighbouring islands.

Dr. Mitchell then spoke of the unsystematised religions of the world. These have generally a vague idea of a good deity, but a very definite and strong belief in the activity of evil spirits. The triumphs of the Gospel have been chiefly among these races in India, Burmah, Polynesia, Madagascar, and many other places. These frightful superstitions gave way more rapidly than the more systematised forms of error.

On the whole, wherever it comes fully in contact with Paganism, the Gospel triumphs. Considering how little man was doing, God is doing much. What the Church needs is tenfold zeal. Doors that have been barred from the beginning of the world are flying open on every hand. God is calling on us to enter. But we are still—as is often truly said—only playing at Missions. We are summoned to "the help of the Lord." But we keep Him waiting for His auxiliaries.

In closing, reference was made to the recent death of Dr. Adolph Saphir, as a man much beloved and an earnest advocate of Jewish Missions.

Dr. Mitchell threw out one suggestion which may, perhaps, bear good fruit. He thinks the time has come when there might be a permanent committee or board to consider Inter-Missional questions.

ADDRESS BY THE REV. DEAN VAHL, OF COPENHAGEN.

THE Evangelical Alliance was formed in 1846. Since that time what has been the progress of Foreign Missions?

In the Turkish Empire, much reduced in extent, the Christian subjects have obtained since 1856 the same rights as the Mohammedans. But it is little more than the name of liberty. The work done is chiefly amongst Christians or Jews, and it is the same in Persia. The native ministers have however increased in Turkey from none to 86, in Persia from none to 41, while the trained agents have increased in Turkey from 24 to 1,032, and in Persia from none to 190. A mission has lately been commenced in Arabia where victims to the climate have already fallen.

In India there have been great changes. The transfer of power to the British Government has given full liberty to all missionaries, but the Government is itself too fearful of changes in the customs of the people. The monotheistic and deistic movement commenced by

Rammahun Roy in 1818 has been carried on by others, especially by Keshab Chunder Sen, who died 1884. But it did little for Christianity. The work of missionaries, especially of medical missions, has been acknowledged as beneficial by the people and Zenanas have been opened to Christian ladies.

Since 1846 the work has grown greatly. In 1845 there was 313 male missionaries in India, 11 female; in 1889, 903 and 522; in 1845, 12 native ministers; in 1889, 746; in 1845, 953 native teachers; in 1889, 11,309; in 1845, 8,549 communicants; in 1889, 161,487. The Christians are most numerous among the Tamils, Telugus, Malabars, and Kohls. East of the Ganges, Burmah has become British; Cambodia, Tonkin, Cochin China, French. The American Baptists have worked successfully in Burmah. They have now 45 native missionaries, 42 female; 521 preachers; 116 native teachers; 29,689 communicants; other societies have followed them. In Siam there is full liberty of preaching but little progress, and in all French possessions no evangelical work has begun. In Ceylon great advance has been made. The Buddhists have begun to publish books and tracts against Christianity. The number of communicants has risen from 2,312 to 10,272.

In the other islands of the Archipelago, especially where the Dutch rule prevails, there has been little progress.

In China and Japan, on the other hand, great advance has been made. In 1845 only a few harbours were open in China, now the whole country. The number of missionaries have increased from 32 males and 3 females, to 594 and 350 respectively. The 6 native Christian teachers have become 208 native ministers and 1,786 native teachers, with 38,593 communicants. Korea has lately been opened with a good and promising beginning. Japan seems likely to accept Christianity as the State religion. It has adherents in every class of society. The president of one of the houses of parliament is an evangelical Christian, and there is a disposition among the different missionary societies to co-operation. There are now in Japan 29,560 Christian communicants, with 139 native ministers and 434 native teachers.

There is no necessity to dwell on the work in Polynesia, America, and Australasia. The discovery of gold and the destruction of slavery have been wonderful events in preparing the way for the Gospel. In New Guinea the advance has been considerable, and there are now, in 1889, 11,098 communicants.

In Africa what changes have been effected since 1845! Full religious liberty in Egypt. Tunis taken by the French, whose rule extends far south, and in Senegal far inland. Morocco open to the Gospel. European influence extending inwards from the coast of Guinea. While the work on the Congo is universally known, and full of promise. In Madagascar there is full religious liberty. Throughout Africa there are many signs of hope, and the dark continent is being enlightened in many places.

Taking a survey of Missions as a whole, the advance is very considerable. In 1845 (extending the work among the negroes of North America) there were 1,293 male missionaries, 52 female, 163 native ministers, 3,016 native teachers, 185,868 communicants; in 1890 there were 11,346 male missionaries, 1,388 females, 3,171 native ministers, 28,782 native teachers, and 751,070 communicants. This is below rather than above the actual numbers. The number of converts won by evangelical missions, is at least two-and-a-half millions.

To this very large progress it must be added that there is a corresponding advancement in the Evangelical Churches themselves, which promises increased power in the future. The missionary zeal of the Churches has increased. Medical Missions, Zenana Missions, have been taken up more and more. A great movement has commenced amongst students. And it must be remembered what statistics we give leave out of notice the missions of Roman Catholics and the Greek Church, and refer only to the labours of Evangelical Christians. The gifts devoted to missions have largely increased as will be seen by the following figures :—

	1845.	1889.
England	£419,813	£1,213,844.
Scotland and Ireland	£22,019	£212,887.
Netherlands	Fl. 64,383	Fl. 230,796.
Germany	Mk. 666,350	Mk. 1,970,701.
Switzerland	Fr. 205,323	Fr. 1,480,040.
France	Fr. 104,174	Fr. 387,360.
Scandinavia	Kr. 10,768	Kr. 909,175.

And to this should be added what is given in the United States, in British North America, in the West Indies, in Asia, Africa, Polynesia, and Australia.

With such facts in view we may well anticipate that the time is not far off when the whole world shall be evangelized, and the Lord shall come in His glory. May God grant that it may be so.

Evangelical Church in Egypt.

ADDRESS BY THE REV. J. K. GIFFEN.

THE first attempt at bringing Egypt to Christ, at least in modern times, was that of the missionaries of the Moravian Church (from 1752—1783). For more than thirty years they laboured without any apparent success, and it was finally abandoned. And with the single exception of the Church Missionary Society, whose efforts were also suspended for a time and only recently taken up, the operations of the "American Mission"—under the direction of the Board of the United Presbyterian Church of the United States of America—is the only purely evangelical work among the native people at large by any formally organized missionary body.

In making this statement we would neither overlook nor ignore the good work done by the Scotch Presbyterians at Alexandria, nor by Miss Whately's School in Cairo. Each have had their influence for good and have contributed largely to help on the great work of educating the masses. But yet I believe the above statement to be the truth, and will, I think, be so acknowledged by all.

It was in 1854 that the American Mission began its work in the city of Cairo, and later in Alexandria and Mansoora, in the Delta, and Assioot and Luxor (ancient Thebes), in Upper Egypt, and with these five mission centres it has worked out until it can number 131 stations, at each of which there is some evangelical agency at work, and these are scattered over the Delta and all along the Nile from the Mediterranean to the first Cataract.

It was, and ever has been, the aim of the Mission to establish in Egypt an evangelical Church, which would have within itself all the germs and elements of perpetuity; looking forward to the day when both the expensive missionary work and the aid of the Church in America could be dispensed with as no longer a necessity. The child that has never been taught to use its feet, or exercise its members, will grow into a big, helpless, useless, body, without beauty of form, and a burden and grief to those who begat it. So the Church that is ever dependent upon other Churches both for its formulated doctrines and teachings and the support of its ordinances, may grow to be an immense body, but it will not be an evangelical Church in the true sense of that word.

The Evangelical Church of Egypt has been taught from its infancy that it was not only a duty but a grand privilege to give themselves and their substance to the support of the Gospel ordinances, and however imperfectly it may have learned its lesson, it certainly deserves credit for having made the attempt. There are now twenty-nine organized congregations and three others that will probably be organized (according to the Presbyterian form of government), during 1891. There are fourteen pastors, six licentiates, and twenty-one theological students, all of whom we hope will be in the ministry before another ten years, and that their places will be filled from among the students now in the Training College, which prepares for the ministry, as well as other professions, educated young men. At the last meeting of Presbytery (in February), there were present fourteen native pastors and about thirty lay members and commissioners, beside the missionaries, and the business was conducted as regularly and decently as in similar Church courts in England and America. From the very beginning, the necessity of educating the masses was recognized, and an effort was put forth to this end. There are now five training schools for boys (including the Theological Seminary and Training College), and six for girls. The Training College, which is the highest Evangelical educational institution in the country, is at Assioot, 230 miles south of Cairo, and, during 1890, there was an average attendance of over 200 pupils, representing many towns and villages from the Delta, all the way to Luxor. The girls' school in Ezbakeeya, Cairo, and both the training college in Assioot, and the girls' school, are boarding schools, and it is in these institutions that we have deeper and more lasting influence on the pupils; but beside these training institutions which are superintended by missionaries and partly supported by funds from America, there are ninety-seven schools in the towns and villages of the different districts which are evangelical in their tendencies and influence, superintended and supported entirely by the people; but these schools are taught by young men and women educated in the training schools above mentioned. During 1890, there were 164 teachers thus employed in the Evangelical schools of Egypt, and in each of them the Bible is employed by all the pupils—with but few exceptions as a reading book.

The different religions too were all represented in the 6,500 pupils, and over 800 of them were Muslims. The girls' schools and the work among the women are most potent factors in the Evangelization of Egypt. The religion of the false prophet does not only neglect woman as an inferior being, but teaches that it is wrong to treat her otherwise. It is only the religion of Jesus Christ, and that in its purer forms, that ascribes to woman her due honour and position. Now we believe there is to be found in the Evangelical Church of Egypt, a power for evangelizing not Egypt only, but also Ethiopia as she stretches out her hands to be saved. This will be, by God's blessing on the means employed, and in His own good time.

International Christian Co-operation.

BY THE REV. DR. G. D. BOARDMAN.

Two great problems are now engaging the attention of thoughtful men all over the world. The first is the problem of secular society, or Sociology. The second is the problem of Christian society, or Ecclesiology. It is to consider this latter problem that we are here gathered.

In treating the subject assigned me—"International Christian Co-operation"—let me speak, first, of co-operation as a principle; secondly, of the Christian Church as the noblest sample of co-operation; and, thirdly, of the application of the principle of Christian co-operation to the nations of mankind.

And, first, CO-OPERATION IS A LAW OF ALL LIFE. It is true of the vegetable world. It is true of the animal world. It is one of the laws of the human world. How does society advance? By the co-operation of capital and labour, intelligence and machinery, production and consumption, men and women, business and conscience.

THE CHRISTIAN CHURCH IS THE NOBLEST SAMPLE OF CO-OPERATION. Its motto is—"We are members one of another." It is the theory of the Son of Man and those who are truly His. It was, in an eminent sense, the theory of His chief champion, the Apostle Paul; especially as set forth in his favourite analogy between the Church, or ideal Commonwealth, and the human body. Let me recall to you this great analogy, particularly as elaborated in his First Epistle to the Corinthians:—

As the body is one, and hath many members, and all the members of the body, being many, are one body; so also is Christ. For in one Spirit were we all baptized into one body, whether Jews or Greeks, whether bond or free; and were all made to drink of one Spirit. For the body is not one member, but many. If the foot shall say, Because I am not the hand, I am not of the body; is it not therefore not of the body? And if the ear shall say, Because I am not the eye, I am not of the body; is it not therefore not of the body? If the whole body were an eye, where were the hearing? If the whole were hearing, where were the smelling? But now hath God set the members each one of them in the body, even as it pleased Him. And if they were all one member, where were the body? But now they are many members, but one body. And the eye cannot say to the hand, I have no need of thee: or again the head to the the foot, I have no need of you. Nay, much rather, those members of the body which seem to be more feeble are necessary: and those parts of the body, which we think to be less honourable, upon these we bestow more abundant honour; and our uncomely parts have more abundant comeliness; whereas our comely parts have no need: but God tempered the body together, giving more abundant honour to that part which lacked; that there should be no schism (dismemberment) in the body; but that the members should have the same care one for another. And whether one member suffereth, all the members suffer with it; or one member is honoured, all the members rejoice with it. Now ye are the body of Christ, and severally members thereof (members each in His part).—1 Cor. xii. 12-27 (Revised Version).

This profound analogy of the body is true only of the ideal Church, or spiritual Church of Jesus Christ. The actual Church, at least in her present condition, is a dismembered body.

Let us attend to some of the lessons which this analogy suggests. I will mention but three.

And, first; As the body, including head and members, forms one physical organism; so the ideal Church, including Christ and His people, forms one moral personality.

The statement is twofold. First, Christ Himself is the Head: " Growing up in all things into Him Who is the Head, even Christ." The Church is no headless torso. Being himself the Head, Christ is, so to speak, the nervous centre of His Church, sharing her sensations, whether of joy or of grief, co-ordinating her faculties, directing her movements, unifying her activities, maintaining her life. As there is but one Christ, so there is but one Head. Being His body, His Church is, so to speak, a part of His own personality, drawing from Him her life, sharing His character, executing His will. As Augustine profoundly says: " Totus Christus caput et corpus est " (the whole Christ is Head and Body). Or, as another Latin saying states it still more compactly: " Ubi Christus, ibi Ecclesia (Where Christ, there

Church). And as Christ is not a monstrosity, in the sense of being many-headed, so His Church is not a monstrosity in the sense of being many-bodied. As there is but one Christ, the Head, so there is but one Church, His Body. Christ and His Church form one personality.

Secondly ; As the body involves diversity of members and functions, so does the ideal Church.

As the body is not all brain, or heart, or eye, or foot, or blood, or nerve, or bone, or cell, so the Church is not all conscience, or reason, or sensibility, or will, or creed, or polity, or minister, or layman, or sex, or sect. The Church has all variety of gift, faculty, grace, temperament, experience, vocation, method, opportunity, conception. And as uniformity is a mark of the lowest stage of existence, so variety is a mark of the highest. The nobler the life, the more complex and differenced. In brief, differentiation is the very condition of life. Dead things are uniform ; live things are multiform. The Church is a myriadfold diversity.

Thirdly ; As the body is diversity in unity, so also is the ideal Church.

For observe precisely the meaning of this word "unity." Unity, I say, not unit. Consider for a moment the difference between them. A unit is a single one, surveyed externally, in isolation from other ones ; a unity is also a single one, but surveyed internally, in its parts, each and every part being in mutual adjustment to a common end. A unit is a bare one ; a unity is the co-ordination of several different ones into a state of oneness. Unity implies something more than harmonious variety of parts ; it also implies the subordination of these various parts to a common end. It is this co-operation of diverse parts to a common end which makes these diverse parts as a whole a unity.

The unity of the body consists in the unified diversity of its parts. And the ideal Church is the noblest specimen of a body, because she is Christ's Body ; He the Head and she the members. Accordingly, the Church, in the adjustment of her own most multiform organs, in the co-ordination of her own most diversified functions, in the unification of her own most heterogeneous elements and conditions, is the consummate, finite (Deity is the infinite) instance of unity as well as of diversity ; of unity because of diversity.

And diversity is as essential to co-operation as it is to unity. Our divine Head does not demand from the members of His Body uniformity of creed or uniformity of polity, for that would be to merge all members of His Body into one vast cyclopean eye, or one vast colossal foot. All Christians of whatever denominational name constitute the one Body of Christ; and each Christian is a functional member thereof. And the Body of Christ is healthy and effective in proportion as each Christian discharges his own organic function—all the members, whether eye or hand, ear or foot, sinew or nerve, bone or cell, working together in reciprocal co-operation.

And co-operation is in a special sense the method of our Evangelical Alliance. We do not propose ecclesiastical union by co-talking, or co-thinking, or even co-feeling. We do propose Church-unity by co-working, even as eye co-works with hand, or ear co-works with foot. This is why we call our Society an Alliance rather than an Association; for while association implies co-thinking, alliance implies co-acting. And observe the purpose of our Alliance. It is not an ecclesiastico-politico concordat, like, for instance, the so-called "Holy Alliance," in 1815, of Alexander of Russia, and Francis of Austria, and Frederick of Prussia, ostensibly formed to guard what they styled a "Christian Brotherhood," but really formed to perpetuate the then existing dynasties. But our Alliance is a sacred coalition formed to join in holy league the Christian sensibilities and the Christian capacities, and so develop and make manifest the unity of Christ's Church. In fact, our blessed legend is, UNUM CORPUS SUMUS IN CHRISTO. England and Italy, France and Germany, America and Switzerland, Christian Commonwealths and Christian mission stations, all become in Christ, in the sphere of His personality, and character and work, one body. May our gathering in Florence give our Alliance fresh impetus and fresh success.

And this leads me to my last point—THE APPLICATION OF THE PRINCIPLE OF CHRISTIAN CO-OPERATION TO THE NATIONS OF MANKIND. For the human race, ideally speaking, is one colossal personality, even Humanity. Here is the culminating application of St. Paul's great analogy of the body.

Each nation has, as truly as though it were a hand or a foot, its own specific place and part in the great corpus or body of mankind.

Each nation has its own role definitely assigned it in the great drama of History. Shem ages ago wrote, as with God's right hand, his Bible of Scripture; Japheth for centuries has been writing, as with God's left hand, his Bible of Science; Ham, it may be, shall ere long join together the hand of Shem and the hand of Japheth, binding God's twofold Bible of Scripture and Bible of Science into one volume—the Book of God. What an insight into the philosophy of history the great Apostle gives us when, addressing the proud autochthons of the Areopagus, he announced: "God made every nation of men for to dwell on all the face of the earth, having determined their appointed seasons and the bounds of their habitation."

On the other hand, the very term "members" implies a common "body." This is what constitutes the nations one vast "solidarity;" the peoples one august body of mankind, the one sublime corporation of the human race.

And the Evangelical Alliance is, under God's benison, doing a blessed service in helping mankind to realize its own unity. By its system of international gatherings, wherein it seeks to maximize the points where the sects agree and minimize the points where the sects differ; by its following after things which make for peace, and things whereby we may upbuild one another; by its championship of the rights of conscience, and of the persecuted of whatever sect in whatever land; by its readiness to co-operate with all branches of the Church in extending and maintaining everywhere the Christian moralities and graces—by all this and such as this the Evangelical Alliance is helping to hasten the day when we shall all attain unto the unity of the faith, and of the knowledge of the Son of God, unto a full-grown man, unto the measure of the stature of the fulness of Christ.

God be praised, we are living under happy auguries. The growing catholicity of the times as indicated in such words and facts as these:—International law; comity of nations; world's fairs; international congresses for securing a common standard of time, of distance, of weight, of money, of signals; a universal alphabet; the world's week of prayer; the international Sunday School lessons; the Young Men's Christian Associations; the numerous union societies; the interdenominational messages and reciprocations; the private conferences of eminent representatives of the various sects; the growing observance of ecclesiastical comity in mission stations and parish fields; the marked tendency toward co-operation in Christian reforms and charities throughout the world; the overtures of a liturgical church, and the reponses of at least some non-liturgical churches; the recent recognition of the Sunday before Christmas as the universal Peace Sunday; the already well-nigh universal observance of Sunday itself as the world's common Sabbath; above all, our own Evangelical Alliance :—all this and such as this is auspicious of the day when Ephraim shall no longer envy Judah, and Judah shall no longer vex Ephraim.

And it is Jesus Christ Himself Who is the unifying principle of mankind. He is the true centre of gravity; and it is only as the forces of humanity are pivotted on him that that they are in balance. And the oscillations of humanity are perceptibly shortening as the time of the promised equilibrium draws near. Heaven grant us the blessedness of seeing with our own eyes what many prophets and righteous men have from the beginning desired to see, namely, One Christian Church throughout the world, even THE HOLY CATHOLIC CHURCH OF THE SON OF GOD.

The British and Foreign Bible Society's Work in Italy.

BY THE REV. SIGNOR A. MEILLE.

THE work of the British and Foreign Bible Society is certainly the oldest missionary enterprise in Italy. It can be said to have begun as early as 1808, when the Society, then only four years old, printed an Italian Testament to be distributed to the Italian soldiers of Napoleon's armies taken to England as prisoners of war. Afterwards a Depôt was established in Malta, from which Holy Scriptures were secretly sent over and distributed in Italy. The late Dr. Desanctis and many other Evangelicals of note were led to Christ in this way. As soon as liberty was proclaimed in 1848, the Society sent the agent for Switzerland to work in Italy, and in 1860 Italy was constituted into a separate agency. The first agent was the late Mr. Thomas Bruce, who organized the work of Bible dissemination in Italy in a way admirable for simplicity and efficiency. At his death, in 1881, he had had the privilege of scattering all over the country nearly 1,000,000 copies of the Word of God in whole or in part.

The advance of liberty of public instruction, and also of safe and rapid communications, has greatly helped the dissemination of the Scriptures in Italy during the last ten years. The total circulation for the last nine years has successively been: In 1881, 58,272 copies; in 1883, 63,594 copies; in 1884, 80,938 copies; in 1885, 95,639 copies; in 1886, 129,038 copies; in 1887, 137,135 copies; in 1888, 139,679 copies; in 1889, 132,750 copies; and in 1890 the unprecedented total of 153,770 copies—nearly three times that of 1881—was reached. Altogether nearly 2,000,000 copies of the Scriptures have now been scattered all over the country.

True, a very large proportion of these sales is made up of small Gospels which the Society allows its agents to sell at one sou each, but there is enough in a single Gospel to teach Christ, and these little books will, it is hoped, give to many a desire for the larger volumes. The best sales are now made away from towns, in the remote districts of the Abruzzi, of Calabria, of Sicily, of Sardinia. The Society's long experience is not in favour of free distribution except in cases of public calamities, or when soldiers start for a far-off destination; but the books are sold generally at half cost price, thus meeting free distribution half-way. It is prudent and right that the people should pay something for the Scriptures they get—this will make them careful to retain the little volumes, and make a good use of them.

The staff of the Society in Italy consists of one agent, six chief depositaries, with a varying number of sub-depositaries, and an average number of thirty-five colporteurs. On the staff are represented all the denominations at work in the country without an exception, and the agent is happy to say that from all denominations have come excellent colporteurs, men evidently raised up of God to do this work. The co-operative union of the Evangelical Churches of Italy can therefore be said to be *un fait accompli* as far as the British and Foreign Bible Society is concerned, for whilst each of the men it employs remains faithful to his own denomination—all work most harmoniously together to the great common work of the advancement of the Kingdom of Christ in this country.

Tract Distribution in Italy.

BY THE REV. O. JALLA.

OUR greatest difficulty has always been to get sales proportionate with the spiritual wants of Italy, and consequently with the financial needs of the Society. The ignorance of some, the reluctance for very serious reading of others, hinder the purchase of our publications in the booksellers' shops, and in our six depôts of Rome, Naples, Leghorn, Genoa, Milan, and Turin. Thirty colporteurs, at the service of the different Italian Churches, are busy to carry our tracts where the pastors cannot reach. But what are thirty colporteurs for 30,000,000 of Roman Catholics in Italy—that is to say, ignorant of the pure evangelical truth? Yet our sales, which for the year 1890 have amounted to 25,229 lire 68 centimes, have proved in many cases followed by a real blessing, as may be seen in the few instances published in our Annual Report for 1890-91.

We are happy to have become acquainted this year with many colonies abroad, where 2,000,000 of Italians have emigrated, seeking for a better, or at least for a surer living. Our weekly periodical *l'Italia Evangelica;* our monthly paper (Children's Friend); our *Children's Annual;* and many tracts have found their way to various countries in the Old World and the New.

The British and Foreign Bible Society have begun in these last years, to publish at our Claudian Press (Florence, 51 via Serragli) new editions of the New Testament, and of separate Gospels. That attempt has proved very encouraging, as Italians buy more willingly the Scriptures when published in their own country, where they had been presented until now as a foreign importation.

But two other benevolent societies of Great Britain have constantly helped us in many ways, to carry on our important work—namely, the London Religious Tract Society and the Italian Evangelization Society in Edinburgh. May the Lord help us to work on more and more faithfully in His service, according with the due expectation of our kind friends and supporters, as well as with the increasing religious needs of our fellow-countrymen.

The Duty of Evangelical Christians in regard to the Slavery Question.

BY PROFESSOR RUFFET, OF GENEVA.

AT the meeting of the International Committee of the Evangelical Alliance, held in Berlin, September 26 and 27, 1888, Dr. Fabri, the venerable Inspector of German Missions, called the attention of his colleagues to the Anti-Slavery Crusade, which Cardinal Lavigerie had some months previously inaugurated. He spoke of the great meeting, held at Cologne, in which he had taken part, and in his enthusiasm he urged the assembled delegates to make their respective branches acquainted with the subject—a subject so momentous and so sad. The result was an invitation to the different branches of the Alliance to take up the Anti-Slavery Question. I can speak for Switzerland. An Anti-Slavery Association was established at Geneva January 7, 1889, and has pleaded the cause of the Blacks before the general public for two years under the presidency of M. Edouard Naville. As a mixed society of Catholics and Protestants it should have been dissolved, for it was evident that common action between them was not possible even in the region of charity.

So much the more reason is there that the question should come before the assembly, and especially as, notwithstanding a general opinion to the contrary, it is an undoubted fact that Slavery carries on its cruelties more fiercely than ever. This I will now show. With a map of Africa before us, we see that it is naturally divided into three parts. To the North, the Soudan, Sahara, and the Mediterranean provinces. In the centre, the Equatorial plateaus, with their great lakes, and the important basin of the Congo, with its affluents. In the South, the countries bounded by the Zambesi and extending downwards to the Cape of Good Hope.

In former times, when the American slave trade carried on its ravages, the Man-hunt was on the West Coast, and Christian philanthropists directed their attention simply to that portion of the sad continent. But since the researches of such men as Barth,

Nachtigal, Schweinfurth, Burton, Livingstone, Cameron, Wissman, Stanley, and others, have opened to astonished Europe the immense regions of the central part, we have learned to our dismay that the oriental trade, though less audacious than the American, was no less active and cruel. Indeed, the slave trade of the past was mere child's play compared to that of the present time. The state of Africa, from the Zambesi to the borders of Algeria, Tunis, Tripoli, and Egypt, that is, with the exception of the Sahara, the richest, most fertile, and most populous portion of the continent, forms the field of this cruel Man-hunt.

Fifty years ago the traders of Zanzibar did not penetrate more than two hundred miles into the interior, and were satisfied with what slaves they could obtain between the lake district and the sea coast. The high road of the traffic was at a distance from the Zanzibar coast; but other routes have been opened in the north and the south—at this time, through immense regions, with millions upon millions of our fellow-creatures, slaves are being carried away by the Arabs, who leave behind them nothing but blood and devastation. Every year, as the testimony of many travellers shows us, nearly a million of the people are carried off, and fertile and prosperous countries are reduced to a desert. Time will not allow me to recite the details of this terrible traffic. Captain Binger has described it in his work on "Slavery, Islamism, and Christianity," and we may refer to the Anti-Slavery Society of Belgium's Report for the year 1890. It is not only the Arabs who reduce the black populations to slavery, but the tribes of Equatorial Africa carry on the same dreadful traffic among themselves. The slave is the African's money. He purchases everything he wants by paying slaves for it. Hence a constant state of war between the tribes, the powerful making raids upon the weak in order to obtain their ebony money, and buy with it the goods of the Arabs, cloth, powder, muskets, and glut themselves on human flesh. "*Yes*," says Mackay, "*Africa bleeds at every pore*"—and as Buxton says, "The cry of the Dark Continent is, *We are the meat, and they are the knives!*"

Friends, what are we to do to cure this terrible evil?

It was in 1876 that King Leopold of Belgium, in the circular which he sent to the Geographical Societies assembled in Congress at Brussels, pointed to the abolition of slavery as one of the principal objects to be pursued in Africa. Two months subsequently the same monarch, addressing the new Belgian Committee of the International Association, put the suppression of the trade in negroes first and foremost in his aims. In 1888, this question, thus prominently brought forward by the King of the Belgians, was carried into a wider sphere. A Conference of the chief civilized States was called together in Berlin by Prince Bismarck to consider the African question. The suppression of slavery, and especially the trade in blacks, was indicated at the first meeting by the venerable Chancellor as the sacred duty of all the Powers, and, with the exception of Turkey, all of their representatives unanimously declared that the new territory of the Congo should not be the route through which the traffic should be carried, of whatever race the slaves might be. All the powers undertook to employ all the means in their power to put an end to the trade, and punish those who are engaged in it. But in spite of all this, the European public generally still remained in ignorance of the facts, and supposed that the horrors of slavery had ceased with the American slave trade.

At this crisis it was that God put it into the heart of a venerable man, head of the Catholic missions in Africa, to come to Europe and destroy this illusion, and *reveal* (the word is not too strong) to a portion of the Western world the miseries of the negro race. He preached his crusade in France, Belgium, Italy and England, and at a meeting in London presided over by Lord Granville a resolution proposed by Cardinal Manning was unanimously adopted, to urge upon the British Government in agreement with the other European powers holding territories in Africa, to adopt measures which should ensure the abolition of this frightful traffic in slaves. Anti-Slavery societies have been established in Germany, Spain, Portugal, Austria, Italy and Switzerland, with most influential persons presiding over them, and the Anti-Slavery Society of Great Britain through Mr. Sydney Buxton, and supported by Lord Granville, have brought the question officially before the Government and Parliament. As a result of this the King of the Belgians called together a Congress at Brussels, in which the plenipotentiaries assembled on the 18th Nov., 1889, and signed an agreement on the 2nd July, 1890. They considered the question in all its details, and agreed to employ remedies against slavery, expressed in a hundred particulars which it is not necessary to enumerate here. Everything which can be done will be done to suppress this nefarious traffic, to civilize the natives, and to encourage those who are labouring in missions and otherwise for their good.

But do not let us think that the work is accomplished. The articles agreed on in the Congress have got to be ratified by the contracting powers, but even if all be consummated, shall we fold our arms? No; the mission of Evangelical Christians in this great question is only just begun. We have only taken the first step. When American slavery was abolished, colonies of freed men were founded in Liberia, Sierra Leone, and only a few years since, Frere Town on the Zanzibar coast, and a home for female slaves has been opened at Cairo. But all such institutions, and the efforts of all our missionaries, all are not enough. They are only the beginning of the work, and Evangelical Christians, on the continent at least, are not doing as much as they ought for their black brethren.

What can we do? We can take up the Propaganda. Some months since, when I met the great traveller, Stanley, in the Swiss mountains, I asked him how he thought we could help the cause of the blacks. He replied, By the Propaganda. We must make widely known the sufferings of the African populations. We must urge the continental press to publish the facts. We must induce our audiences in frequent meetings to touch the hearts of our Sunday School children, to appeal to the devotion of our Young People's Christian Associations, so that associations may be formed to set up refuges for freed men in Africa, asylums for children, agricultural colonies for adults, in short, to labour in every possible way to stop the plague, and to staunch the flowing blood. There should be a national society formed in every country, and all such societies should form themselves into a federation for co-operation and mutual assistance, waking up public opinion, keeping vigilant watch upon governments, and constraining them to persevere in fulfilling their promises.

I have one more word to say. There is an enemy rapidly advancing in Africa, threatening our missions and protecting slavery with all its horrors; I mean *Mohammedanism*. It is impossible to draw too much attention to this fact: the revival of Islam. There is no fact more significant in this nineteenth century. Mohammed is regaining in Africa what he has lost in Europe.

The future of the black race is involved in the struggle between Christianity and Islam, and depends upon the vigilant and heroic efforts of Christians. Two-thirds of Africa, geographically, belongs already to Mohammedanism. The fetish worshipping negros are being compelled by force and fear to accept it, and it ministers to their carnal desires. There is a confused awakening, a desire to rise, among the black races; Mohammedanism appeals to this. Even the European colonies, Sierra Leone, and Liberia, show an increase in Mussulmen; where there was not one to be found, there are now fifty thousand. Wherever Mohammedanism goes it carries slavery with it, which is necessary in order to maintain its polygamy.

Let us not depend on Governments and carnal weapons. We need them in their way. The Mussulmen will never accept Christian rule. England and France must include political reasons in their efforts. But we must rescue the souls of these black people from Mohammed; for on them also the Sun of Peace has risen. Missionary work and Anti-Slavery work must go hand in hand. We must carry to these people not the sword and the fire, but the whole Gospel—that Gospel which heals the wounds of humanity, and carries to men the Word of eternal life.

Let us keep in mind the last words of the dying Livingstone, and engraved on his tomb in Westminster Abbey—" I have nothing more to wish for as I die, than that the most abundant blessings from Heaven may rest upon all those, whoever they are—English, Americans, or Turks—who will help to banish from this world the frightful plague of slavery." Evangelical Christendom, I confidently believe, will accept this legacy of Livingstone, and receive the blessing which he prayed for on the saviours of the black people.'

AFTERNOON MEETINGS.

THERE WERE TWO SECTIONS; LORD KINNAIRD PRESIDED AT THE FIRST, AND M. SARASIN-BISCHOFF, OF BASLE, AT THE SECOND.

Our Young Men and Young Women.

ADDRESS BY THE REV. PROFESSOR CHARTERIS, OF EDINBURGH.

IN 1844, the *Young Men's Christian Association* was founded by Mr. George Williams, whose absence from this meeting we greatly regret. In March, 1891, it had 4,063 branches and 364,934 members, with fields of labour in every quarter of the globe. It has 38 branches and 600 members in Italy. It seeks to unite young men in efforts to extend Christ's kingdom. In 1855, the *Young Women's Christian Association* was originated by Miss Roberts and Lady Kinnaird, and I rejoice to address Lord Kinnaird when I speak of an Association which owed its best impulses and wisest guidance to his mother for many years. Its branches and members are also found everywhere over the globe, but I do not see any statement of the number of its members. Its central principle is stated as "A living union with Christ."

Kindred in some respects to this last is the *Girls' Friendly Society*, the aim of which is to raise the standard of moral character, by uniting those whose moral character is beyond reproach. Like the Y.M.C.A., it also aims at associating for their mutual benefit ladies of Christian experience with young women of their own sex. In England, it is a Church of England Society; in Scotland, it is entirely undenominational. I might speak of several other unions of young men, such as the *Sabbath Morning Fellowship Union*, which may be taken as representing the strictly religious side of the Y.M.C.A., and I observe that in Scotland the Associations are now united.

Except the Girls' Friendly Society in England, all the foregoing are non-ecclesiastical organizations.

There has been of late in Great Britain a large development of another kind of society closely connected with the several Churches. I think they all bear the name of *Guild*, in this, as in their constitution, following the example of the first of them, the Church of Scotland *Young Men's Guild*. The object is to unite the young men in every congregation in mutual helpfulness and good works, and to unite the various parochial and congregational branches thus formed in a Church Guild. In practical methods the Guild closely resembles the Y.M.C.A., but it is in connection with the Church : a part of its organization, and subject to its authority. It has not been found that there is in this connection any restraint upon the liberty dear to youth : or on the other hand any disloyalty to the Church which is Christ's ordinance upon earth, and which shelters its young men in their Guild. Many Presbyterian Churches and the Congregational Union have now such Guilds.

In some respects similar is a method of the *Organization of Woman's Work in the Church*, of which the General Council of the Presbyterian Churches unanimously approved in 1889. It aims at the same objects as the undenominational Associations already mentioned, but is an attempt to make those who worship in the same sanctuary recognize their obligation to mutual helpfulness as well as to united service of the one Lord. Without entering into details, I may say that it gives to every female member and adherent of the Church a place in its general grade or Woman's Guild, and assigns to those who have given several years of service a right, as members of the Women Workers' Guild, to be leaders of the others, while on those entitled by longer service or by special training the Church confers the degree of Deaconesses.

Equally with those last-named Guilds connected with the Church, but composed of both sexes is an American Society, the growth of which has been absolutely phenomenal. The Society of Christian Endeavour dates only from 1881, and already it has 13,000 branches and a million members. Its object is to unite all young people of both sexes in each congregation on the basis signified by its name. Its active members declaring that they are Christians, and that they seek to promote the glory of Jesus, bind themselves as the mark and bond of union to attend without failure (unless their reason for absence be such as they can expect to satisfy Christ Jesus) the weekly Prayer Meeting of the Society, and to contribute to the proceedings of that meeting by statement, suggestion, question, quotation, prayer, or praise. There is also a monthly meeting, at which the active members give their experience by statement or descriptive text for the encouragement of the others. In addition to those active members others are joined as Associates, who do not profess actual union with Christ Jesus, but are possessed by the desire to be found upon His side. While thus a part of the congregation and of the Church, like as Guilds are, this remarkable Society has one distinctive feature, which makes it somewhat resemble the older and undenominational Societies, viz: There is an Annual Conference, to which all the Congregational Societies of all the Churches are invited and expected to send delegates.

There is another largely successful Society in America with the quaint name of *The King's Daughters*, whose distinctive outward feature is that every group consists of Ten. Its motto is as quaint as its title: Look up and not down: look forward and not back: look out and not in: lend a hand.

We thus complete our survey, and now we ask what conclusions force themselves upon us.

First of all, we see here, as may be seen in foreign missions, that the first movement did not come from the corporate Church, but from groups of *individuals* possessed by a kindred aim, and impelled by a like ardour. The representatives of Churches and the leaders of Associations are anxiously and successfully making arrangements to promote mutual understanding and harmony by interchange of deputies to their respective Annual Meetings, and by facilitating the enrolment of local societies as branches of more than one union. The fact is that the Church has adopted the principles, or rather have undertaken to do the practical work of these Associations, and therefore the Associations cannot find it so easy to proceed without any regard to the Churches as it was forty or fifty years ago. If it be said, Why should the Churches not leave it to the Associations to work out the principles? we must say—

2. *The idea at the basis of the Associations is an essential part of the Church.* Nor is this all. The Church can do more in the good cause than any undenominational Association. Instead of the

exceptional few, she can reach and invite all the youth. She can provide means of intercourse and good influences with infinitely less trouble than it can. Her men of position, her women of experience, are but doing the most obvious commonplace of Christian duty, when, as members of the congregation, they make themselves friends and counsellors of the young people who grow up by their side, and worship with them. The associate and the member of a Girls' Friendly Society have no previous bond of acquaintance, and it is not easy for them to arrange even an occasional meeting; but the mature Christian lady in a Church and the eager young life that is trembling into womanhood in the adjoining pew have been in the Master's presence together, and they meet every time they pass in by the same door to stand up and praise Him in the congregation. When St. Paul instructed Timothy to tell rich men how to use the riches, and aged women how to guide young ones, he never intended that the blessed functions to which those happy possessors of talents were called should be outside of the Church of Christ. I have recounted with pride the present numbers in the Y.M.C.A., but what are they among so many? I know Scotland best. The Y.M.C.A. in Scotland is admirably managed and wisely guided; but it has only some 25,000 members, and the Guild of my own Church, ten years old, has already 20,000. The corporate Church, now awakened, can stretch out wider, and penetrate deeper than any other agency; and the future will be hers.

3. *The Churches ought each to have a Young Men's Christian Association, and a Young Women's Christian Association, and a Children's Christian Association:* the Churches ought each to have one (perhaps with sub-divisions for sex and age) and *the Churches ought all to have one.* The Church Guild seems to me to be a step in the right direction: the conference of delegates of all Churches in the annual meeting of the Society of Christian Endeavour is another right step. For the oldest Church Guild I think I can promise that we are ready to enter into that Federal Union. I have long dreamed that it would be possible to see *the* Y.M.C.A. composed of all the Church Guilds and Societies for Young Men, bearing the same relation to them that this Evangelical Alliance has to all the Churches represented in it. The same, and yet different; for the

delegates to the Central Society would be officially delegated by the Societies of the Churches. Aye, and perhaps our own Alliance will be enabled to take that further step, and keep up with the young people's pace: so that from every General Assembly, Synod, Consistory, and Convocation we shall be sent by our Churches to say we are one body in Christ Jesus. Perhaps we may see the young people lead the way, for they have no history to develop, no awkward old pledges to modify; they are coming untrammeled into the great arena, round which hovers the cloud of many witnesses waiting to see us begin the unity which is their glory up above.

4. *There is in this a combination of unity with diversity, of law with freedom, which might for the time we live in be the realizing of an Ideal of Church Life;* of the Life of the Body of Christ. By Church I, of course, mean any band of believing people organized for service and worship. The Body of Christ has been far too long concerned about the subordination of members; it is according to the answers to a question as to the law of subordination that our various denominations are distinguished, and so Churches are Episcopal, Presbyterian, Congregational, and what not. To hold the Head, even Christ; to belong to the Body of Christ, *i.e.*, to be of His Living Church; to do the work of Christ in the world as a part of that Living Body; that is what men are coming to in our day. And so men and women will not, do not, wait for clerical leading as they used to do. Such and such a work is to be done, and if our clergy will not lead us, and our Church does not give it a place, we shall do it in Christ's Name, and it is done. And rightly too. No doubt in another sense Christ's Church is an army, and there must be leaders under the One Great Captain, but in these democratic days, "bayonets think," and the bayonets will not be fixed and charge under the rule of officers who are unfit to be leaders, no matter how high their titles sound. And so there is in the multiplication of Societies as part of the Church just what we need in our time. "Unity without diversity is tyranny; diversity without unity is anarchy," said Pascal; and what is repose without labour but iniquity when there is so much work to be done? To avoid tyranny, anarchy, and selfishness, the Church of Christ must have many departments of labour, in which those Associations have pointed and are pointing the way.

Christendom is full of corruptions, and will never be free of sin until the labour of Hercules is repeated. Into that Augean stable we have to turn the river of God's good pleasure. To *do good* and to *communicate*, forget not, for with such sacrifices God is well pleased. To talk of the self-sacrifice of our religion is not enough. There must be sacrifice, which means dedication of our powers, help of others with our work. I see this in all the Associations. The missionary spirit is spreading. It is not really much to say that so and so, once members of some of those Associations, has gone to the foreign mission field, for one can scarcely imagine that anyone would be fit for a foreign mission if they were not taking part with the foremost at home. But a spirit of missioning at home is growing. The young people are giving personal trouble to bring out others, and to keep them up to the mark. And this is as it should be. But it is only to a weak and small beginning. Till we recognize that a congregation is not an instrument to be played upon, to make reposeful music, a harmonium that goes very slow and has many stops, but is an instrument to work with, to guide, to direct, the sword of the Lord and of Gideon, there is no hope for corporate humanity in this redeemed world. There is this transubstantiation needed: the bread and wine of the Christian life to be turned into flesh and blood, the very flesh and blood of the Lord Jesus, that His work may be done in the world.

It is Christ the Life we are looking for, and, God be praised, are realizing. The reformers proclaimed Christ the Way; and our divines and apologists have shewn that Christ is the Truth; but it needs the living Church to shew that Christ is the Life. As those days pass and the old things fade away with them, the Church must become more of a social force, elevating, consecrating, using social influences. I know those Associations are doing Christ's work, and I cannot forbid them merely because they follow not with us; but He Who told His disciples that, also so founded His Church that those out-workers—never forbidden—were welcomed and incorporated in the great organization whose portal was baptism, whose reunion was at the Communion table, and whose function was, and is, to make up that which is behind of the sufferings of Christ, and so complete the redemption of man.

Young Men's Christian Associations in Switzerland.

ADDRESS BY M. TOPHEL, PASTOR AT GENEVA.

In 1855 at Paris, M. Perrot stated that he represented 338 Young Men's Christian Associations in union with one another, with 20,600 members, spread over eight countries. In 1879, at Basle, M. Fermand represented 2,400 Associations, and now twelve years later I am the delegate of 4,063 Associations, spread over twenty countries and including 365,000 enrolled members. Glasgow is the largest of these united Associations with its 9,000 members. They wield an influence over millions, and extend their operations even into the remotest eastern world. It is hoped that when in 1894 the Jubilee of the Young Men's Christian Associations will be celebrated, a complete history of their wonderful progress will be given.

By the side of this advancement in numbers there has been an advancement in organization. The local Associations have been combined into district and provincial unions, and at last into a great international society, the committee of which considers the widest interests of all the Associations. In this respect a beautiful example has been afforded of the possibility of a great and comprehensive religious federation, uniting in an evangelical faith representatives of all the churches, and combining order with liberty.

The objects of these Associations are twofold. The primary object is the salvation of the young by the efforts of the young—their conversion, regeneration, progressive sanctification and perfection for the service of Christ. The secondary objects are moral, social, intellectual and physical. Now as to the primary end of our endeavours, the salvation of the young, many of us must confess that we are not as zealous as our predecessors. If we were fuller of the Holy Spirit we should have more success than we have among certain classes of the young, such as students, the wealthy, and the lowest social and moral grade in our great cities. Nor is it merely our deficiencies that humble us, but the dangers we have to meet, the sensible weakening there is in faith and piety. Our members have many other designations, and with the idea, correct enough in itself, that God saves the whole man as well as the soul, worldliness creeps into our associations. Nevertheless, with all our anxiety we can say that the Spirit of God is at work in the present day in the midst of us.

He it is, the Holy Spirit, Who gives success to all the various operations of the Young Men's Christian Associations. How much our family life and the progress of society itself depends upon their work.

Brethren, let us join in this work. Like Elijah on Mount Carmel we have with our weak hands raised an altar to the glory of God, composed not of twelve stones, but of four thousand. It is the fire coming down from Heaven that we desire to see. It is the Lord Himself, His own Spirit, that we ask for and wait for so earnestly. What are our Associations without Him? It is "the Spirit that quickeneth." Oh, let us ask for a fresh baptism of the Holy Ghost.

Sunday School Work.

ADDRESS BY BISHOP WALDEN, D.D., METHODIST EPISCOPAL CHURCH, U.S.A.

THE centenary of the Sunday School has been celebrated. During this first century the demand for utility has become more and more exacting. To find at this time, when everything is judged by practical results, that there are in Christendom 183,390 Sunday Schools, with 1,999,569 officers and teachers, and 17,716,212 scholars, is a sufficient evidence of the high estimate placed upon this form of Christian work. Laboured arguments in its behalf are no longer required. The Evangelical Alliance must regard the Sunday School work with a deep interest, because more than nine-tenths of the Protestant Sunday Schools in the world are under the auspices of Evangelical Churches—the Churches represented in this Alliance. There is a seeming propriety in opening this discussion in English, as of the 19,715,781 officers, teachers, and scholars in the world, about 17,000,000 use the English language, and more than 9,000,000 of these are in America, which in part I represent.

The theme, "Sunday School work," is, of course, to be treated in its relation to the aims of the Alliance. The Sunday School is not only so denominational, but so identified with the local Church, that, at first thought, its work may seem quite apart from the scope of the Alliance. It has been clearly maintained by one of the speakers that foreign missions are cultivating that spirit of unity which has its highest expression in this body. May not this be affirmed of the Sunday School with even more confidence? There is in foreign mission fields a trend toward co-operation, in which we may well rejoice, but Christian workers in the Sunday School have already come closer together than this in the home field. The Churches have not even taken counsel with each other how to best occupy heathen countries, but Sunday School workers of various denominations often meet in County and State Conventions (I speak of America) to discuss their great work in all its varying features. From this commingling of earnest Christians has arisen much of the good fellowship among the various branches of the Church in America.

A blessed fruit of the Alliance is the Week of Prayer—a concert of prayer that belts the globe. Much of its power at the Throne, as well as of its unifying influence among Christians, is from their lifting thought and heart to God at the same time—asking for the same mercies and blessings. Not unlike in its effect is the turning of the heart and thought of teachers and scholars to God's own Word each Sunday the world round. In America, where is found one-half of the Sunday School army of the world, through the uniform lesson, their thought is engaged with the very same divine lesson. Each Sunday the teachers and scholars on the Pacific slope know that God has spoken to those on the far-off Atlantic slope in the same words they study, and this creates a community of interest never known before. Such an interest is the very spirit of the Alliance, and will reinforce its blessed work.

The purpose of the Alliance is not merely to cherish beautiful sentiments, develop good fellowship among Christians of different communions, but to cultivate that unity of spirit which will insure honest, earnest, active co-operation in the evangelization of the world. As the Sunday School tends to this end we may properly and profitably consider its work, and ask how it may be made more effective in its high mission.

The Sunday School educates the conscience. The establishing in society of what is right, is only the correspondence of what has been wrought in the conscience of the people. The most difficult and involved social problems may thus be solved. The relation of the Christian Church to all social reforms has been forcefully stated by your speakers. She does her most effective work in these elevating movements by educating the conscience. In America, where the saloon is the bane of society, the people have knowledge of the magnitude and prevalence of the evil; when a public conscience reveals responsibility and enforces duty, the days of the saloon will be numbered. The labour question involves right and wrong. An enlightened conscience will harmonize all the relations of capital and labour.

The means of educating the conscience is God's Word—"the entrance of Thy Word giveth light"—and this Word is the text-book of the Sunday School. The conscience is not educated in the public school—at least not in America. The conscience is not educated by the public press; it records current history, discusses current questions with a politic wisdom, but this scarcely touches the public conscience. In too many homes, rich as well as poor, the conscience is not educated. The Evangelical pulpit is coming more and more to so preach the Gospel as to reach and rectify the conscience, and the world's hope must centre here. But next in power to this are the Sunday Schools in which 18,000,000 youth and children study the Word of God. This emphasizes the place of the Holy Scriptures in the Sunday School. They should not be merely read but studied— precept as well as promise—the Law as well as the Gospel, the Old Testament that exalts God's justice and righteousness as well as the New that exalts His mercy and love.

Sunday School work belongs to that multiform Christian service classed under the term evangelization. The Sunday School is not an adjunct to but a part of the Church. The Church is one body in Christ but many members—members besides individual persons and distinct communions. The Christian Mission embracing those who work in mission fields and those who give and pray for their success, is a member; organized societies for church building, and the Christian Press disseminating Christian thought and the facts of Christ's kingdom, are members of the one body. If Christianity be a force every agency connected with the Church by which this force operates is a member of that body, and such is the Sunday School. The end toward which this force ever moves, by all agencies, is the evangelization of the world, and toward this end all Sunday School work may be—should be drawn.

Hence this should be held in harmony and conjunction with every other member of the body. (*a*) The pastor should be the spiritual director of the Sunday School; (*b*) the teaching should reinforce, not substitute the teaching of the pulpit; (*c*) the devotional exercises should not excuse the scholars from public worship, but rather prepare them the better for it. The spirit and power of public worship is needful to secure the highest ends of Sunday School teaching. Thoughtfully, carefully, conscientiously, I say that where Sunday School attendance keeps or excuses scholars from public worship, more is lost than gained. But where the Sunday School is kept in harmony with the Church, it enhances her Evangelistic power.

The great fields for Sunday School work are the great cities—those growing aggregations of people which present the most difficult problems to the Church of to-day. The darkest feature of our great cities is not the hard-working, poorly-paid men and women—not even the idle and dissolute men and women, but the youth and the children in the homes of poverty and haunts of vice. Thousands of boys and girls in London and New York have never heard the name of God except in profanity—know no more of the loving, helpful Christ, than the children of darkest heathendom. In our great Protestant cities are fields for the co-operation of the best, most experienced Sunday School workers, and a loud call to-day is for a united movement to evangelize Protestant cities.

The Churches in the past have been working apart in these waste places in our cities, and the results show nothing more plainly than that these divided efforts cannot succeed. There must be co-operation among the Churches; co-operation that expresses a true unity of spirit. The preparation for other co-operation may be best preceded by the co-operation of God's chosen Sunday School workers in gathering the neglected youth and children into Sunday Schools—yes, into *Union* Sunday Schools, in these waste places in the great cities—teaching the neglected ones the Word, teaching them spiritual songs, familiarizing them with the voice of prayer. Let the hearts of our Sunday School workers be drawn to these greatest mission-fields, and let them feel that here they are to lead in that community of Church work by which the most difficult problems of the age are to be solved. As we carry the spirit of this great meeting of the Evangelical Alliance to our several countries and Churches we may greatly encourage this needful and hopeful co-operation.

ADDRESS BY MR. THOMAS EDWARDS, of the Sunday School Union, LONDON.

THE Sunday School Union was established in 1803, on truly Catholic principles. Its very first circular (prospectus) declared that "its purpose was to promote the founding of Sunday Schools, not in connection with one religious body only, but to unite all Evangelical teachers in a bond of Christian activity for the universal establishment of these institutions." This is the spirit in which it has always endeavoured to carry on its work from the very beginning. It is, and always has been, an absolutely unsectarian Society, representing every section of the Christian Church of the Protestant order. It is thus, in itself, a veritable Evangelical Alliance, and is doing a work in the furtherance of God's cause among the young, which is in entire harmony with the spirit and the aims of your Society. I claim, therefore, dear brethren, a position among you at this important Conference as the representative of an Institution which is kindred to your own, and helping with you to foster that "unity of the Spirit in the bond of peace," which St. Paul so strongly commended, and for which God's true people in all lands earnestly labour and pray.

The special objects which the Union has steadily kept before it are—

1. *To stimulate* and encourage Sunday School teachers to greater exertions on behalf of the religious instruction of the young.

2. *To improve* in every way possible the methods of teaching.

3. *To ascertain* the localities, both *at home and abroad*, where new schools are needed, and assist their establishment and development.

4. *To supply* suitable literature and school requisites at greatly reduced prices, and

5. *To carry out* these objects *without interfering* in any way with the internal managements of individual Schools or of affiliated Unions.

After nearly ninety years' labour, we can add, on its behalf, that harmony of feeling or effort has, under the Divine blessing, been constantly preserved, while the thoroughly representative character of its General Committee or Council has faithfully embodied the views and aims of its large constituency through that long space of time.

The Union is divided into three great Departments. 1. *The Home Department*, which deals with the work in Great Britain. 2. *The Colonial and Indian Department.* 3. *The European or Continental Department;* with the last of which I have the privilege to be specially connected.

From the commencement, the Home Department has promoted the organizing of local or district Unions, not only in large towns or cities, but in country places also. Some are for a single town or city with its immediate suburbs; others take in the scattered villages and hamlets within a certain radius, while others again include a whole town or province. There are now 222 of these Unions affiliated with us in England alone, having 5,224 Schools, 138,487 teachers, and 1,246,963 scholars, which have assisted in establishing new Schools, and our land has become so well covered that there is scarcely a spot with its dozen or score cottages that has not also its Sunday School.

The Home Department is again sub-divided into ten principal Sections. 1. For supplying Schools with suitable literature and material of all kinds. 2. Organizing normal classes for the training of teachers. 3. Classes for the study of Hebrew and Greek. 4. Illustrated Lectures on Biblical, Historical, Geographical, Social, and Religious subjects, an average of nearly 1,000 being given yearly. 5. Promoting of Bands of Hope (Temperance) and of Christian Bands among the Young. 6. The International Bible Reading Association. 7. Yearly Examinations for Teachers, on the Principles and Art of teaching; Evidences of Christianity, and Scripture History and Doctrine. 8. Yearly Examinations of Scholars on the International Lessons studied in School between certain dates. 9. Visitation of Provincial Unions. 10. The collating and certifying of Sunday School Statistics. You will thus perceive that the work of the Sunday School Union is of a very wide and varied character. Most of the improvements which have taken place in Sunday School organization, methods and material have been directly owing to its initiation and effort. In England, *we believe in union*. I do not hesitate to affirm that in nearly all cases those Schools are the most prosperous and effective that are most loyal to the Union, whose influence and guidance tend greatly to give method and concentration to their work. I draw this conclusion from very numerous and wide-reaching opportunities of observation during many years.

Our Continental Mission was inaugurated in 1864. Its sole purpose from the first has been to foster and assist the Sunday School enterprise of this Continent in every way possible. All that time there were, comparatively speaking, very few Schools; many Churches had not risen to any true conception of the work, nor of their proper relation to it; there were only two United Committees, in Paris and in Lausanne. There were no missionaries and no means for putting forth organized, sustained effort in the way of extension or improvement. Since then, however, there has been enormous progress in these respects. There are now, at the lowest computation, close upon 20,000 Sunday Schools in these Continental lands, with 70,000 teachers and nearly a million and a quarter of scholars. There are 20 missionaries, several score Unions, a steadily growing and useful literature, and the work at large is increasingly obtaining a composite, organized character, that adds greatly to its strength and value.

The work of the Sunday School was never more important than it is to-day. It appeals to parents, for its one purpose is to secure the godly education of their children. It is a work for teachers, bringing them into closer contact with the truths of God's Word, and with the fresh, young hearts of the little ones. It is a work for the Christian Church, since the Church can only live and grow as she is built up from among the ranks of the young. It is a work for the State, as the grandeur and safety of any nation depend upon the moral character of its people. "The strength of Christianity, humanly speaking, in any land," as Rev. H. Woodruff, of America, very aptly said at the World's Sunday School Convention, in London, in July, 1888, "consists in the hold which it has on the popular heart. The most prominent feature of the Sunday School," as our experience in England has abundantly proved, "is its tendency to embody Christianity in the national life." Our country owes a debt which is simply incalculable to the sound, thorough, earnest religious work which has been done by three generations of Sunday School teachers. The influence of that noble band of self-denying workers, in making Christianity the power that it is among us, cannot possibly be overestimated. That influence has, again and again, saved our country from revolution during the past one hundred years. Our leading statesmen, our principal writers and interpreters of public opinion, irrespective of political or ecclesiastical distinctions, agree in acknowledging that the Sunday School has been the greatest factor in working out the social and moral improvement of our people. The greater part of our pastors have come out of the Sunday School; the majority of our Church officers and members, especially among the Free Churches, have come out of the Sunday School; many of our philanthropic institutions have taken their rise from the Sunday School. The Sunday School amongst us has been and is the great training ground for Christian work and Christian workers of every kind.

Our Christian philanthropists have observed with much satisfaction a very sensible diminution in the number of our criminal population during the last ten years. There is now an average of 28 per cent. fewer male prisoners and 45 per cent. fewer female prisoners than there were ten years ago, and the diminution among young people consigned to prison under sixteen years of age is still more remarkable. Out of 113 principal prisons there are to-day 57 that are closed for lack of criminals. These gratifying results are attributed in great measure to the good influence of Sunday School teaching upon the rising generation. We believe, therefore, that what the Sunday School has done amongst us it can accomplish everywhere. Convinced of this it is our ardent desire to do all that we can to bring the same source of blessing to, and help in producing similar results in all other lands. It seems to us that true patriotism demands, and that all true Christians will gladly seek to advance a work so excellent, and that can produce such results. The Sunday School Union, however, has never sought to impose an institution, which is peculiarly English or American, always and everywhere in exactly the form which it takes among ourselves. Its great commendation is its flexibility, its capacity to adapt itself to every variety of circumstances and surroundings, to all the diverse conditions, exigencies, habits, and needs of various lands.

The future of the State, it has been well said, is in the cradle. The happiness, the prosperity, the social and moral greatness of any nation will always depend upon what its youth will become, and as with the individual so with the State, it reaps that which it sows. The French Statesman Gambetta, once said, "I have an idea for my country, and it is this, that whenever I look at a child in the cradle I can say, There shall be a soldier for France." We, dear friends, have a better idea than that, much higher, worthier, and nobler; and our idea is that when we see a child in the cradle we can say, There, with the help and the blessing of God, shall be a soldier for the Lord Jesus Christ. As workers in God's Kingdom we profess much anxiety for the salvation of the world. If we would save the world, dear brethren, we must first save the children.

Our population in England is growing yearly at the rate of 13 in every thousand, but our Sunday School scholars have been increasing at the rate of 23 per thousand. In my native county of Yorkshire they have multiplied three times as fast, or 39 per thousand, while in the south-west part of the country, the district which I come from, the increase is at the rate of 65 per thousand, or five times as fast as the population. If that rate of increase were to continue, and could be equally operative all over the county, then, in course of time, our idea of the Sunday School would be realized, for, in our estimation, it is not for young only, nor for the poor merely, but for everybody—the place provided by the Christian Church for Bible study on the part of all. As Dr. Pelmbel said, at the International Convention, in London, "We want all the Church in the Sunday School, all the Sunday School in the Church, and everybody in both."

It seems to me, dear friends, that we who labour in connection with the Sunday School Institution may largely contribute to the accomplishment of this idea, first, by giving ourselves to our work with greater earnestness, zeal and prayerfulness, and secondly by a more real and thorough union among ourselves for mutual stimulus, instruction and encouragement. We need more personal consideration on the one hand, and more cordial, fraternal co-operation on the other. Among the tendencies in the Church life of to-day, at least in Great Britain, perhaps one of the most remarkable, hopeful and healthy is the movement towards unity. We see signs of this tendency in the closer drawing together of Congregationalists and Baptists, of the various sections of the great Methodist body, of the Churches of the Presbyterian order, and in the manifest desire on the part of certain leading bishops and clergy of the Anglican communion to find common ground upon which the adherents of their Church and of the Free Churches may more largely and freely join together in common work for the Master. May we not hope that Christ's true people, of all communions, are becoming weary of those things which divide them, often so unnecessarily, and are longing and striving for the nearer fulfilment of the prayer which our dear Lord Himself offered,—"That they may all be one, even as Thou, Father, art in Me and I in Thee, that they also may be one in Us." This, at any rate, is the desire and purpose both of the Evangelical Alliance and of the Sunday School Union, which have ever made it their special endeavour to unite Christian people in common work for common ends. But whatever distinctions and differences may exist between various sections of Christ's Church on earth these need have no place so far as work amongst the young is concerned. All may combine, if they will, in making known to the children the simple truths of God's Word, and the lessons of obedience and charity, of truthfulness and purity, of temperance and self-denial, of reverence and love towards God which that Word inculcates. Professor Drummond relates that when he was leaving Japan the native ministers sent a message by him to Europe to this effect, "Do not send us more doctrines, for we are tired of them; send us Christ." That short but highly suggestive sentence expresses the deepest need, not of Japan merely, but of Europe at large. Whatever our doctrinal divergencies may be, dear brethren, we will at least join together in teaching the young about Jesus, the children's best Friend.

For many years past our society has been helping to promote Sunday School work in Italy, but such help has only been fitful and partial, according to the few opportunities which here and there have presented themselves, we have a growing desire to do much more than we have hitherto done. We sincerely trust that the Lord, in His great mercy, may soon raise up some servant of His to do for the Sunday School cause in this country a similar work to that which the late Dr. Stewart was called to do for the Waldensians, and our dear brother, Mr. MacDougall, for the Free Evangelical Church.

We wish to be "all things to all men"—Waldensian, Free Church, Methodist, Baptist, Presbyterian—"that by all means" we may win you to a larger conception, a deeper consecration, a keener apprehension, a more resolute determination with regard to the God-given work of strengthening His Church, of regenerating the State, of redeeming the world by saving the children.

ADDRESS BY THE REV. EDWARD CLARKE, OF SPEZIA.

IT is with no feeble sense of the responsibility of my position that I respond to the call to say a few words relative to Italy as a mission field, especially to the young. In the memory of not a few attending this Conference, Italy was sealed against the public teaching and preaching of God's Word. But God's providence was working, and the thoughts of Mazzini, the *finesse* of Cavour, the courage of Victor Emmanuel, and the sword of Garibaldi, all were combining to open up a pathway for the reading of God's Word in the family, and its being taught in Day and Sunday Schools. My acquaintance with Italy as a mission field extends over a period of more than twenty-five years. When I arrived in Spezia in 1866, I found I had entered on an undertaking more arduous than that of Napoleon, when he had to contend with all the power of Austria, for I saw the serried ranks of hoary superstition and antiquated customs stretching out to oppose me in such a determined manner, that for a time my heart sank within me, and I cried out to God for His omnipotent aid to help me in the mighty struggle. For the welfare of the dear lads and maidens of Italy, my heart vibrated with tender pity, seeing them the slaves of ignorance and superstition; but while deeply oppressed in spirit I did not despair—yet nothing less than confidence in the God of my salvation could have kept me in Italy. I was, however, remarkably encouraged in my efforts for Italy's evangelization by the kindness and loving counsels of the Rev. R. Stewart, D.D., of Leghorn, who, learning the circumstances connected with my coming to Italy, and that my steps were bent towards Spezia, said: "Now I see how God answers prayer. Go, and whatever I can do to assist you in your work, I will do"—and thus was begun a friendship which, without a break, lasted during a period of over twenty years. After much thought and prayer, it was resolved to begin a Bible Day School in Spezia, and my sister opened it with one child. The rage and opposition to which this movement gave rise, were all the more persistent as the school movement was supported by a free distribution of the Word of God. Happily, the government authorities on all occasions stood by the work, when needful for us to apply to them for their necessary assistance. But if this demonstration of hatred to the instruction of youth in Bible Day Schools was so evident, what could be expected in Sunday School work?

The *Bible Day Schools* (in connection with the Spezia Mission) now numbering over 500 scholars, have been a vast help to our Sunday Schools. The important position which our Day Schools have taken in and near Spezia give the friends of truth and Italy ample encouragement for renewed energy in the support of them. The children have been gathered almost exclusively from Roman Catholic families of the working classes, who have had but scant opportunities of intellectual improvement. In the daily routine of these schools an earnest effort is made diligently to train the young for the stern business of life; and so to instruct them that they shall not only be saved from the slavery of evil passions, but also be led to trust in the redemption by Jesus Christ. Nor have these efforts been in vain, as the remarkable experience of the dear youth of our schools in the time of great bodily suffering have testified. One dear girl, eight years of age, who died at Spezia, may be specially mentioned. She knew a very large portion of the hymns sung at the school. During her illness she excited the attention and wonder of many as they heard her so constantly speak and sing of her Saviour. She exclaimed: "*Behold Jesus comes! I come, I go—I go to Jesus.*"

Beside the opposition to Bible truth, there is also this difficulty in Italy to the advancement of Sunday Schools—the mode in which the Italians have been taught to regard the Lord's day. This at present is a mighty barrier; but we are aiming to accomplish by Bible Day schools, Sunday Schools and Orphanages, founded on Evangelical lines of action, a complete change in the lives of the people. The various Sunday Schools in connection with the 24 stations under my care number 214 scholars; the Day Schools, 500; the Girls' Orphanage, 20 orphans.

At present the Gospel in Italy is especially the Gospel to the poor, the rich as yet standing aloof; but we live in the hopes of seeing rich and poor embracing the only panacea for earth's woes. Italy has the benefit of a king who has not been afraid to give to the Evangelical Alliance his hearty welcome, and some time since, when having a special occasion to telegraph to him, I took occasion to add "and may Italy live by means of the Bible," he manifested in his reply his real sympathy with the tenor of my despatch. Not long ago a poor woman, a member of the Church of which I am pastor, sought of the King a favour for her husband; the King graciously signified his approval of the woman's request, but bade her to arise, adding—" Kneel to no man, kneel only to God." There is much also to encourage us to hope that in the higher circles in Italy Bible truth will yet become powerful. When the Venerable Leo, startled in the Vatican by the progress of the Gospel in Italy, shall say —" If this is the sentiment of the Italian people my presence in Italy is useless," then, indeed, may we expect Bible Day and Sunday Schools to flourish, and to hear from many thousands of Italian youth: " Hallelujah, the Lord God Omnipotent reigneth!"

EVENING MEETING.

THE REV. H. J. PIGGOTT, OF ROME, PRESIDED.

Christian Work among Soldiers and Sailors.

Report of the Military Evangelical Church in Italy.

BY THE REV. CAV. CAPELLINI.

FOR more than eighteen years an important Mission of Evangelization has been carried on among the soldiers of Italy. Such a work demands not only zeal and untiring activity, but tact and prudence, on account of the extreme jealousy of the Italian government, as to the relations between civilians and military.

It was in the year 1872 that by the grace of God this work was founded in Rome. It began with the distribution of books to the garrison, then in gathering together those who received the Word of God with joy, and as the meetings daily increased in numbers a larger Hall was engaged. At the beginning all sorts of difficulties arose, notably from the landlords of the houses, who, urged on by the priests, refused to allow their rooms to be used for the preaching of the Gospel; but God, Who was the Director of the work, defended it, aided it in its difficulties and distresses, and at Easter of the following year a small number, twenty-five only, first-fruits of the mission, celebrated the Lord's Supper, thus laying the foundation of the Military Church. From that day onward the work has gone on increasing, and up to the present time, the nineteenth year of labour, not less than 1,604 Italian soldiers have publicly confessed their faith in Christ at the Lord's Table.

This does not represent more than a fraction of those who have been brought by their comrades to hear the Word of God.

The changes in the stations of the different regiments, and the termination of the period of service of the various classes, open a fresh field of Evangelical labour every year, while the return to their homes of those soldiers who have finished their military career, sows the seed of the Gospel in the cities and villages throughout the length and breadth of Italy.

A colporteur, who acts as door-keeper, and an Evangelist, who is an ex-soldier, converted to the Gospel in this Church, aids the Minister in his work, and the meetings are never interrupted; but every evening, those soldiers who are free and can come, meet during their short hour of liberty, hungering and thirsting after the Word of God.

Besides the Church, with its daily conferences, there is instituted in a suitable locality, in three large rooms, in Via Pouro delle Cornacchie 14, a club for the non-commissioned officers, which has taken the name of the Y.M.C.A. Martin Luther. In these rooms, besides the reading-room, with books and newspapers, there are night schools for Italian, French, English, and Stenography, and by means of these classes, by means of conversation with the soldiers, by means of visits to the Hospital, and by the distribution of the Holy Scriptures and tracts, the seed of the Word of God is diligently sown in all sorts of ground.

But the work is not limited solely to the garrison of Rome. Every summer, when the troops are sent for their military manœuvres, we go to the camps with as many books, Bibles, and Testaments as we can gather together. We visit regiment by regiment, distributing books, and speaking to them the Word of Eternal Life, so that, in the nineteen years that the Mission has existed, we can safely say we have assisted at all the grand manœuvres that have taken place in the various provinces of Italy, and that we have visited all the encampments.

Besides this there have been established small branch congregations, dependent on the Church at Rome, which I can visit every three or four months, holding services and administering the Lord's Supper. These Churches, each with its deacon at the head, at Viterbo, Spoleto, Perugia, Civitavecchia, Capua, and Caserta, are composed of the brethren in the various regiments which were formerly in garrison at Rome. To these also must be added the correspondence carried on with those who have been transferred to cities at a greater distance; with the garrisons in Africa; with those who have attained the rank of officers, and with those who have returned to their homes, whether in villages or towns, or small isolated cottages on some high mountain, where no one is near who cares for their soul.

When the garrison is entirely changed, the Church naturally is quite deserted—and therefore with the new regiments, one must begin the work all over again from the beginning—but, between the preparatory work of the summer manœuvres and through soldiers sent to the Church by friend or relative who has formerly been a member, and now returned home, one soon arrives at refilling the meetings, and re-forming the Church, and the work goes on its way, as in years past.

In the course of the year, after due preparatory instruction, a certain number of these soldiers, who were all formerly Roman Catholics, publicly profess their faith by taking part in the Lord's Supper.

The adherence of the soldiers to the religious services has been shown in many ways; more than once, there have been those among them, who after a fatiguing march of twenty miles or more with their knapsack on their back, hardly returned to barracks, tired, dusty and dirty—have given themselves a little tidying up and gone out again to the services, perhaps two miles distant from their quarters, having just time to sing a hymn, join in a prayer, hear a part of the sermon, and then hurry off to be in time again in barracks for the roll call.

I might also speak of the time of Carnival and other public Fetes, when the soldiers prefer to come and hear the Gospel. It is on these occasions that the men, having extra leave, profit by the liberty granted them, to come in larger numbers to the services, so that every evening whilst in the street there is riot and uproar, the Military Church is full from end to end, of healthy, hearty, young men, representatives of all the provinces of Italy, singing the songs of Sion, and listening with hungry ears to the exposition of the Word of God.

In the same way, every year on the King's birthday, a special meeting is held, in which the soldiers themselves make splendid speeches concerning their King, their country, their religion, and prayers are offered to the Most High, for the King, Queen, and Country, and if His Majesty himself could be secretly present at one of these meetings, he would see how it is the Gospel alone that makes true Italian soldiers, good subjects and good patriots.

Hearing of these things, the clerical party began anew its fierce war against the Military Church, sometimes sending gentlemen and ladies to the neighbourhood of the entrance door, who, with flattering words, tried to prevent the soldiers from going in, or by means of their religious newspapers, *l'Osservatore Romana, Voce della Verita*, &c., putting all the relations of the soldiers on their guard, so that they might demand from the Government that their sons who had come up for military service, to serve their country, should not be led astray and forsake the religion of their fathers. But the Military Church did not fear the thunders of the Vatican, neither did the soldiers the menaces of their parents. They were deprived of their dear home letters, and even of the little money help which fathers generally send to their sons (and be it noted that a soldier has many wants, and that his pay is two halfpence per day, and only one if he is punished for any breach of discipline).

But the Church was more filled than ever, and the testimonies to the truth more frequent, and the soldiers themselves applied to their captains to be taught as to their liberty of conscience and to obtain justice.

Now one sees at the meetings not only non-commissioned officers, corporals, and soldiers, but officers also; the captain, who will receive a book, and give it to his soldier servant to carry home; the major, who sits among the men to hear the same word of truth; a colonel, who put his head in at the door, looks at the meeting, but, fearing to make the men uncomfortable, stays at the door throughout the whole service; another, more courageous, enters, sits down on the last bench, and remains to the conclusion. And, all the time, in Rome, the men are being sought after, in their quarters, in the Piazza d'armi, in the guard-room, and in the prisons; and soldiers and officers, prisoners and prison-guards, are being converted to the truth. In all other parts of Italy, Sicily and Sardinia also, new Churches are formed by the home-returned soldiers, like the Romans found in Jerusalem on the day of Pentecost, who, returning home, were the first to establish Christianity in this city, so these soldiers, who, in Rome have received the Gospel, returning home, have first introduced the knowledge of the truth, as it is in Jesus, into their native villages, and so from this beginning Churches are formed which increase from day to day.

If I were to narrate the facts and conversions which occur in the story of the Military Church every year it would take me far too long, but as I wished only to give a very short account of this important work I think I have said enough, and I will close this relation with saying that it is most needful in these present times, when Catholicism tries in every way to destroy us, to labour more and more. And in order that the military mission should not decline, in order that we may work freely and conquer in our warfare against our various enemies, it is most necessary that all Christians throughout the world should support us with their prayers and with their sympathy, it being a work which embraces the whole of Italy, and therefore has a good right to be called the Evangelical Italian Church.

Work among Sailors.

BY THE REV. DONALD MILLER, OF GENOA.

This has been emphatically a century of Missionary effort. But there is a class of men which the Church has, until very recently, neglected and practically ignored. It is the sea-faring class.

The history of the Church's efforts in behalf of seamen may be told in very few words.

So far as I know, nothing special was done for sailors before the Reformation. In the beginning of the seventeenth century, the Danes, whose flag went to all parts of the world for commerce and conquest, appointed special chaplains for their seamen. Wherever they established colonies, pastors were settled whose duty it was to minister not only to the colonists but to the crews of the numerous Scandinavian ships which traded with them. From 1619 to 1637 twenty-two ministers were ordained with reference to the spiritual care of the sailors alone in the East and West Indies. The Society of Church History in Denmark has very rightly published the names of many of these pioneers of the Church's work among the men of the sea. But with the close of the eighteenth century the list ends, for under the blighting influences of Rationalism in Denmark all such work ceased.

In Britain, isolated Christian efforts for the spiritual benefit of sailors may be traced as far back as the middle of the seventeenth century, but no organized and systematic work was undertaken till the beginning of the present century. To the Rev. George Charles Smith, a dissenting minister, once a sailor, and Tebulon Rogers, a Methodist shoemaker, belongs the honour of establishing prayer meetings for sailors in the Port of London, the first of which was held on board the brig *Friendship*, on 22nd June, 1814. Three years later the first " Bethel " flag was run up to the mast-head of the *Zephyr*, a flag which is used to this day, both ashore and afloat, to indicate the sailors' place of worship. In 1818 "The Port of London Society" was organized, and a Floating Chapel provided for seamen on the Thames; and the following year "The Bethel Union Society" was formed, with a view to extend the work to other British ports, and maintain correspondence with godly seamen in foreign lands. These two societies were subsequently united to form "The British and Foreign Sailors' Society," which is thus the oldest existing society in the United Kingdom for the prosecution of Gospel work among seamen. Since the formation of this society others have been organized in Britain for the same end, and there is hardly a port all round the coast of Britain where a Mission to Sailors is not to be found.

In the United States of America also, societies exist for promoting the Gospel among seamen, which had their origin about the same time, and of which "The American Seamen's Friend Society" is the most efficiently equipped and most widely operative. In more recent times similar societies have been organized in Sweden and Norway. It is unnecessary to enter here on any detailed history of these societies. Enough to bear in mind that they have all come into existence within the last eighty years; and that before that, if we except the work of the Danish pastors already referred to, no organized effort had been previously made to save the souls of the men of the sea.

At the beginning of this century the moral condition of sailors was sad in the extreme. The ships of Christian Britain, which then, as now, outnumbered those of any other nation, were familiarly known as "floating hells." Blasphemy, drunkenness, impurity, and insubordination abounded. Religion was laughed at. The man who dared to profess it, or show any aversion to the dissolute practices and filthy conversation of his shipmates, was considered unfit to be a sailor. The idea of making sailors Christians was ridiculed by those who had to do with them, and the few Christian philanthropists who attempted to stem the current of evil found that their efforts were of little avail. And the state of things on shore was even more deplorable than on board ship. Sailors returning from long voyages abandoned themselves to the gratification of their appetites and lusts, and professing Christians regarded them as too dissolute in character and habits to be reformed. I have no means of knowing what the condition of sailors was at the beginning of this century in Roman Catholic countries. Possibly there may have been less drunkenness among them than among the sailors of the northern nations which profess Protestantism, but there is no reason to suppose that in other respects they were better.

Now, thank God, a great change has come over the character of sailors in Protestant countries, and it is not too much to say that that change is to a great extent due to the *special* efforts made on their behalf. Wherever the sailor lands he is almost sure to find an Institute, a Rest, a Boarding House, a Hospital, where he is made welcome and surrounded by Christian influences. His physical, intellectual, and spiritual necessities are provided for, and every effort is made to keep him from temptations and shield him from the land sharks who are ever ready to prey upon him. And when he sails he is furnished with Bibles, carefully-selected books and periodicals, by which he can carry on his intellectual and moral culture when at sea. At the present day thousands of ships have Loan Libraries placed on board by various societies, which can be passed on to other ships, or exchanged at the societies' headquarters. Savings Banks have been organized in many ports, to protect the sailor's hard earned wages from robbery and abuse, or to facilitate their transmission to his family. In short, the Christian Church, or rather, I should say, the Evangelical Church, has now begun to care for the men of the sea, treat them as brothers in the common family of humanity, and preach to them that Gospel by which they, as well as other classes of mankind, may be saved. And though the amount of good actually accomplished is proportionately small, it is in the aggregate incalculably great. The converts of the sea can be counted by thousands. Indeed, it may be well questioned whether in the whole range of Christian husbandry any field is at present yielding, in proportion to the efforts put forth, a richer or more abundant harvest.

But these efforts are capable of great development, and there are many reasons which should impel the Church of Christ to give them more of her attention and a much larger measure of her liberality. Let me refer briefly to some of these reasons.

The dangers to which sailors are exposed and the privations they have to endure, are of themselves a strong reason why the Church should extend to them her special sympathy and care.

Again, sailors are men on whom vast responsibilities rest. Think what an enormous amount of property, what countless numbers of human lives are intrusted to their care. Without them the commercial traffic of the world and intercourse between nations could not be carried on. Is it not, then, of the utmost importance that, instead of having on board our ships men whom dissipation and vice have rendered physically and morally incompetent for their work, we should have sober, steady, God-fearing men, who will realize their responsibilities, and discharge their duties to the world and to the Church in the Spirit of Christ! On these grounds alone, the sailors' claim is one which cannot be considered with cold indifference in any country where Christian charity and brotherly love exist.

But there are stronger reasons why the Church of Christ should give to the men of the sea her most earnest and solicitous attention, reasons which arise from the consideration of the place assigned by God to sailors in His great plan for the redemption of the world.

The sailor needs the Gospel; yes, but it is equally true that the Gospel needs the sailor! Let the Church turn her attention to the men of the sea, and convert them, and then she will be better able to convert the world. She must make it her aim and endeavour to turn the mighty energy, which is now employed for the diffusion of evil, into a force for the extension of the Kingdom of God. Sailors are indispensable to commerce and to civilization, and they are equally indispensable to Christianity. It is along the lines of commerce, as a rule, that Christianity propagates itself. There is a Society in New York which places on board every vessel that leaves the port a packet of Bibles, Testaments, and tracts, in the language of the country to which the ship is bound. The results have been wonderful; but how much more wonderful would they not be if the seamen to whom the distribution is entrusted were all truly Christian men! There is not an agency which the Church has devised for the spread of the Gospel which would not find in the men of the sea a powerful auxiliary if they were only men of God. For the sailor does nothing by halves. When he is converted, he is thoroughly converted. When he becomes a true Christian, he is an earnest, witnessing, working Christian. Such are the men the Church needs to aid her in christianizing the world. Oh, if the 3,000,000 men of the sea were converted to God, how quickly would the Gospel be spread throughout the world!

Another reason why the Church should seek the co-operation of sailors in the work of spreading the Gospel is, that both the declarations of Scripture and the example of Christ show plainly that God has assigned to them a most important part in that work.

Let the Church ponder well the example of her Lord, if she would understand the important part sailors must bear in the evangelization of the world. His labours when on earth were confined to a small and comparatively insignificant country, and yet in those labours the little Sea of Galilee, with its shipping and its sailors, played no unimportant part; and if, as we believe, everything He did was done for a wise and deep purpose, and as an example to His followers, it cannot be without significance that He *began* to teach and to preach by the seaside at Capernaum. Did He not intend that His Church should understand that sailors are indispensable to the evangelization of the world? I cannot doubt it.

And then, lastly, there are analogies in nature and facts in Providence which seem also to indicate that, in the Divine plan for the world's redemption, sailors are destined to bear a most important part, and which should therefore suggest a further reason why the Church should labour and pray for their conversion and co-operation.

And the teachings of Divine Providence point to the same conclusion. Since the Reformation, the commerce of the world, so far as the sea is concerned, has, to a very large extent, passed into the hands of Christian nations professing Evangelical truth. The great maritime powers are the Protestant nations of the world; and surely that fact should be regarded as indicative of the purpose of God in relation to the spread of the Gospel.

I cannot now dwell on the many important considerations which this fact suggests, nor will time permit me to indicate other arguments which might easily be drawn from the teachings of both Providence and Revelation.

Enough has been said to establish a definite conclusion.

Considering the present moral condition of sailors, the dangers to which they are exposed, the privations they have to endure, the responsibilities that rest on them, and the vast power they possess to influence the world;

Considering that the efforts made in recent years to improve their moral and spiritual condition, though far from being proportionate to their numbers and necessities, have nevertheless been crowned by most encouraging success;

Considering that the declarations of Scripture and the example of our Lord teach us that in the Divine plan for the world's redemption a most important and indispensable part has been assigned to them, and that, until that is carried out, the Church has no right to expect that the world will be evangelized;

And, considering that the analogies of nature and the facts of Providence confirm the teaching of revelation in regard to this subject;

We are led to the inevitable conclusion that the Church of Christ, deploring her past neglect, and realising that her work in the world cannot prosper as it ought without the co-operation of the men of the sea, is bound to turn her attention to them, and use every possible means for their conversion to God, so that they in turn may aid her in spreading the Gospel throughout the world.

When the Church shall have done her duty to sailors, the apocalyptic vision of the new heaven and the new earth will soon be realized, and then "there shall be no more sea."

SATURDAY, APRIL 11, 1891.

COUNT KNOBELSDORFF PRESIDED.

CHRISTIAN FAITH AND CHRISTIAN TESTIMONY.

How the Power of Faith is perfected in Love.

BY PROFESSOR DR. FABRI, OF BONN.

THIS subject belongs to the very central sphere of Christian thought and life. It concerns the individual and the whole Christian community, and it is vitally important, apart from all Creeds, Churches, and parties. We shall all agree that both Faith and Love are fundamental to the spiritual life, and that Love is the greater of the two. The little book which Professor Henry Drummond has just published, "The greatest thing of the world," has been universally read, and helped us all to feel our unity in its world-wide acceptance. Our subject, to-day, touches closely the same truth, but it is not quite the same. Rather we take up that which is complementary, or if you take it better, preliminary to the Divine celebration of Love. For our subject is more directly how we reach the fulfilment of the royal precept of Love. Is Faith necessary before it? Has it power in itself to subdue our selfishness, and to lead us into the path of Love? Love is, in fact, a universal moral law, which makes itself felt in every human heart. Even those who have no faith acknowledge the obligation to cultivate friendliness, kindness, and good will in commercial intercourse. Still, valuable as this moral impulse is, it falls far short of the Divine precept. Selfishness, egoism, is the root of all evil. Estrangement from God is, we might say, the tragedy of the world's history and of the history of man. Our greatest question, then, must be, How can we escape from this slavery to self? The answer is twofold. Man's answer for his own side, and God's part in the work.

The first thing is to obtain a true, unprejudiced knowledge of ourselves, our errors, our sins, our inward discontent, the vanity of all earthly things, the restlessness and fleetingness of all joys and sorrows of this life, the fear of death, all show us that we are not in our true element; we are in a strange land, and therefore miserable. We need something to make us complete, to renovate us, something which can come only from above. Man can find out as much as this, at all events in his best state, by self-study and observation : the law of the knowledge of sin works within him (Rom. iii. 20), he may be receptive of the help which a higher hand offers him and may desire it. Such a help we know is offered, and millions of men have already found it. It is God's work, accomplished in Jesus, and brought to us in Him. Cleansing from all sins, peace with God, joy in the Holy Ghost, and a living hope for the future, that is the substance of it. How do we become partakers of these things? Through faith. ·Faith is the organ, the medium, by which we are included in Christ's salvation. Hence it must be both distinct from and higher than any mere acceptance of propositions and dogmas. However important this may be, that which brings us into vital union with God and His life is something greater. This is what the Church of the Reformation made a fundamental truth.

Where then is the place of Love? Faith is the means, Love is the proof and aim of Salvation, as appropriated by Man. Hence they are inseparably united, and demand and conditionate one another. Love appears in the very first act of faith. *God's* Love; for Salvation is the announcement of it. *Man's* Love; for immediately the divine Love is shed abroad in our hearts. (Rom. v. 5.) Love is the eldest and most excellent daughter of Faith. It is not the foundation of the new life, but it is necessary to its development and perfection. (The paper expounded this view at considerable length by scriptural proofs.)

But in all periods of the Christian Church the fact is more or less plainly seen, that the degree in which Love reveals itself, as the proof of the power of Faith, varies much and is often very small. Burning zeal, we find in many instances, has not been directed to subdue the power of sin and unrighteousness and to guard and defend the Faith itself, but to maintain theological or even philosophical speculations, calling fleshly lusts to its help, and preventing fanatically with fire and sword those who were of opposite opinions; not to mention the Inquisition, the trials for witchcraft, and other outbreaks of an evil spirit. Orthodox Pharisaism has, alas, played a sad and momentous part frequently in all periods and among all ecclesiastical parties. The world has too often exulted in the contrast between such facts and the claims of Christianity to be the religion of Love. The real explanation of such facts is that the natural man cannot receive the Spirit of God. The Guardians of the Sanctuary have set the example of carnal zeal, what wonder that the unconverted mulititude have followed it! They have not understood that Faith works by Love. Hence it cannot too often and too loudly be proclaimed in our own times. It is especially the duty of learned writers and those who are in spiritual office to do so. We must destroy Pharisaism by the power of the love of Jesus. There were many perils besetting the kingdom of God in these days, not only in particular nations, but wherever there is the life of culture. It is perfectly true, as it is said, that Christianity alone, that is, Faith working by Love, can save us from these dangers. Each individual believer has therefore a great work to do.

The perfection of Faith in Love is the realization of the believer's present experience in the fulness of eternity. God is Love. Eternal blessedness therefore must be the everlasting, free manifestation of divine Love in and to the whole redeemed and saved creation, God's Light flowing through all countries, and uniting them into an eternal and holy society with its peaceful glow of warmth and with unbroken serenity. That is the highest conception we can form of Faith perfected in Love.

We are here met together in a great gathering of the Evangelical Alliance. In such a union there are two chief thoughts suggested. We meet together not as attempting to unite all the divisions of Protestantism in a new form of ecclesiastical union, but as one in a fellowship and love which is rooted in a common faith.

And again, the Evangelical Alliance has set before it the aim to show the value and truth of the great principle of toleration and religious freedom. However good, useful and even necessary this object may be, and we cannot forget at the present time the lamentable state of things in Russia, which has already drawn our attention, still it is the first of these aspects of our Alliance which appears to be the greatest. Everything which promotes true fellowship on the ground of Truth itself, has the promise of an immediate Divine blessing resting upon it. Our subject, therefore, has a direct bearing on the objects of the Alliance. Even the defence of religious liberty is eventually a work of brotherly love. The irregularities of religious zeal have frequently been hindrances to religious liberty. Priests and preachers have often been, and sometimes still are, its most intellectual opponents, in league with the powers of this world, lawyers and the representatives of human ideas of right. It is not in obedience to the Gospel and under its influence, but still in the spirit of it that the so-called modern enlightenment has been working, and it is the principle of religious toleration for which it has claimed an open path among civilized nations. For once Love has won its victory without the power of Faith being its instrument. The propaganda of Love has preceded that of Faith. The almost innumerable labours, and the fervent and happy zeal of the inner Mission is a similar instance of the same. But undoubtedly our object must be to work the work of Love in the power of Faith. The more by God's help we succeed in this, the more influential will our Alliance prove itself, and the more blessed will be the results of it. It is our common desire and prayer that we may so succeed, and that the Lord may pronounce upon our work His Yea and Amen.

The Presence and Power of the Holy Spirit in Christian Life.

BY THE REV. H. W. WEBB-PEPLOE, M.A., OF LONDON.

WITH regard to the *universal endowment* of God the Holy Ghost as a gift, God's Word made it clear that once for all there had been bestowed that gift of the Holy Ghost *as a Person.* But this would not prevent a constant repetition of earnest prayer for the experience described in Luke xi. 13 : " If ye then, being evil, know how to give good gifts unto your children : how much more shall your heavenly Father give Holy Spirit to them that ask Him ?" There was no article "the" quoted in that passage ; the word was partitive, not personal : it is " Holy Spirit." None of us had realized the fulness of the possibilities that might be expected concerning the gift or powers, or qualities of this " Holy Ghost ;" the very holiest would always be conscious of needing more. It was one thing to recognize that we had failed to take and to use what our Father had bestowed ; it was another thing to charge our Father with not having bestowed what He says He has given.

The Holy Ghost has already given as the universal income of the Church, "the earnest of our inheritance : " the earnest, because a man may possess a splendid income and yet never have seen his magnificent property. What we enjoy of our income is the measure of holiness which we really possess, or exhibit in this life. Hereafter the inheritance will be ours in its fulness. The promises in the Old Testament distinctly marked God's intention to give the Holy Ghost. There were several texts that spoke of God's "pouring out" of His Spirit, and the passage in Joel ii. 28-29 : " I will pour out My Spirit upon all flesh," *et seq.* was the key text to the whole, because in Acts ii. 16 the Apostle Peter says : " *This is that which was spoken* by the Prophet Joel." That was a most remarkable expression. Great authorities sustained the view that the term " upon all flesh " did not mean upon each individual man, but that the descent of the Holy Ghost was to be on human flesh as a whole. This was the character of the promise; had it ever received any distinct fulfilment? We had an historical fulfilment in Christ at His baptism, when the Holy Ghost descended and lighted upon Him; and then the historical fulfilment for the Church in the day of Pentecost, with its glorious results.

We had these remarkable facts. First, the Holy Ghost descended upon the Lord Jesus, as representative *Man*. Then Christ went back to Heaven, and, at Pentecost the Holy Ghost descended as a Person, and became the absolute gift of God *to men*. There was a generic fulfilment of God's promise upon the Israelite, the half-breed, and the pure Gentile. Thus were all mankind included. This was the universal endowment or gift to man, of God, *the* Holy Ghost.

Individual enduement was a totally distinct thing. The first fact already mentioned was one in which man was in no wise concerned, God acting alone. In this second stage there was partly the work of God and partly the work of man. When any man was dealt with by God, the Spirit came to work in him a process of conviction of sin, of righteousness, and of judgment. The very moment the man received the blessed truth that God was in Christ saving him, he was given a new life. At that moment there was in him, first the old natural life which remains with us to the end of our existence, and secondly—the new spirit life which God the Holy Ghost bestowed: "If any man have not the Spirit of Christ he is none of His." All the Church, therefore, were at one upon the simple fact that when we believe we are partakers of the Holy Ghost and the life of the Spirit is put into us. As Christians we are not "waiting for the promise;" but we *have received* the blessed spirit of liberty and of power; the individual enduement has taken place. There was a most solemn distinction between the actual endowment, or the enduement, by God, with the gift of the Holy Spirit, and man's *personal enjoyment* of that gift from the moment he received it. The Holy Ghost is to the soul what pure air is to the body. The only real question now to be answered is, "What can we do to be filled with (or in) the Spirit?" In the days of Hezekiah, when the temple had been allowed to have all kinds of iniquity brought into it, the priests came and purged out all the filth. In Nehemiah's day when Tobiah had filled God's chambers with household stuff, the prophet cast it all forth. When the temple was filled with money-changers and sellers of merchandise, the Lord

Jesus made a scourge of small cords and drove them all out. That was the first step to be taken by us; and that first step taken, the Holy Ghost would rush into our hearts as air does into a vacuum when opened, or as water into a vessel when placed under a fountain.

Between the Old Dispensation and the New there was this difference. The Old Testament prophets were borne along by the Spirit. He never drives now. The Gospel is not a driving dispensation; you must be willing to be led. There were *negative* results of yielding to the Spirit. "Walk in the Spirit, and ye shall not fulfil the lust of the flesh." (Gal. v. 16.) The lust of the flesh was in all men to the last. The flesh was there, and what was the Christian to do: "Walk in the Spirit," because willingly led of the Spirit, and stay there all the days of your life; if you do you will never fulfil the lust of the flesh.

What were to be the *positive* results? The answer was in Gal. v. 22: Do not let us talk of the fruits of the Spirit; it was the fruit of the Spirit—nine grapes in one bunch. It was all of one Spirit who desired to work one and the same blessed fruit in us all. Nine beautiful grapes they were, and all relating to character rather than to conduct. You are wanting to go and do some great works; God wants you to begin with character. The Holy Ghost works character; then He can fill for service. It was no man's special prerogative, or gift, above his fellows, to be filled by the Spirit; but a child of God may grieve and quench the Holy Ghost. A command of the Lord to each one was this: "Be filled in the Spirit," and then "Yield yourselves as those that are alive unto God!"

ADDRESS BY PROFESSOR BARTH, OF BERNE.

WE believe in the Holy Ghost, the characteristic sign of the children of God; and in His work, the conversion and sanctification of sinners. But how are we to conceive His working, and whereby do we recognize His presence? Some see Him whenever men are filled with enthusiasm for anything, taking Him to be the human spirit in an exalted condition. It is, however, a limited empiricism to find spirit only in the human life, since the same, on the contrary, is ruled by the flesh, as long as there is no second birth. Others see just the reverse. They only see the Holy Ghost when the activity of the human spirit ceases, therefore, in the supernatural; they emphasize the gifts of grace, prophecies, tongues, the healing of the sick, deplore their extinction in the Church, and desire their revival by a new outpouring of the Holy Ghost. But the Apostles warn us from an over-estimation of these wonderful gifts, and find in daily life the apocalyptic territory of the Holy Ghost.

By what do we now recognize Him in daily life?

The Holy Spirit is the Spirit of *Christ*. The first Adam had Spirit by the breath of God the Creator; but became flesh by His disobedience. The second Adam had flesh by His human body, but became Spirit by His obedience unto the death of the Cross. He introduced the Spirit of God as a uniting power into the life of man. The new humanity receives from Him the Holy Ghost, who, through the second birth, sanctifies body, soul, and spirit of man. The Holy Ghost is thus the Divine Life-power which appeared in Jesus as the principle of the human life, and now also brings to bear upon His disciples a divine law of life upon the human period of life. Their signs of recognition are, as with Jesus, the form of a servant, and the form of the Crucified. The Holy Ghost works mightily, but imperceptibly. He gives to man an ethical gravity of life, as Jesus suffered the Cross to remain obedient to God. He gives a loving devotion to man for his fellowmen, as Jesus has suffered for us. He gives a mind of patient bearing, as Jesus bore to the very cross. He gives the glance into the invisible, with which Jesus has passed through the Cross to the Throne. Man receives the Holy Ghost through *faith in Jesus*, which results in Communion of Spirit with Him. But "faith cometh by preaching, and preaching by the Word of God." The more we rest upon the Word of God, the more we become spiritual men, and our Evangelical Church is the Spiritual Church, because she is the Church of the Word. Therefore we pray for the Holy Ghost, but also labour for His increase through searching in the Word of God, and the use of its treasure for the spiritual life of our nations in order that the Reformation may remain permanent amongst us by God's Word and Spirit. Then we may also in love say to one another: "Ye have the same Spirit with us."

AFTERNOON MEETING.

M. LE PASTEUR DR. LELIEVRE, OF PARIS, PRESIDED.

The True Unity of the Christian Church.

BY THE REV. DR. GERTH VAN WYK, OF HOLLAND.

"I BELIEVE in the Holy Catholic Church, the communion of saints." Such has been for ages the Creed of the Church in all parts of Christendom. Notwithstanding many elements in the atmosphere of the present time, hostile to the Church, it is yet a force which reveals itself always. What is the Church? The many terms by which it is described in Scripture cannot be applied to what we see as the visible Church of Christ. We must distinguish between that which is visible, and that which is invisible. This distinction has been chiefly insisted upon since the Reformation, but it was recognized by the fathers, as *e.g.*, by Augustine. It was John Huss who clearly announced that the Church is a spiritual body, the company of the elect of all ages. Separation from Rome led to the distinction being still more clearly enunciated. The Heidelberg Catechism has defined the Church as "the Society which the Son of God has elected to eternal life out of the whole human race, in the unity of the true Faith, and which by His Spirit and His Word He has gathered together from the beginning of the world to its end, and which He protects and supports through all time!" Such a description pre-supposes the invisible side of the Church.

Some may say such an invisible Church is a nonentity, but as Melancthon has said, it has a real existence in opposition to a merely ideal Church. Man is not two beings because he is body and soul. He is the same one being, now regarded as visible and then as invisible. So there are not two Churches, but one Church, both visible and invisible. The mystical body of Christ has its external manifestations. It appears to the world in the assemblies and institutions of the Church, and in the confession of faith which it publishes, as well as in the life which it prescribes. But as the snow becomes defiled by lying on the earth, so the visible Church contracts defilement by contact with the evil world.

In the Scriptures each manifestation of the mystical body of Christ is called a Church, that is, a company of those who are called out of the world. The Holy Spirit unites them. But they do not, properly speaking, make up the Church which is spread all over the world. However we may desire in our own neighbourhood to hold fellowship with other Christians, the Christian Church itself is larger than our town, or country, or nation. But as local Churches increase, they are very apt to lose their purity, especially their unity. The Scriptures give us principles of organization, but not a detailed system. Hence one Church may adopt what another rejects. In times of persecution the Church has been less worldly; in times of prosperity the Prince of this world has directed his assaults upon its inner life, sowing tares among the wheat.

Rome has charged Protestantism with the divisions of the Church, but there has never been a period when there was not schism. Episcopacy did not heal the divisions. The division between the Eastern and Western Churches, between the Greek and the Latin, preceded Luther by many ages. Rome tries to preserve unity by excommunications and anathemas, but it is inconsistent, for it recognizes the baptism of Greeks and Protestants, and yet cuts off many whom it thus recognizes. In my country for almost two centuries, there is an absolute schism in the Roman Catholic Church. Two archbishops of Utrecht are directly opposed to one another. One of these represents the ancient episcopal clergy, commonly stigmatized with the name of Jansenists, but because they are not in accord with the Papacy, regarded as worse than the Protestants.

Protestantism has indeed separated itself from Rome, because it could not be faithful to Christ and remain attached to so corrupt a Church. But from the beginning there have been sub-divisions among Protestants themselves. They are Lutherans, Baptists, Anglicans, or Reformers. There has been too much separation between these different sections. Luther would not unite with Zwingli, Calvin could not bring together the Lutherans and the Reformed. The pious Elector Palatine risked his crown because he would not renounce the Heidelberg catechism. Holland failed to secure the assistance of

Germany in her war with Spain because she had adopted the Reformed confession and not the Lutheran. As there are divisions in the Greek and Romish Churches so there are among Protestants more than two hundred denominations.

And yet we still say we "believe in the holy Catholic Church, the communion of saints." There is one Church militant on earth, one with the Church triumphant in Heaven, one bride of Christ, one "Church—which is His Body." We mourn over its imperfections, but we still keep before us the promise of the Saviour, "one fold, one Shepherd." The Apostle Paul insists upon unity—"one Lord, one faith, one baptism," and calls upon the Ephesians to preserve it in the bond of peace. Providentially, no doubt, our divisions may sometimes work for good, but they are a principal witness against us.

Now in this individualistic and unspiritual age we must beware of a false unity. We must distinguish between sections of the Church with historical and national endowments, and those which originate in mere individualism, a Donatism or a Montanism fighting for independence in an egoistic spirit. We cannot transfer the customs of one country to another. What must we do? My brethren, we must believe in the Unity of the Church, and we must act as those who do believe in it. Unity is *His* unity Whose Kingdom is not of this world. It is unity, not uniformity. It is not in ceremonies, or in external organizations, but in the Holy Ghost: a unity built upon the foundation of the apostles and prophets, faithful to the Apostolic doctrine, and aiming at one end. We must include in our unity of faith, as essential, our love to the One Lord, Who is the object of faith, but we must not exclude diversity. We repeat the well-known words, "In things necessary unity, in things doubtful liberty, in all things charity."

We must not, as desiring the unity of the Church, act as though our portion of the Church were the whole Church. We are, as the Apostle Paul says, members of the body, and all the members together form the body. If we must bear witness against the corruption of any Church we must do so because the love of Christ urges us to do it. Rome, with its pretended Papal infallibility, separates from us more and more. We must fight against superstition as well as against unbelief. But never let us forget that the nearer we come to Christ the nearer we shall be to one another. Already there is a part of the Church of Christ in Heaven. But the Church on earth is still militant, and the more it takes to heart the duty to be militant against Satan, the more its unity will be manifested. The Evangelical Alliance, as it has been well said, is itself a prophecy of unity, a unity which shall be more and more realized on earth, which shall be fully enjoyed in the glory of the Church triumphant. Let us take fresh courage as we meet together thus, and affirm with stronger and stronger faith, " the communion of saints."

ADDRESS BY THE REV. DR. L. T. CHAMBERLAIN, OF PHILADELPHIA, U.S.A.

THIS Conference of Christians is to reach its largest usefulness, is to accomplish its noblest mission, by giving to Christendom the assurance that, so far as in you lies, our present unhappy divisions are to be rendered less obtrusive; that, God helping, our present hindering alienations are to be put in the way of gracious removal, and Christendom will be filled with devoutest thanksgiving.

And to this blessed end I invoke the recognition anew of the absolute unity of the Holy Invisible Church. The ideal ever underlies the actual. The unseen is ever beyond the seen.

From the Church invisible comes the meaning, the measure, of the visible Church, and in the Church invisible there are no schisms! Time and space make no divisions there. Before the song of the glad morning stars, antecedently to the shout of the unfallen sons of God, it was ordained that into essential harmony should be gathered a company that no man might number. The great enumeration still goes back to the first soul that under the first dispensation repented and believed. It widens to embrace all who in these present days love the Lord Jesus Christ in sincerity. It advances to include all who in the ages to come shall be born from above. It ascends to take within its claim all those on high who walk in white and are named with the new name. True to the letter are Wesley's grand words:—

> " One family, we dwell in Him,
> One Church above, beneath,
> Though now divided by the stream,
> The narrow stream of death.

> One army of the living God,
> To His command we bow,
> Part of the host have crossed the flood,
> And part are crossing now."

Encompassed, therefore, by the eternal oneness of the invisible Church, incorporated for ever into its essential unity, are we, my brethren, so as we also have been regenerated by the Spirit and truth of Christ. God grant that, standing on that transfiguration height, we may see with anointed eyes. In the presence of the bush that burns and is not consumed, may we have grace to put the shoes from off our feet. As with the prophet, when the door-posts moved, and the voice cried, and the temple was filled with smoke, may we be ready to say most humbly, Woe unto us! because we also are men of unclean lips, and we dwell in the midst of a people of unclean lips; for, in the glorious form of His Church Universal, our eyes have discerned the King, the Lord of Hosts!

But, my brethren, there is also the Visible Church, and even in its visibility it is still the Holy Catholic Church. The visible Church is made up of all those on earth who, at any given time, profess the Christian faith. The true members of the visible Church are members of the invisible Church as well; yet there may also be false members, which are like the vine's fruitless branches, whose destiny is to be severed and destroyed. The doctrine of the visible Church is substantially the doctrine once for all delivered—the inspired authority of Scripture, the absolute divinity of the Son of Man, the free atonement through His blood, the renewing power of the Holy Ghost; yet there may be sad departures from the pure faith, and a "teaching for doctrines the commandments of men." The mission of the visible Church is generically to foster the true piety of its members and to win all men to Christ; yet worldliness may hinder spiritual growth, and delay the world-wide triumph. None the less, it was the visible Church of which the Saviour Himself declared, "On this rock, I will build My Church, and the gates of hell shall not prevail against it." It was the visible Church to which three thousand were added on the day of Pentecost, when the Spirit descended in power. It was the visible Church which Christ loved and for which He gave Himself, " that He might sanctify it, having cleansed it by the washing of water with the Word, that He might present it to Himself a glorious Church, not having spot or wrinkle or any such thing." It was the visible Church to which He Who ascended far above all the heavens "gave apostles, prophets, evangelists, pastors, teachers, for the perfecting of the saints, unto the work of ministering, unto the building up of the body of Christ." It was to members of the visible Church that the Apostle wrote, "Now ye are the body of Christ, and severally members thereof;" and again, "There is one body and one spirit, even as ye are called in one hope of your calling."

Brethren, as I lay my poor heart against the great heart of Christ, I seem to find there, still, the passionate, supreme desire for the complete unity of those who profess to be His. It is as if I could see that those gentle eyes were weeping, and the five wounds bleeding afresh, because of the evident divisions among those who call Him Lord. Breathing His Spirit, I cannot do otherwise than deplore the separations which are so inconsistent with the perfect ideal.

I love, and shall ever love, that fellowship whose distinctive name I bear. Dear are the inspirations which come from the deeds done, the truths upheld, by those with whom I am thus akin. Those also are "trophies which will not let me sleep." Yet, far above all that, do I prize my membership in the world-wide Christian body. It is by virtue of that greater membership that I inherit all things. To me, in that larger Union, belong the wonders of all Scripture, the triumphs of all believers, the testimony of all confessors, the witness of all martyrs, the grace of all liturgies, the truth of all creeds, the glory of all reforms. Wherever there are those who accept the Bible as the true Word from Heaven, and Christ as the Saviour of the believingly repentant, these are my spiritual kindred. Wherever there is a holy ministry reverently ordained, the faithful proclaiming of the Gospel, the worshipful administering of the blessed Sacraments, there is my loved, my welcomed sanctuary. I say with Whitefield, "Do they profess repentance towards God and faith towards the Lord Jesus Christ? If so, they are my brethren." I say with one of the most devoted and honoured of the Episcopal Bishops of my own land—in words which were applauded to the echo, in the great General Convention in which they were uttered,—"There is not one in the vast company who have washed their robes white in the blood of the Lamb, who is not my kinsman in Christ."

I confess that the word of the noble Döllinger does not suffice me,—" Let us, in the great garden of the Lord, shake hands over our confessional hedges." Yea, rather, let us somewhat remit the exclusiveness, even as in the fine treatment of landscape the due rights of inheritance and possession are maintained, in the absence of bristling barriers ; or, as in the mapping of the globe, equator and meridian are lines of reckoning which, along with their exact designation of boundaries and localities, give purposed assistance to survey and travel alike. For myself, I would rather the Presbyterian name, dear as it is, were surrendered and for ever forgotten, than that its retention should, for one moment, hinder the perfect fulfilment of our Saviour's prayer. Nor, in saying this, do I at all forget the sacredness of individual conviction. I do not in any wise overlook that Scripture which says, " Let every man be fully assured in his own mind," even adding, " first pure, then peaceable." Not for an instant do I cherish the notion of mere ecclesiastical uniformity. The dream of such uniformity has already borne monstrous fruit in the history of that Church whose head presumes to the vice-regency of God on earth, and wherein the rights of conscience are persistently denied. True unity has place for variety. True unity is perfected in organisms whose constituent parts are both numerous and distinctly differenced. The Apostle, accordingly, sets forth the Church, the body of Christ, as having " many members." The Master Himself portrays the one flock as including many folds.

What, therefore, we are directly to seek is not the sudden, violent removal of denominational distinctions. The removal of those distinctions will never come by one denomination's absorption of the rest. It will not be realized through any coercion of external power. No ! the end will be gained, to such degree as pleases God, by the filling of Christians, of Christendom, with the mind of the Master and the grace of the Spirit. The great resolvent will be the supreme love of God, with the love of the neighbour as oneself. The resultant union will be simple oneness in Christ Jesus, rather than in the Church, as the Papacy affirms, or in the Book, as Protestantism is said unduly to maintain. Believe it, through Christ alone will the faith be held in the unity of the Spirit, in the bond of peace, and in righteousness of life. In the day thus ushered in, will the churches that maintain the few great essentials thoroughly honour the common bond. Among those churches there will be those unrestricted courtesies, those reciprocal ministrations, which bespeak full confidence and full esteem. In those churches the Scripture will be fulfilled, "One Lord, one faith, one baptism, one God and Father of all, Who is over all, and through all, and in all." There and then coldness will be turned to cordial recognition ; rivalry will give place to co-operation ; lack of mutual understanding will be succeeded by alliance offensive and defensive, an alliance whose one object is the hastening of the kingdom's advance !

Moreover, good friends, though I am no alarmist, and though I can never make despair my inspiration, I perceive that the existing urgency is very great. There is peril in each instant's delay. Imperative is the call for the closing of ranks and an unbroken front to the foe. Heathen darkness cries aloud for light. Those at home who are bound as in iron, stretch out hands for deliverance. That humanity which the Church is set to save, is assailed as never before. The visible Church herself is plotted against in constant plots.

> "The wicked now
> Are winged like angels. Every knife that strikes
> Is edged from elemental fire to assail
> A spiritual life."

Astronomy tells us that as our earth swings through space in annual and diurnal round, baleful meteors are shot at her from all the compass' points. Aimed at earth's centre, earth's very heart, those missiles fly ; more than 400,000,000 each twelve-month, more than a million every twenty-four hours, more than a dozen a second. Our planet is literally bombarded as she moves ! Similarly, the world of souls is under ceaseless assault. Oh that the Church were manifestly one, that thus, herself defended, the shield of her protection might be over all ; even as against our planet's encircling atmosphere the meteors dash, to ignite in harmless splendour, and then to fall in dust and ashes on the sheltered soil ! Should the dangers, the crises, of this century's close help to bring Christians into co-operating, federated, loving nearness, it would be but the fulfilled assurance that all things work together for good to the friends of God.

You may recall, Mr. President, that when the merciless conqueror burned ancient Corinth, there was afterwards found in the ashes, by those who came in tears to mourn their loss, such an amalgam of metals as had never before been known. Statue of bronze, and shrine of silver, and coin of gold, and household utensil of copper, had been blended in that incomparable Corinthian brass, whose secret, thus learned, went far toward that restoration in which the "eye of Greece" gleamed with more than its former brightness. So, too, I am told that at Government arsenals they are welding great bars of steel by means of electricity. It is said that at the point of otherwise cold, unyielding contact, the current is applied, and that, swifter than the lightning's gleam is the resultant fusion. Particle blends with particle, mass with mass, and the homogeneity is complete.

I would, therefore, that the friends of Christ, amalgamated, if need be, in the hot flames of evil's fires, practically welded in the fusing current of danger's flash, of danger's bolt, might present themselves henceforth in a complete oneness, most gracious and abiding. Such manifested, effective union, is the article not only of a standing or falling Church, but also of a standing or falling commonweal!

It is asked when the longed-for end will come? Brethren, on you, in goodly measure, on your holy love, your holy daring, depends the answer. I am confident that you will not prove false to your trust. History records that on the night of the battle of Novara, when the last hope of Italian independence was apparently lost for ever, the defeated but heroic Charles Albert exclaimed, "L'Italia sara!" In less than thirty years, Italy free from the Alps to the Adriatic, was united under one government, with Victor Emmanuel as king. Standing on this soil, it surely is impossible that we should either doubt or falter.

Mr. President, when, two years ago, Germany's Emperor visited the seven-hilled city, and stood by night on the Palatine mount, Tiber and Via Sacra, Capitol and Coliseum, arch of Titus and arch of Septimius Severus, Forum and Temple of Peace, hidden in darkness, the whole was suddenly made visible. Floods, corruscations, of light, of apparent flame, turned arch and temple, palace and ruin, into one vast, resplendent glory. Then, when the coloured gleams had begun to fade, there rose from the Capitol's summit a majestic star, pure and white—emblem of Italy's union—its beams shining far out over both land and sea, still steadfast, even when all other lights had paled and disappeared!

Thus shall it be with the Church of God, when, at last, denominational differences are rightly subordinated to central truths, and the Spirit of peace descends again in power. Christ, the star of the Church's hope, the seal of her oneness, and an evangelized world the consummation of her earthly life and work!

ADDRESS BY PASTOR L. MONOD, OF LYONS.

Is the unity of the Church a realized fact, or is it ideal?

The Church is one. Yes, notwithstanding all appearances to the contrary.

There is a unity which upsets all our organizations, forms, Churches, sects, and parties. It is essentially a unity of aim, the unity of all those who seek after righteousness, truth, the kingdom of God; it is unity of Spirit; unity is fellowship with the life of the Lord Jesus. We hear those who are separated from us in a thousand different ways, speak in language which makes our heart thrill with love to the Saviour, and we recognize a brother in the stranger, we see in him that our common Lord and Master is amongst us.

Unity is not of our creation or manufacture. We recognize it and proclaim it in the ancient creed, "*I believe in the Holy Catholic Church.*" Our endeavour is to manifest this real unity in its completeness and its true nature. Is that a contradiction? It is a contradiction which pervades all Scripture and the whole spiritual world. "*Do what you can.*" "*Be what you are.*" That is in fact the Evangelical proclamation—uniting human effort with the divine gifts. "*You are saved,*" nevertheless, or rather, because it is so, "*work out your own salvation,*" and so in many other instances.

Unity is the ideal end to be reached; the fruit of the Spirit; but the development of unity must necessarily be difficult at the first; no respect for liberty, and the diversities which liberty promotes, is an essential condition of realizing the true unity. We are rightly warned against needless separations and infinite sub-divisions. They destroy our strength. They are inconsistent with that subordination of personal professions which, when conscience is not violated, is required of all of us, that generous breadth which is truly Christian. But sometimes those who complain most of these evils of division are the most responsible for them.

We must distinguish differences of organization from real divisions. There are spiritual affinities deeper than traditional bonds, which unite us in spite of differences. We may have different ideas of Church government, and yet we may in the sphere of activity work together without division of feeling and without destroying unity. Some cannot worship without a liturgical service, others cannot believe prayer to be heartfelt which is not free and spontaneous. Why should there be uniformity? Why should we doubt that we worship the same God, and in the same spirit, in the variety of forms?

To suppose that these differences will soon be lost in an absolute uniformity is to keep up a delusion injurious to true unity. Such a mere phantom of external union is the principal obstacle in its way. To give up all idea of bringing every other Church to identify itself with our Church; to recognize frankly and openly the rights of others to be faithful to their Church as we are to ours; to put down the sectarian spirit by showing the unsectarian; that is the only way in which we can realize the true unity of the Christian Church.

This is the spirit in which the Evangelical Alliance works as an association of Christians among themselves. If the Churches would form such an association, sending representatives who should have it as their object to remove the differences which human passion produces, and bring into proper order all that concerns the common interests of the Churches, that would be an evidence in the eyes of the world that the Church is really one.

The Church is really one. The unity of the Church is the Church's aim. Let us go then from unity to unity, from the unity of *spirit*— continually possessed anew in the communion of the life of the Saviour—to the unity even more and more abundantly *manifested to the world*, in fraternity of intercourse and the fruitful activity of the kingdom of God.

SATURDAY EVENING.

Farewell Meeting.

The final meeting of the Conference was a very impressive one. The platform was crowded with the principal delegates from various countries; on the floor of the Theatre not only were the seats all filled, but every inch of standing room was occupied, the three tiers of boxes were filled beyond their sitting capacity, and the gallery was thronged with an eager and attentive crowd of listeners, many of whom were content to remain standing for over two hours. It was most gratifying to have such a proof that the interest in the proceedings so far from diminishing had steadily increased.

The chair was occupied by the Rev. Cav. Dr. Prochet (Rome), and after a hymn had been sung by the audience in four languages, prayer was offered by Signor Silva.

It was arranged that brief parting words should be spoken by a few representative members of the Florence Committee for whom no other place had been found in the programme. These brethren— Rev. Signors Ravi and Stagnitta, Pastors Fischer and André, and the Rev. J. H. Eager, together with the Revs. J. R. MacDougall, Cav. Fera, and others—had taken a very active part in the local arrangements for the Conference, and the appropriate words of parting which they uttered were very warmly appreciated. After this the

CLOSING ADDRESS

was given by the Rev. Cav. Prochet, D.D. (President of the Roman Branch), who said:—

Speaking first in Italian.—And now we have reached the end of the work we had set before us. These days have passed like a dream, yet they will leave an imperishable memory behind them. Time will not allow me to give expression to the thoughts and feelings which crowd into my mind and heart . . . but one thing I earnestly long

v

for: That our Lord and Father, who knows all our weaknesses, may so act upon and around us by His Holy Spirit that the devil may not take away the blessed seed which has been abundantly sown during these past days, and that, not many years hence, another invitation may go forth from this land to brethren of other lands to come and see "the great things the Lord hath wrought." One last word to the brethren that have come to us from other countries.

Then speaking in French.—To you who have come to us from the noble and free Helvetia I do not say good-bye. We are so near. By the Canton trains you penetrate into Italy as a wedge, but by that wedge we hold you. There are no Alps between us; there are only the custom agents of Chiasso, who have never thought of levying a tribute on the tokens of affection, on the tangible proofs of Christian sympathy you have lavished upon us. Thanks to you for all you do in favour of our compatriots who go to Switzerland to earn their bread. We do not forget it, and He does not forget it, He in whose name you do it, and who will give it back to you a hundredfold . . .

And you who are going back to your great and beautiful France. It has been a delight to *see* you, and a greater pleasure still to *hear* you. Politics will never break the ties which bind us together. We shall in the future, as in the past, divide your joys and share your sorrows. When the news came that Edmond de Pressensé had been elected Senator you might have seen beaming on our faces the joy and the legitimate pride which filled your hearts; and the other day we have mourned with you, when we heard that this great champion of truth in France was no more. May God give you many a Bersier and many a Pressensé; may He bless abundantly your efforts, and hasten the day when crowning them He will give to you or to your children the sweetest, the grandest joy, that of having led France to the feet of Jesus.

Speaking next in Spanish.—To you beloved friends of Spain one word is sufficient. *We are brothers.* We *knew* it, but now we have seen and heard you, now that our hands have clasped yours, we *feel* it. For you our best wishes, our most fervent prayers are that Spain may join Italy in the way of liberty, and the two, hand in hand, may march on to the conquest of the most precious of all liberties, of that liberty which, alas! our nations do not know as yet, and which the Son of God gives to anyone who believes in Him. "If the Son maketh you free, you will be free indeed."

Again speaking in French.—And you, brethren from Belgium— you also, like us, a small minority in your country. Perhaps someone has said in Brussels what has been said of us in Rome, we are a "minoranga trascurabile"—*i.e.*, a minority not worth taking into consideration. Courage, brethren! there is One who takes you into consideration, yea, who cares for you. Permit a brother to repeat to you the words of Him, in Whom we are one: "Fear not little flock, for it is your Father's good pleasure to give you the kingdom."

Continuing in French.—Brethren from Holland, God has granted you many privileges, and you have made a noble use of them. Your homes, your hearts and your purses, you have thrown open to those who needed your help. I wish I had more time to speak to you, but I can only give expression to the ardent wish that from my heart rises to my lips: May our Heavenly Father grant you the grand blessing to appear one day in His presence, and to say: "Lord, Thou deliveredst unto me five talents; behold, I have gained besides them five talents more."

Then speaking in German.—You who have come to us from mighty Germany, with what joy have we hailed your coming, your presence amongst us! The time was when at the mention of your name there was but a cry from north to south of the great Peninsula: *Va fuori d' Italia, va fuori Stranier*—Away, out of Italy you foreigners. Praises and thanks to God! The times have changed—to-day we say, and we say it with warm hearts: Come, ye friends, come, ye beloved brethren, twice our allies. The alliance which here unites us is far more precious than the other. This made by men can be broken by men; man cannot unloose the former. The ties of love which bind us God keeps in His own loving hand. The past is a sure warrant for the future, you will not forget us. We are still few and weak, engaged in unequal struggle with the Roman Colossus. But our struggle is your struggle as we fight for the same great end. May Luther's fatherland remain and become more and more a strong bulwark for the eternal truth as it is in Jesus Christ our Lord—God bless you!

Speaking in Swedish.—A word also in a northern tongue to you dear friends and brothers, who come from the far north. How glad we should have been and how happy had we had the privilege to welcome many more of our Scandinavian brethren among us! God bless Denmark, Sweden, and Norway, and make them to be a great light to the salvation of many souls.

Now speaking in English.—To you, my brother from Greece, I cannot speak in your own language, but we have first met on an English-speaking land, and in the language we have used I say how much it cheers us to see you, and what warm wishes we form for the success of your endeavour to bring to Christ the noble people you represent.

[Here Dr. Prochet wishes to express his profound regret not to have mentioned the delegates from Bohemia and Moravia, an oversight which he laments the more deeply, because his heart feels very warmly towards the churches of those countries, with which his forefathers had such strong and intimate relations in the ages gone by.]

And now to you that have come from England, Scotland, Ireland, America, Canada, Australia, and other English-speaking countries, to you I could speak for any length of time; but I cannot detain this assembly, and so I reserve the greater part of what I should like to say, to say it in your own countries. We have given you the greatest proof of affection that we could afford. We have invited you to come to see us and have allowed you to bring your dinner! It behoves me, on the part of my Christian brethren to return our sincere thanks, especially to the London Committee, and I charge our beloved friend Mr. Arnold, to whose indefatigable activity and practical common sense we are so much indebted for the success of our Conference, to express our gratitude to those he has so nobly represented. Just one word more. These Conferences will have attracted the attention of our fellow-countrymen upon us more than heretofore. They will expect great things from us, and we are so small, so utterly weak; do not forget it, and tell it to your brethren of the various countries you come from. We owe much to all the friends here; but it is but just to say, and the others will not take it amiss, that you have done more than any to bring Italy to the point of having these Conferences. *Noblesse oblige*, and by your coming here you have morally pledged yourselves to stretch forth your strong hand and to help us on. . . Indeed, you have identified yourselves with us, as never before, in the eyes of the Italians, so that our victories will be your victories, but our failures will also be counted as your failures. . .˙ Without blushing, and without any false pride, we say to you: To carry on, to follow up the blessed results of these Conferences we need your sympathy, your prayers, and your *help*. Let these be such as the cause deserves, and we have faith enough to believe that fifty years hence your children will receive another invitation from our children, and that they will not then be obliged to bring their dinner with them.

RESPONSIVE WORDS.

The responsive words spoken by the Foreign delegates were models of brevity. For France, Pasteur Lelievre replied; for Germany, Pastor Baumann; for the United States, Rev. Dr. Chamberlain; for Spain, Rev. Señor Cabrera; for Switzerland, Pastor Hugendubel; for Holland, Rev. Dr. Gerth van Wyk; for Belgium, Pastor Rochedieu; for Greece, Dr. Kalopothakes.

PARTING WORDS.

On the opening night of the Conference, the first to respond to the Address of Welcome was a delegate representing the British Branch. At the closing meeting of the Conference it was arranged that a British delegate should speak last in the responses given by various delegates to the farewell address. The following is the substance of the brief address of Mr. W. E. MALCOLM, of Burnfoot, who spoke in the name of the British Branch :—

MR. PRESIDENT AND CHRISTIAN FRIENDS,—When word came that the way was open to you to invite the friends of the Evangelical Alliance to meet in Florence, a thrill of gratitude was sent through many more hearts than those of the few members of the British Branch who have been enabled to accept your invitation, and whom I now represent. In their name, I tender you our sincere thanks for your warm welcome.

While we have enjoyed the surroundings of your beautiful Florence; while we have admired the works of art with which your city is adorned; while we have had the historical associations renewed with which your past story is replete; still more, and above all, we have rejoiced in hearing within this theatre Gospel truths proclaimed, remembering former visits when even your Italian Bible was contraband.

Of the many who have visited your shores, I have thought of one traveller who trod the Appian Way, prisoner as he was, on his way to Rome, how he delighted in Evangelical Alliance. Listen to the ring of his favourite expressions: "fellow citizens," "fellow heirs," "fellow labourers," "fellow soldiers," "fellow servants," "fellow prisoners." And let me remind you how God cheered His servant's heart by this very instrumentality, the Christians of Rome coming out as far as Appii Forum and the Three Taverns, "whom, when Paul saw, he thanked God and took courage."

May we all enjoy more of this communion and fellowship, remembering that wherever Christians meet, brethren meet, and return to our homes with more gratitude to God and more courage for His service.

I will not say "Good-bye," but rather commend you to Him who never says "Good-bye."

A hymn having been sung, the closing prayer was offered by the Rev. Dr. Geymonat. The Benediction was pronounced, and thus ended the Ninth General Conference of the Evangelical Alliance.

APPENDIX.

Resolutions Adopted on the Recommendation of the International Committee.

AT the first session of the Florence Conference, a general committee was appointed to consider several questions of interest to the whole Alliance. This Committee was composed of delegates from the various branches represented at the Conference. On the closing day, the following report was presented to the Conference by Monsieur Edouard Naville, LL.D., of Geneva, who had been selected to preside over the deliberations of the committee. The resolutions thus submitted were unanimously adopted by the whole Conference.

M. NAVILLE, in presenting the report of the committee said:—

DEAR FRIENDS AND BRETHREN,—The general committee which you named at the first meeting of this Conference, has had to examine several resolutions bearing on very different subjects. Most of these have been adopted. We now submit these to your approval after prefacing each of them by a few short words of explanation.

Each of these resolutions was carefully discussed in a large committee composed of representatives of all the branches which had sent delegates to Florence. We trust we may prove that your confidence was not misplaced, and we now ask you to adopt the outcome of our deliberations without entering on new discussions which might lead us far beyond the bounds or limits of this Conference.

I.—We begin by a resolution which affects the constitution of the Evangelical Alliance. You may not know that at the Conference of Copenhagen, it was decided that measures should be taken to keep up, as far as possible, an International Union. In the interval of our conferences, its existence might have seemed to be nearly, if not entirely, lost sight of. We felt that we should seek to prevent the breaking up of a union apparently so strong and well knit together one day, then dispersed again for many a day.

The Conferences held by your delegates at Geneva in 1886, and at Berlin in 1888, have attained this most desirable result, which has been definitely embodied in the following resolution :—

First Resolution.

1. "Every two years a Conference for consultation, composed of the President and Secretary of each Branch or of Delegates named *ad hoc*, shall meet in a town previously chosen. In the event of emergency, other meetings may be called at an earlier date by the concurrence of at least three Branches of the Alliance."

2. "The resolutions of the Conference are not binding on each Branch, but are recommended to the approval of each of them."

As soon as this resolution had been voted, our brethren of the French Branch of the Alliance expressed their desire to receive the next Conference of Delegates at Paris in 1893. We heartily thank them for this proof of their sympathy with, and affection for, our Alliance. Their proposal was unanimously adopted by your committee.

II.—Our second resolution is intended for the guidance of the committee which will have to organize the next General Conference. Its two component parts explain one another. Its object is to diminish the number of addresses or prayers to be read at the Conference, to encourage fraternal discussions on the subjects treated at these, and to give more time for prayer and mutual edification.

Second Resolution.

"The Committee recommend that in any future General International Conference of the Evangelical Alliance, the formal addresses or papers at any one session be limited to two in number, and that a proportionate time be allotted for brotherly discussion."

"The Committee also recommend that additional opportunities be found for prayer and spiritual conference, and that, so far as the laws and circumstances of any country may permit, open meetings for evangelization purposes be appointed for two of the evenings during the week of the General Conference."

III.—All questions referring to religious liberty have always been actively taken up by the Evangelical Alliance. Even in countries which pride themselves on their advanced civilization, the time has not yet come for saying no more about oppression of conscience, and for speaking of this as of a sad reminiscence of the past.

The steps taken by the Alliance in behalf of Christians persecuted in Russia, such as the Lutherans of the Baltic Provinces and other Evangelical denominations—the Stundists, Molokani, &c.—appear to have been fruitless. An address signed by all the branches of the Evangelical Alliance was forwarded to the Emperor of Russia. He ordered the Procurator-in-Chief of the Holy Synod to send us an answer, to which we felt bound to reply. What has been the result?

Two eye-witnesses have given you heart-rending details of the sufferings inflicted on our Brethren in the Faith. On the other hand God has clearly shown us that all appeals to the powers that be are useless, and that we must cry to Him alone. To these Russian brethren we say, "Wait on the Lord, though He seem to tarry," for their case is in His hands, and we will say to Him in the words of the Prophet King, "Remember, O Lord, Thy tender mercies and Thy loving-kindnesses; for they have been ever of old." (Ps. xxv. 6.)

Third Resolution.

"The Ninth General Conference of the Evangelical Alliance wishes to express its deepest sympathy with the Christians of the Russian Empire, who are persecuted for their faith; prays earnestly that God's grace and mercy may be manifested to them, and commends them to the prayers of their brethren in Christ in every Church and nation."

IV.—In quite another part of the world, in Peru, Signor F. Penzotti, a colporteur, Italian by birth, but a citizen of the Argentine Republic and agent of the American Bible Society, has been imprisoned at Callao ever since the month of July, 1890, and a telegram announcing his release has just been received. He was falsely accused of holding public religious meetings in opposition to the Roman Catholic Church; all bail was denied him, as though he had been a criminal; acquitted again and again his case was slowly dragged from court to court! During all this persecution he showed a most Christian spirit, and was full of courage and submission as well as a remarkable

humility. The Committee proposes the adoption of the following
resolution :—

Fourth Resolution.

"Resolved that the Ninth International Conference of the
Evangelical Alliance records its sincere and prayerful sympathy
with Signor F. Penzotti in his long imprisonment in Peru,
for the Gospel's sake, and also expresses its hope that the
Peruvian Government may soon grant as much religious liberty
as most of the nations of mankind now enjoy."

V.—The Methodist Episcopal Church in Saxony has informed
the Alliance, through its American Branch, that its meetings had been
closed in several places, its pastors fined, and that meetings at which
prayer and praise were offered up had been several times treated as
illegal. The Methodist Episcopal Church requests the Alliance to
take up this matter, and the following resolution was adopted :—

Fifth Resolution.

"The request of the Methodist Episcopal Church in Saxony is
referred to the North German Branch of the Evangelical
Alliance."

VI.—In Schleswig, the Danish Branch requests us to act in
behalf of those Danes living on German territory who do not belong
to the established Lutheran Church there. Their complaints are
two-fold :—

1. Their services are forbidden before 4 p.m., and their pastors
may not hold private meetings even when invited to do so.

2. Government requires that all instruction in the schools be given
in the German language. Great injury is thus done to the religious
instruction given by the Danish pastors.

These complaints had been already remitted to the German Branch,
and although on the first head the Danish Branch admits that an
answer was sent by the German Branch—it was decided to remit the
two questions again to some neutral branch, and the following
resolution was passed :—

Sixth Resolution.

"The complaints of the Danish Branch are referred to the Swiss
Branch."

VII.—In Bohemia, notwithstanding great progress made, to the kindly influence of his Majesty the Emperor of Austria, to whom a deputation was sent after the Bâle Conference, complete religious liberty has not been granted yet. An American evangelist informed us that children are not allowed to accompany their parents to the Bible meetings. The parents alone can enter the place of meeting, their children must remain in the outer hall. Resolved :—

Seventh Resolution.

"That this Conference records with thanks the gracious action of his Majesty the Emperor of Austria in the development of religious liberty, and trusts that his Majesty may still further see fit to promote this cause by the removal of restrictions still existing."

VIII.—After the paper read yesterday on the abominable cruelties perpetrated in Africa on the poor blacks, one of the hearers rose and proposed that the Alliance should take up the question of the liberation of slaves and should not abandon the care of the bodies and souls of these unfortunate beings to the Church of Rome alone. Your Committee proposes the following resolution :—

Eighth Resolution.

"The Ninth General Conference of the Evangelical Alliance met in Florence requests the different branches of the Alliance to encourage National Anti-Slavery Associations on the basis of the Gospel, and expresses its desire to see such associations working, as far as possible, together and in a Christian spirit."

IX.—Lastly, we come back upon a question which has often been raised in our Conferences, that of the opium trade. We hope that some united expression of feeling by Christians of all lands, when conveyed to the British Government, may possibly help our English brethren in their persevering efforts to abolish it. They therefore resolve :—

Ninth Resolution.

"Christians of all nations met in the General Assembly of the Evangelical Alliance desire again to state that the opium trade, carried on by the Indian Government with China, is contrary to the principles of the Gospel and is injurious to the progress of Christian missions. They earnestly request the British authorities to take necessary measures for the suppression of this trade, which is a blot on the great and blessed work carried on through the zeal and devotion of British Christians."

On Sunday morning, April 12, a goodly number of the members of the Conference of various nationalities assembled in the Swiss Church for a United Communion Service, which was conducted by the Revs. Dr. Geymonat and Dr. Stöcker (Berlin).

On the afternoon of the same day, a large gathering of Sunday School children and their friends was held in the Theatre. Several addresses were given.

In the evening the Theatre was thrown open for an Evangelistic Meeting. It had been announced that Lord Kinnaird would preside, and that Addresses would be given by the Revs. Signor Fera, H. J. Piggott, and Signor Luzzi, Lord Radstock and the Rev. Nevile Sherbrooke. An effort was made to bring in only those who do not attend any of the Churches or Chapels, and this was crowned with complete success, for the vast congregation, which speedily filled every seat in the theatre, was made up almost entirely of the very class it was desired to reach. The choir, whose services had been so valuable in leading the singing during the Conference, were again present on the platform; but this time to sing to the audience, who evidently enjoyed this part of the proceedings. It was most gratifying to observe the rapt attention with which each of the speakers was listened to; and, during one of the addresses especially, the silence was almost breathless.

As the Theatre had been leased for the whole month of April, it was arranged to carry on, several times a week, these evangelistic services, and they were continued till the end of the month of May.

During the days of the Conference meetings for prayer were held in the early morning at eight o'clock, and were largely attended by Christians of many nations. On Sunday morning, April 5th, a goodly number met together in the Scotch Church—kindly lent for the occasion—at eight o'clock, and a delightful Service of praise and prayer was held. The meetings which followed on each morning of the week in the Lower Hall of the Salvini Theatre will never be forgotten by those who took part in them. There was a very full attendance from the first, and a deep feeling of the blessedness of such a prayerful fellowship of many nations seemed to fill every heart, and express itself in the earnest prayers which were poured out before the Throne of Grace. It was like a renewal of Pentecost. France, Germany, Scandinavia, Great Britain, and Italy seemed to be all lifting up hands together to the God and Father of all through the one Saviour and Mediator. Sometimes as many as twenty short prayers were offered in six or seven different languages, full of fervent feeling, calling for a blessing on the Conference and on the world. The attendance increased day by day until after the first three meetings it was found necessary to hold them in the large theatre itself.

There were also very largely attended meetings held in the Lower Hall in the evenings, when earnest practical addresses were given by the Rev. H. W. Webb-Peploe and others on spiritual religion.

Several distinguished friends of the Alliance were prevented by different causes from being present at the Conference. Count Bernstorff of Berlin, was at one time expected to preside over the first meeting, but was unable to leave Germany. The Alliance, while deeply regretting his absence, were thankful that they were able to secure the valuable assistance of the Hon. and Rev. E. V. Bligh, M.A., whose interesting address with its striking reminiscences of Florence and the Madiai forty years ago will be greatly appreciated by all who read it. The Rev. Dr. Schaff was also unable to be present. His most able and instructive paper was read in summary by the Rev. Signor Luzzi. The venerable Dr. Stoughton was unequal through the infirmities of age to undertake the long journey to Italy, and forwarded his address to the Conference. A summary of it was given in Italian to the audience by the Rev. Signor A. Meille. Sir J. W. Dawson, K.C.M.G., D.C.L., F.R.S., Principal of Magill University, Montreal, was not able to leave Canada to attend the meetings, which he very much regretted. His most important and interesting paper was read to the Conference in portions by the Rev. Dr. Donald Fraser, of London.

In addition to those whose papers or addresses have been given in the preceding pages, many other brethren from various countries took part in the proceedings of the Conference, and among them the following may be mentioned:—M. le Pasteur Recolin, M. le Pasteur Rougemont, and Professor Raoul Alliee, of Paris; Revs. Senor Cabrera and F. Fliedner, of Madrid; Count F. Van Bylandt, of the Hague; M. le Pasteur Senft, of Berne; Pastor Weitzsecker, of South Africa; Rev. Dr. Stuckenburg, of Berlin; Count St. George, of Geneva; Lord Radstock and the Rev. Neville Sherbrook, M.A., of London; the Rev. P. Colborne, of Birmingham; the Rev. J. R. MacDougall, Dr. Comandi, and Signor Bianciardi, of Florence; Pasteur Felix Boret, of Neuchatel; the Rev. P. Johnston Irving, of Naples; the Rev. Dr. Teofilo Gay, of Rome; the Rev. Drs. Graham and Mead, from the United States; the Rev. Dr. Muller and Pasteur Correron.

As we have entitled this volume, "Christendom from the Standpoint of Italy," we append a few extracts from Evangelical newspapers published in Italy.

The Rev. Signor G. LUZZI, writing in *The Italia Evangelica*, says:—

Let us lift up our hearts to God in faith and hope, and record our thankfulness for what He has done for us; and in order that our sacrifice of thanksgiving may be real and heartfelt, as well as acceptable to Him, we desire to acknowledge the benefits received in the past, and to recognize the duties devolving upon us in the future. Among other blessings which God has bestowed upon us through the International Conference of the Alliance, the following should be especially kept in mind :—

1. He has caused us to see with our eyes, and realize in some degree, the grand evangelical idea—unity of spirit—under variety of denominational forms, unity in diversity; the unity which allows of liberty; the unity which demands a sincere communion of heart and soul, and leaves to each and all the right of putting forth his own

religious sentiments in that manner which he deems the most convenient. The spirit and the heart are independent of all external circumstances; but forms are not. They will necessarily harmonize with the inclination of the individual, with his surroundings, and with the historical traditions of the nation to which he belongs.

2. The Conference has also produced a powerful testimony in favour of the Evangelical Church: a testimony splendidly complete and ample. "You are a mere handful," say some. "On the contrary we are many," replied the representatives of twenty different nations and millions of Evangelical Christians. "Others say, oh you are poor." The noble, the rich, and the great, who have formed part of the Conference have shown that, after all, the Evangelical Church is not exclusively made up of the poor. "The Gospel is for us all," said a famous German theologian, "for by it alone can we hope to arrive at the solution of those problems which are urging men on almost to desperation." Again it is said that we have no future. This assertion is as false as the rest. As one of the most celebrated theologians in America and in Europe has asserted, "the Gospel is well to the fore in the conquest of the world." An authoritative echo of this declaration comes to us from Italy, where also the Gospel must go on conquering, and to conquer.

3. There is a third benefit. The Conference has proved once more the power of faith. What was the secret of that energy by which the Moravian Missions were the advance-guard in missionary work? Faith. What is the secret of these marvels of which one hears so much in connection with evangelizing efforts throughout the world? Faith. How is it that certain churches continue to exist, which, owing to the sword being cruelly unsheathed against them, and at every onset of their enemies, cry out, "It is of the Lord's mercies that we are not consumed?" By Faith. And what is it that sustains and comforts those exiles who have left all for the love of Christ? Again it is Faith: faith that comforts and sustains under their bitter trials and hardships.

4. The Conference has also proved the efficacy of prayer. Most remarkable have been the answers to prayer which stand upon record in the annals of the Evangelical Alliance; but the early meetings for prayer held during the Conference have been, as it were, a prelude to

the work of the day, and fell like a spiritual dew on the souls that were hungering and thirsting after righteousness. How sweet it was to listen to those prayers offered up to God in so many different languages! . . . . Diversity of tongues was no obstacle to union, for the heart of one and all was the dwelling-place of that living and heavenly interpreter—the Holy Spirit.

And what are the duties which the benefits which we have received call upon us to fulfil?

1. The first duty affects us as individuals. Is it not true that the Conference has, morally speaking, given us an impetus and made us feel that we must aim higher and attain to higher things, that we must awake out of sleep, must grow in faith, in knowledge, and in sanctification, and must strive more energetically to realize that idea which the Gospel projects on the horizon of our spiritual life?

2. The second duty touches ourselves again, not as individuals only, but more particularly as churches. The Conference has brought out in strong relief faults and failings in our ecclesiastical life which it is our duty to overcome, if we desire to take seriously the friendly criticisms offered, and regard them as so many intimations of the divine will. The remarks made urge us on to judicious organization, and in this way to demonstrate that when we are weak then we are strong, for our strength must come out in our unity.

Another fact the Conference brought out unmistakably : the desirableness of calling in the aid of all our brethren and sisters in the great work of evangelization. Monopoly in such work in the Christian Church tends to that Levitical sacerdotalism which Christ has abolished. If this sacerdotalism is showing itself in any degree, it is surely the fault of the laity, who deliberately stand by and renounce their privilege of being workers together with God, for the advancement of His Kingdom! The pastors have no right of monopoly, and they only, as it were, become initiators of action, owing to it being a part of their duty imposed upon them in the nature of things.

3. We owe a debt to our brethren in the faith. A cry of suffering has reached us from Turkey, where the Evangelical Church, insulted by the Government journals has not even the right of justifying

itself in the sight of the nation. Another cry of distress reaches us from Russia, for exile and Siberia are the penalties which those who confess Christ have to pay for being faithful to their convictions. Spain, too, is under the yoke of repressive tyranny, and, earnestly looking into the dark and cloudy night, is waiting for the dawning of the day of full liberty of conscience. And shall we say that we can do nothing for these our brethren who are going through a great tribulation? Is the Christian brotherhood only a phantasm—only a dream? Has the prayer of faith lost all its energy? Brethren, let us pray, believing that the heart of our heavenly Father is not closed against our cry, or against the cry of these sufferers who are indeed His children.

4. There is yet a fourth duty which we owe to the world at large. That we should especially think of our brethren is legitimate, but if we confine ourselves to these only, we are guilty of a deplorable egotism. The Conference has come down among us as an angel, to break down the wall of selfishness which tends to separate us from the rest of humanity, and to open up to us a new and far-stretching horizon. Lying out before us there is the vast expanse of missionary operation and fields white unto harvest, waiting for the Lord to send forth more labourers. We are called upon not only to pray, but also to make sacrifices, both with regard to personal dedication and money. Then, again, there is the great anti-slavery question, in regard to which we are bound to take united action. In the near foreground are the masses lying around us, with immature problems which so nearly affect them waiting to be solved. There is the social question with its economic phases; there is profanity and foulness to be assailed and driven from our midst; there is the sanctification of the Sabbath to be insisted upon, and public morality to be upheld. What have we done in matters such as these, and what are we going to do in the future, the Conference asks? It is from the Gospel alone that true light and wisdom can come. These, then, are indeed *our* problems. Let us cease living up in the clouds, and come into close contact with the pressing needs of humanity. Let us be a little less transcendental, and more thorough and practical. Let us go out free, free to revive among us that living and divine Christianity—the Christianity of Christ Himself, who went from place to place announcing the Gospel

with divine simplicity, and doing good to all; who not only preached, but healed; who fed the hungry, and filled men's hearts with the joy of His salvation.

We quote the following from *Il Testimonio*:—

The event which all Christians, and especially the Christians of Italy, have been looking forward to for many months has become a fact. And as all have been praying that God would give it His blessing, so it becomes us now to record our thankfulness to Him for having heard and answered our prayers. The sittings have been edifying and instructive to all those who were able to be present, and we trust that the effects will be felt among the Churches of the various denominations which were represented. No one who was present at the morning prayer-meetings—a privilege indeed—and experienced the result of that intimate communion with God, and with one another—that fulness of joy which filled the heart—can ever forget it. If we could, throughout our country, have such earnest gatherings among the different Churches once a week, we should indeed have fresh occasion to render thanks to God. The curse inflicted at the building of Babel—the curse of the confusion of tongues—seemed lifted from us, as we listened to prayer offered in various languages to the common Father of us all; and the "Amen" pronounced at the end of each prayer was evidently not a simple formality, but something which came from the heart and the understanding. The proposal put forward and carried out to hold a prayer meeting for the Italians only, to us appeared an earnest of blessing for our Churches. May God grant it!

But not in prayer alone was it found possible to have union in common, for in the meetings of a general character the fraternal feeling was evident, and showed itself in its thorough unity. The interest shown in the various subjects treated of evinced how much there is which can unite us, and upon which we are agreed, rather than upon those on which we differ. The address of Professor Mariano, as the expression of an independent evangelical thinker—independent of any Church, and of any ecclesiastical questions—awoke the applause and admiration of the whole assembly. We hope that the printed address will be largely circulated, especially among students. It is not a trivial thing that a man of culture like Professor Mariano should declare publicly in the language of the Apostle, "I am not ashamed of the Gospel of Christ." We do not believe in the infallibility of anyone on earth ; however, we do believe that there is a word for all the Churches (a word by which they may all profit) in the address of Mariano when he speaks out candidly on our divisions and strifes.

* * * * *

The meetings, in which the representatives of various sections of evangelical work spoke, were among the most important. In these it was clearly proved that if the brethren would come together more frequently, determined to work together for a common end, conscious that the eyes of the world were upon them, misunderstandings and contentions would cease, and these obstacles—for they are obstacles to the work of converting the world—would no longer be an impediment thereto. The sentiments expressed by the various representatives gave the impression that each one was animated by a feeling of charity and fraternal kindliness to the other. This is surely a proof that all regard such feelings as a duty, and it is to be hoped that after such a public admission of it there will never be an occasion to say of the Evangelicals, as is said of the priests in the Church of Rome : "They preach well enough, but do not practise what they preach."

We were somewhat concerned to see (if we do not mistake) that there was but a very inadequate interest shown with regard to Sabbath observance. Notwithstanding the magnificent discourses of Signor Meille and Signor Sciarelli, there was not that enthusiasm shown which might have been expected. It may be that the influence of the Church of Rome is still affecting our people, although they may hardly be conscious of it. However, it is a question which should be very dear to the heart of all those who have the triumph of the cause of the Gospel as their watchword.

The speeches and addresses on evangelization given and translated in the evening meetings, were listened to with the greatest attention. It would be impossible to give an account of all that was said, or even of the subjects touched upon. If something was said which did not please everybody, it surely will be well for us to dwell upon that which gave satisfaction, remembering that imperfection is attached to everything here below; and that the best thing to be done is to treasure up all the good we can rather than to dwell upon the evil which we cannot help.

It has been good for us to have been gathered together. The fact that we can henceforth hold similar Conferences in Italy is a sign of great progress in a right direction, and is an omen for good that the full liberty which we in part now enjoy, will become a legally acknowledged and approved status of our national life. The day will come when our people, fully conscious of the true dignity of man, will formally abolish the first article of the "Statuto" (Constitution), and when the Italians, having their consciences awakened, will turn to the Lord, who, "if we confess our sins, is faithful and just to forgive us our sins, and to cleanse us all from unrighteousness."

A feeling of gratitude is due to Mr. Arnold, the Secretary of the Alliance, who devoted himself to the work, heart and soul, sparing neither time nor trouble, and whose love of fair play and disinterestedness showed itself on every occasion, and not unfrequently at moments when the situation was a very difficult one. We owe also to the central committee in London a debt of gratitude for the generous aid which it has given, and without which it would have been impossible for so many evangelical ministers to enjoy the privileges of the congress. Above all, we thank God, who has so graciously blessed us with His favour. Let us ever continue instant in prayer, one for another, and earnestly entreat Him to hasten the coming of His Kingdom.

Il Bolletino, has a long article on the same subject, from which we extract the following sentences:—

At the Conference held in Florence, 600 delegates, representing twenty nationalities, were present. Papers were read of the very utmost importance on the religious condition of Italy, on the truth of Christianity, on the application of Christianity to those problems which are agitating public opinion at the present moment, on missions, and other branches of Christian activity.

We, evangelical Italians, cannot, however, allow such an auspicious event to pass without making some special reflections, and on this occasion we may well repeat those words of our Lord which He spake to His disciples : "Blessed are the eyes which see the things that ye see."

1. Above all other matters this Congress has been a monument of the power of God. Like Samuel, we would raise up a pillar and call it Ebenezer, and say: "Hitherto hath the Lord helped us." Looking back upon the last forty years we have much to record about what God has done for us. In 1851, a young Waldensian, Paolo Geymonat, was arrested for having preached the Gospel. To-day this same Signor Geymonat solemnly inaugurates the world-wide Congress of the Evangelical Alliance, in this same Florence, sending the expression of its homage to the King, who receives the same with satisfaction. Before this century closes it will stand recorded that the classic soil of the Inquisition, and the sheep of the Lord's little flock thereon, have been so conditioned as that Christians from all parts of the Protestant world come together with perfect freedom for deliberation and action. Forty years ago, Italy had only about twenty pastors of avowed evangelical principles grudgingly tolerated in the valleys of Piedmont, whose race neither Pope or Prince, or Louis XIV. even, could extirpate. To-day, 150 pastors from all parts of Italy have come together in Florence, to welcome Protestant Christians from all parts of the world. Who has brought about this change? God, doubtless, who has also brought about our national resurrection; and so evident is this, that even atheists acknowledge it, although under a pagan formula calling Him, "The Star of Italy." The Lord reigns and has done great things for His faithful in Italy; let us, therefore, trust in Him, and take courage. Such is the watchword that sounds out from the Congress at Florence.

2. Jesus has said that the world will recognize His divine mission when His disciples are one, even as He and the Father are one. Well, this spectacle of Christian unity, unhappily but too seldom seen in individual churches, has been set before the world openly, and in a wide and imposing sense in the Florence Congress. Who will now think of those differences of which so much circumstance has been made, when they see Christians united to proclaim the only true and living faith? The real unity among Evangelicals appears to shine forth in the Œcumenical Congress of the Evangelical Alliance. Our

King has now understood that there is only one religion among the Protestants, and not several, as the priests insist upon giving out, since he calls those who met at Florence "representatives of one faith alone." From his point of view Evangelicalism is not a religion of division, not a Waldensian faith—a Lutheran faith—an Anglican faith, or a Wesleyan religion. All these denominations represent one faith only, as the crowded audiences which filled the Teatro Salvini time after time must easily have perceived, as they listened to the speakers belonging to the various denominations of the Protestant world—"the Protestant sects," as the priests choose to call them. How otherwise can it be explained that bodies of men associated together, all independent of each other, as bodies without any pope or head or central committee that could hold them united—jealous of their liberty, and having a tendency to make use of it, even to produce divisions down almost to exaggerated fractional minuteness—keeping closely in view their own standpoint, and yet maintaining a fundamental unity, in the midst of their immense variety of forms and absolute autonomy? How can this be accounted for, we repeat, if there be not an invisible Head who is directing and bringing it about?

3. The Conference teaches another lesson. As Elisha said to his servant—"They that be with us are more than they that are with them"—so it has been with us. We feel ourselves to be numerically weak in Italy. We are regarded as a minority, and that "so small and insignificant as to be of no account." But here, in the face of all Italy, come the representatives of the wealthiest, the most enlightened, and the most powerful of the nations, and they come and call us brethren. The greater part, if not the whole of the population of these countries, are "of us," that is, profess our faith—the Christian faith—and not only are they with us in belief, but one in heart also, bearing our burdens with us, and remembering us in their prayers at the Throne of Grace. Besides all this, we have had in our midst an illustrious professor from the University of Naples, R. Mariano, who came to deliver his most able paper on "The State of Religious Thought in Italy," and who bore this flattering testimony: "Now one can understand that the only people in Italy who have grasped the problem of justice between man and man, and who are setting

themselves seriously to the task of solving it are the Evangelicals. Their principles fit and qualify them for it. Few in number they may be, but they are the pillar of fire in the midst of the desert. These men who stand out alone and who have a quiet conscience, know how to practise a morality which accords well with the Christian faith, and find no difficulty in respecting liberty, in developing culture, and in exercising all those duties which they owe to their country as patriots. These men are not one thing at home and another in the market place, but feel that, as true believers and true citizens, it is their duty and privilege to be genuine and thorough. They have repudiated the perilous maxims of Machiavelli that those citizens only are truly great and noble who set a higher value on their patriotism than on their souls. For the Evangelicals it is evident that however high their country ranks in their estimation it does not rank higher than their soul; for they feel that the country without the soul—without the needs and aspirations of the soul—is reduced to a mere abstraction. I cannot imagine any movement more commendable than the missions for the evangelization of Italy."

It is said that there is no longer faith put in the Old Gospel, that science has destroyed the faith, and that only a few credulous individuals have any belief at all. How untrue this is, the Florence Conference has proved. Here were gathered together illustrious professors, noblemen of the first rank, famous scientists, enlightened statesmen, all come together to proclaim that the Christian faith is valiant and strong, and more than ever ready and able to go forward to the conquest of the world.

We thank God that He has so greatly favoured His little flock in Italy, as to bring about among us this great gathering at Florence; and we heartily greet the Evangelical Alliance, which He has seen fit to use as an instrument for its realization.

Some of the speakers have not been able since the Conference to send a full report of their addresses, and we have, with their consent, inserted in this volume the summaries which have appeared in the numbers of *Evangelical Christendom*. This was the case with the valuable address on Missions by the Rev. W. Park, Moderator of the Presbyterian Church of Ulster. The Rev. Dr. Murray Mitchell, of Nice, and the Rev. Dean Vahl, of Denmark, also read comprehensive papers on Missions, which are given in summary. Since the meetings Dr. Mitchell has been too ill to be able to give a fuller report, but has himself corrected that which is inserted. The Rev. Professor Dr. Fabri, of Bonn, was too ill to be able to be present to read his paper. He was detained on his journey at San Remo, and sent his son, Vicar Fabri, to read the beautiful address on Faith and Love, the greater part of which appears in the foregoing pages. Since the Conference we are grieved to learn that his illness terminated fatally, and the seal of death is upon his last utterance of Christian sentiments.

During the Conference, several telegrams and letters were received from friends of the Alliance in various parts of the world, expressing regret that they were unable to be present. Among these the following may be mentioned:—

The Rev. C. H. Spurgeon wrote: "Dear Mr. Arnold—After having been absent so long in the winter, I could not again leave home even to attend the meeting of the Evangelical Alliance; I would, however, send my brotherly love to the assembled friends. Happy are they who can share in the feast of fellowship! May the Lord Himself be among you by the power of His Holy Spirit! I rejoice greatly that so many believers from so many countries are united in the faith of the eternal verities, in these days of doubt and departure. It is delightful to think of these men of many tongues and of one faith meeting in Italy to hold a Council. Thank God for the freedom which allows this, and for the Christian zeal which carries it out. God bless Italy! May it have not only an united State, but an united Church. If we cannot become one Church visibly, let us be one spiritually. The times are such that all who believe the inspired Scripture must rally for the defence of the faith once for all delivered to the Saints. May every hour of your Conference be warm with prayer and bright with praise. May every meeting be instinct with life divine. God bless all the assembled ones, as He alone can do!—Yours very heartily, C. H. Spurgeon."

The Rev. Wm. Arthur, whose state of health forbade his being present, wrote: "May the Lord be with you all and fill the souls of His servants with grace and power." Count A. Bernstorff and Count

Lüttichan (Germany) and Count Korff sent telegraphic messages. The Italian Methodist Church of New Orleans sent its salutations by telegram. Messages were also read from Branches of the Alliance in China, Australia, and other countries. A message expressing sympathy with Dr. de Pressensé, of Paris, in his serious illness, was sent by telegram, and a reply was received from him a few hours before he passed away.

An interesting address was delivered on Friday afternoon, by M. LE PAST. HOLLARD, of Paris, on *The Revival of Moral and Religious Feeling in the Rising Generation in France*. The Editor deeply regrets that he has been unable to procure a full report of M. Hollard's words, but as this has not come to hand, he cannot conclude this Appendix without a brief reference to some of the facts to which so capable an observer referred. He remarked that a revival of moral and religious feeling is more especially noticeable in that section of the population which is the more highly cultured, and the evidences of this revival have become marked of late years in an unmistakable manner. Among other proofs might be mentioned, the success which such a book as "le Bonheur"—from the pen of the poet, Sully Prudhomme—has had; the fame which has surrounded the romance of the "Deciple," by Paul Bourget, a work which professes to point out the fatal consequences of mistake and error in life, and the present day theories of positivism. Also there must be noted, the conference held by a student with his comrades, on "Romances of a Naturalistic Character;" the passage from a discourse by Mons. de Vogue, at a banquet of the Students' Association, held in Paris. Then again, there may be taken into consideration the opinions on the subject of men of mark, and noted men of letters, such as MM. Faquet, Lavisse, Janet, Desjardines, &c. The admission of all those who come in contact with the youth who frequent the great educational establishments in France is, that positivism no longer suffices and satisfies the best thinkers of these schools—it seems to them to stifle thought; they appear to want something more and something better than that which positivism gives, something upon which they can build up their ethical life and their hopes for the future.

Having pointed out some evidences of this movement, Mons. Hollard then spoke of the chief causes of it; be it in a reaction, which some call natural—but which he rather designates as *supernatural*—or the new phases which the social question has assumed in some minds; or, further still, the incapacity which is felt in the political world to cope with the actual condition of things, in order to raise the masses in a moral sense, and to establish that union founded on justice and right feeling, which is so much to be desired.

As to the importance and drift of the movement, it is only prudent not to exaggerate. For the moment it is only, as it were, an admission of dissatisfaction and the expression of a want. Sometimes, at the most, it is a tribute rendered to the Gospel; at others, and more often perhaps, an act of homage to their party of ethics. But this movement is a grand call to the Christians of France, especially to Christian young men. It is for them to follow the example of St. Paul at Athens, who, after having looked upon the altar dedicated to the unknown god, said, "The God whom therefore ye ignorantly worship, Him declare I unto you."

The following is a fuller report of the address on Religious Thought in Italy, by Dr. PAUL GEYMONAT, of Florence, which came into the Editor's hands too late for insertion in the proceedings of 6th April.

HONOURED AND BELOVED BRETHREN,

Italy has a splendid sky. She is still more brilliant in arts and letters, by her beautiful and harmonious language, the genius of the nation and the learning of her laws. But to our eyes she does not shine in the purity and truth of her religious thought, however true it be that she has in her midst that Holy See to which the world looks, from beyond the mountains and seas, for light and grace.

We have preferred that the aspect of religious thought in Italy should be stated by the learned professor of the University of Naples, a fervent Catholic prior to his enlightenment, and at the present moment unattached to any communion. By his own experience, and studies, and meditations, and social relations, he is the fittest to give a satisfactory account of the real thought of the country. The picture which he has presented to you is one that appears quite in conformity with the sad reality.

We have reserved to ourselves the part of putting before you official Roman Catholic thought, which is always that which is nominally supreme in our nation though it may not direct and govern it, and which, having its seat in Italy, stretches itself into all your countries, having a hand in all councils and in all diplomatic intrigues. In opposition to this thought, really more political than religious, we place evangelical thought, which has come from the pure fountain of the Gospel, and is represented in the different denominations, which, as the decided and salutary antithesis of the Roman Catholic, spreads itself and declares itself only by peaceful methods. There is the contrast, on one side, *Catholic Thought*, producing profound division under the appearance of unity, by craft and policy ; on the other side, *Evangelical Thought*, producing real unity under various denominations, without craft and without political intrigue.

1. We have no intention to enter upon the subject of doctrine, the variations which have arisen from period to period in the history of the Church and of dogmas, though not from one Pope to another. We are concerned with *Thought*, which we know has varied from one Pope to another. Doctrine is, so to speak, consolidated Thought. Thought is doctrine moving upon the world, to lead it or to follow it according to the times and humours. This movement of Thought should be observed to-day more than ever ; because in consequence of the proclamation of the dogma of Infallibility, the Thought of the Pope and his word have acquired a kind of dogmatic force.

Pius IX. was little of a thinker, but felt and spoke much. Leo XIII. is a thinker and a writer, but feels less. Pius IX. a soldier in his youth, at first in love with liberty which he afterwards betrayed, was a militant Pope. Leo XIII. is a theologian and a diplomatist. Pius IX. formulated his thought in the Syllabus in sentences which denounced all modern liberty ; Leo XIII. diffused his thought in numerous encyclicals, already more than a score in number, upon matters more or less practical. Pius IX. proclaimed the dogma of

Infallibility, and made out of it an offensive weapon. Leo XIII. quietly brought it into use. Pius IX. showed the negative side of Infallibility by launching constant anathemas against all liberty. Leo XIII. has kept the Syllabus in hand, has shown the positive side of Infallibility; even has taught liberty and called it a most excellent gift—"*præstantissimum donum*"—and commended universally, and especially to Italy, the blessing of an infallible direction such as his own. He has called into use reasoning rather than the anathema, which has become harmless. To the infallible authority with which he is invested, he adds the equally infallible method of proving everything that is wished, "*sic et non*," the scholastic method, formal logic. To give the form of science to theology, he recommends the study of philosophy, but meanwhile adding that philosophy must regard herself as most honoured by being a humble handmaid ("*Summi honoris loco habeat quod tibi liceat in morem ancillæ formulari*"). As the Archbishop of Perugia, he founded there the Academy of St. Thomas, the greatest philosopher and theologian. Now raised to the Holy See, he has ordered the study in all the colleges of the theology of the Doctor Angelicus, as that which best of all reconciles together the lines of Reason and of Faith; then binds them closely to the fulfilment of his orders, calling together solemn assemblies for discussion.

The aim of the Pope in thus giving a philosophical order to the studies in Theology, is not so much to give it a scientific form, but to give to the defence of Catholicism one single thought and method. Unity of study gives to different minds a unity of thought.

"Catholic forces," said a Catholic review, "seem to be a little scattered. We should draw the threads together."

In the time of Pius IX. certain questions remained in suspense; certain propositions of Rosmini were passed without observation. Leo XIII. has had them examined by the Cardinals of the Inquisition; the "Supreme Congregation" has decided that forty-two of them ought to be refuted, condemned, and proscribed. Leo XIII. has issued the decree of refutation, condemnation, and proscription. Rosmini had many adherents in Lombardy and in Piedmont; the word of the Pope seems to have reduced all thoughts to a single thought. As an act of authority the thing is imposing enough, but in itself is it not a mere suppression of thought?

As a result of the proclamation of the dogma of the Infallibility of the Pope, it is not so much in dogma, or in faith, that unity is sought; there must be one thought alone—that is, the thought of the Pope. *Catholics* generally have become liberal enough, but *Catholicism*, the Catholic system, is more rigid than ever; only as the support of states is refused, or by their opposition, it is in practice more elastic and free.

It is not only philosophy which the Pope adopts for the triumph of his thought, but history also—the history of the Popes, history made by the use of Papal archives, and for the glory of the Papacy. By the Brief of August 13th, 1883, he authorized Cardinal Petri of Luca, Hergenrötter, to publish the Registers of the Vatican. From these must be drawn universal ecclesiastical history, embracing the history of the Papal jurisprudence, the Papal diplomacy from Martin V. to our own times, the Papal biography, examples of the principal controversies, the history of the University, Scholastic Theology, and the Pontifical chancery. That history is to serve as the source from which the Catholic Schools are to draw, in polemics and in popular narratives. The Vatican history will be for the Roman Catholics of the future what the sacred Scriptures were for the ancient Catholics, what they are and always will be for Protestants. Instead of leading the nations to the fountain of living water, they have "hewn out for themselves broken cisterns that can hold no water." (Jer. ii. 13.)

The unity of Thought being shown by the acts of the Papacy, there is still to be sought unity of action. Such a society exists as is required, with a powerful discipline, absolutely devoted to the Papacy—the Jesuits are as strong for action as St. Thomas for doctrine. It is well to unite that which is completest in doctrine with that which is most able in action. Boldly defying the public sentiment, Leo XIII. has openly granted them his full favour. By the Brief, "*Inter alia dolemus*," issued July 18th, 1886, he has solemnly approved and confirmed all the privileges, powers, and dispensations they have ever enjoyed. The Jesuits are not said to hold, properly speaking, the doctrines of St. Thomas; but if the Pope wills it so, and if it is suitable, they will even teach that doctrine.

An ideal drawn from the middle ages, and worked out by the

Jesuits—such shall be the religious thought of Italy, and if the other nations and Italy allow it, such will be the programme of the Vatican.

On the strength of that very modern liberty which he has anathematized in the Syllabus, and which he would deny to those who have generously conceded it to him, the Pope issues his orders to his devoted legions in Protestant countries, in Germany, in England, in the United States—to his religious corporations, his beloved Jesuits; and what if, at last, a preacher in the Cathedral has already proclaimed the conversion of Geneva, the conversion of the Emperor of Germany and of Germany, the conversion of the Queen of England and of England, and of the United States! As the turbid waters of Socialism are said to increase, the Pope, to use the expression of one of the Cardinals, has begun to lead and guide and fashion that movement, in favour of States or against them, in accordance with the interests of the Holy See, and for the advantage of the Romish Church.

Continually harping on the subject of the temporal power the thought of the Pope is continually in collision, in Italy, with the natural aspirations of to-day, and it is for this reason perhaps that he has less influence in Italy than elsewhere. Why are our Italian patriots disturbed? Because their conscience is not at rest, because it is not all in God, simply in God!

2. Religious Thought, if it is to be wholly true, must be both real and ideal. The highest and fullest truth is that which defines the real from the ideal. We must oppose to imaginations and illusions reality, to the imaginary ideal we must oppose the true and real ideal. What is that one, holy, infallible Church, directed and governed by a mortal as Head? It is an imaginary ideal, accredited by ancient traditions, and by wonderful monuments, by an imposing order, but disfigured by errors and arbitrary conditions, by dissensions and hatred, by political and perfidious subterfuge; a covering based upon texts wrongly interpreted, and which sustain nothing more than false and vain pretensions.

To all such fictions we must oppose the reality. Protestantism has done so, by a solid exegesis, an accurate history, a criticism ever more minute, a freedom of examination ever more bold. We have gained by this immense labour, "proving all things, holding fast that which is good." There exists in Italy the committee for religious publications, with its centre in Florence, and its own printing press; which hitherto has printed translations more than original works. From us has really commenced critical, exegetical, and historical study. We have had excellent leaders in De Sanctis and Gavazzi. Ribetti, Theophilus Gay, Sciarelli, and others of every denomination, have proved themselves by word and pen. But we are really critics and polemics only that we may affirm the real truth, not that we may shake it.

The true ideal cannot be opposed to the imaginary ideal. Has not Protestantism wandered a little from its true aim? Is it not the aim of an ideal to unite minds and efforts to one end? As in God's order and Nature's order we make true progress by preserving that which should be preserved and overcoming evil with good. The true ideal is not the Church, or the reign of the Church. It is not the Catholic Church, nor is it any Protestant Church; it is neither the visible nor the invisible Church. There is no Church which can say, I am the Truth. It is enough if it can say, I follow and obey the Truth. It is the greatest error of Catholicism to put the ideal in the visible Church, that is to say, in the Romish Church, and it is an illusion of Protestantism to see it in the invisible Church where no one can see it.

The true ideal is not the Church, but the faith of the Church and its mission. The Church has to represent the ideal and to go after it. Its mission is in that respect clearly distinct from that of the State, and one is the complement of the other if they keep distinct. The Church aims at the ideal, and should teach and exhort to practise righteousness by love—the State aims at the real, prescribes righteousness by laws and maintains it by force.

The true ideal is not of the fancy, but of the heart. Jesus Christ has imprinted it there by His prayer, which is employed by all Christendom. The true ideal is simple and easily understood by all, it is human and divine at the same time, as Christ is Man and God. But we must distinguish between the ideal already realized and the ideal which has yet to be realized, a distinction easy, convenient and helpful.

The ideal *is* realized in the person of Jesus Christ, in Whom we see perfected the personal unity of God and of man, and in His work which is the fulfilment of the "Law and the Prophets, the example of all righteousness in the expiation and remission of our sins and the whole world." Behold the Man! the Man Who by the perfection of His person, and by the holiness of His life is the living and real image of the invisible God. Behold Him on the Cross, crowned with thorns, and bleeding unto death to make peace between Heaven and earth, then crowned with honour and glory, and humanity in Him justified, sanctified, glorified—that is the perfect ideal realized.

The ideal has yet to be realized in the union of God with men as the Father with His children, and of men with one another as brethren in the universal manifestation of all righteousness, whose fruits are peace, prosperity, security, order, and liberty. The ideal to be realized is the reign of Heaven on earth as in Heaven, as the prophets have already foreseen in their visions, as it is set forth in the Gospel, as we see it in part realized in the Christian life. The ideal is divine charity in the human life as in Christ, as to a certain degree already here and there in individuals, in families, in Churches truly Christian.

The ideal is the element of religious thought, it is its basis and its end, its resting place, and at the same time its constant object of endeavour.

The ideal realized is the living substance of the faith and of thought likewise; it is the object of speculative study which formulates truth in precise dogmas, and it may also be the object of æsthetic study which reproduces truth in forms more vague and attractive.

In this country of the Arts, which idealizes objects or things of the fancy, and is the servant of the imaginary ideal, we must not venture to set forth truth in its naked and bare simplicity; nor must we neglect æsthetic study, and disdain to use the help which can be attained from eloquence, poetry, music, and those fine arts which are more spiritual, more conversant with the religion of the Spirit and consecrated by the Word of God.

The end of religious thought is to teach the ideal; that is, its aim and the object of practical studies may exist; the chief is morals, the science of the good. But whether it be science or the arts, whatever may be found to be the foundation, the forms, and the laws which affect the welfare of mankind, they must all bear upon and tend to the glory of God and the making of His Will to be done in earth as it is in Heaven.

On such a basis as this, with such an ideal before it, evangelical thought, free and apparently divided, can yet go forward in unity. Already that unity has been seen when, in 1883, a Congress was held for the union of the different denominations, and without difficulty a " Consensus Evangelicus " was agreed upon. The obstacle to the attainment of the object has been the worship of names and of denominations too dear to each one.

Where is the opposition? Not with Catholics, who recite with us the same Lord's Prayer. The opposition remains inevitable and irreconcilable with the Catholic system, in the absolute and exclusive thought of the Vatican, which has for its basis Romish dogmas, for its rule the infallibility of the Pope, for its end or ideal its own universal domination, proclaiming as its object a kingdom which in the form of the Romish theocracy would organize all kingdoms about itself. We all, on the contrary, in all countries, among all nations, seek the Kindom of God and His righteousness, which is the ideal of the Gospel.

"I saw an angel flying through the midst of Heaven," so says St. John, "having the everlasting Gospel to preach to all the inhabitants of the earth, to every nation, tribe, people, and tongue." (Rev. xiv. 6.) We have seen him passing through our beautiful sky, settling over Florence, and even over Rome on the opposite side to the Vatican, spreading his wings over all Italy. And you all, brethren from every country of Europe, and you from America, and you from Africa, and you from Asia and from Australia, you have all seen him in your heavens. The divine sign is at this day universally verified by the spread of the Gospel. Ah! through all my mountains, and throughout Italy as well as my mountains, in all your countries as in our Italy, the angel with the everlasting Gospel to preach still spreads his wings, declaring to all men the eternal love of God, and turning the wandering ones to the Shepherd and Bishop of their souls—Jesus Christ our adorable Saviour. (1 Peter ii. 25.)

x

www.ingramcontent.com/pod-product-compliance
Lightning Source LLC
Chambersburg PA
CBHW030317240426
43673CB00040B/1194